Research Methods for English Studies

Edited by Gabriele Griffin

Edinburgh University Press

© in this edition, Edinburgh University Press, 2005
© in the individual contributions is retained by the authors

Edinburgh University Press Ltd
22 George Square, Edinburgh

Typeset in 11/13 Ehrhardt by
Servis Filmsetting Ltd, Manchester, and
printed and bound in Great Britain by
MPG Books Ltd, Bodmin

A CIP record for this book is available from the British Library

ISBN 0 7486 2154 7 (hardback)
ISBN 0 7486 2155 5 (paperback)

The right of the contributors
to be identified as authors of this work
has been asserted in accordance with
the Copyright, Designs and Patents Act 1988.

Contents

Acknowledgements

This volume has its origins in a regional seminar on research methods training for postgraduates, held in 2002 and involving representatives from humanities subjects from the universities of Sheffield, Manchester, Leeds, York, Leeds Metropolitan, Newcastle-upon-Tyne and Sheffield Hallam, and the University of Hull whose Faculty of Arts and Social Sciences funded that event. The focus of the seminar was a discussion about the implications of the then just-published Postgraduate Review by the Arts and Humanities Research Board (2002) for postgraduate research training. That discussion highlighted the absence of writing on research methods in certain humanities subjects, including English. Following this meeting, the University of Hull sponsored a year-long research seminar series on research methods in which many of the contributors to this volume took part. I would therefore like to acknowledge, in the first instance, the support of the Faculty of Arts and Social Sciences in enabling this project to take shape, and in particular its now-retired Dean, Alan Best, who recognised the timeliness of this project and agreed to the funding of the seminar series. Secondly, I would like to thank all the people who participated in the seminar series, both as speakers and as listeners – the discussions we had fuelled this volume.

I would like to thank all those who commented on this volume, offering advice and support. They include Ben Knights, currently Director of the English Subject Research Centre, whom I consulted about contributors, and Lucie Armitt, Head of English at Bangor University, who invited me to one of their research seminars where a lively discussion took place. My colleagues in English at the University of Hull – in particular Valerie Sanders, Patsy Stoneman and Katharine Cockin – as much as my colleagues in Gender Studies – Rachel Alsop, Suzanne Clisby, Kathleen Lennon and Stella Gonzalez-Arnal – were the source of useful discussions and supportive input. I would also like to thank my Masters and PhD students past and present whose work has influenced my thinking on research methods and kept me on my toes intellectually, theoretically and practically. My visiting professorship at Monash University, Melbourne, Australia, during the summer of 2003 enabled me to work on this volume, and special thanks go to Maryanne Dever for making that time possible.

During the development of this volume I obtained a three-year EU-funded research project grant (DG XII Research, European Commission) to work on 'Integrated Research Methods in the Humanities and Social Sciences'. My sincerest thanks go to my project partners – Harriet Silius, Abo Akademi University, Finland; Isabel Carrera Suarez, University of Oviedo, Spain; Karin Widerberg, Oslo University, Norway; Ulla Holm, Goeteborg University, Sweden; Jasmina Lukic, Central European University, Budapest, Hungary; Silke Wenk, Oldenburg University, Germany; Ursula Apitzsch, Frankfurt University, Germany; and Nicky Le Feuvre, Université de Toulouse Le Mirail, France – with whom I continue to be engaged in intensive and productive discussions about research methods. Working with them is one of the joys of my professional life.

I should also like to thank Edinburgh University Press, and in particular Jackie Jones and Bob Morris, for supporting this project and for inaugurating the 'Research Methods for the Arts and Humanities' series of which this is the first volume. Their recognition that research training in the Arts and Humanities in Britain and across Europe is undergoing significant changes has been key to making this volume possible.

Last but not least, I would like to thank my husband Simon Gunn for his support, good humour, perspicacity, willingness to share ideas, comment on drafts, and make lemon and ginger tea – all vital ingredients in the research process.

CHAPTER I

Research Methods for English Studies: An Introduction

Gabriele Griffin, University of Hull

THE CONTEXT

Until very recently, research methods were not widely discussed in English studies.[1] In the 1980s, when I was a postgraduate student, they did not figure at all – research was what you did, and the best you could hope for was a brief introduction to the vagaries of the library. There was no sense that you needed to know about the process of conducting research, or that how you did it might influence the outcome, though you might find yourself held to account during your *viva* for the sources you had used as the basis for your research.

During the second half of the 1990s, when the issue of research training began to creep up on public and institutional agendas, research methods were what you asked other people to deliver to your students, mostly in the form of a basic library introduction (always unwelcome to those who had used that particular library already and felt they knew it), and basic computing skills (also frequently unwelcome, especially among younger students who had grown up with computers and had basic word-processing skills).[2] The ethos remained that research methods – more properly, skills – were divorced from the academic enquiry into the subject; that it was librarians' and computer technicians' job to deliver any relevant training (the word 'training' itself being viewed as detracting from higher-order intellectual endeavour);[3] and that it was a necessary evil rather than a positive good.

This is strange considering that significant numbers of English studies academics in the UK[4] are active researchers who clearly employ research methods to produce their often stunning and paradigm-shifting results. Yet they have remained surprisingly in- or possibly non-articulate about what they do to achieve these results. One prevailing view is that 'A lot of research methods can't be taught. You pick it up by doing it' (Williams 2003: 27). Unsurprisingly, the corresponding view from a student who had undertaken research methods training was: 'Everyone in my group hated it and didn't learn anything. The only thing you learnt was from working with my supervisor.' And from another: 'The most useful part was going around by myself, finding out what I needed to know . . .' (Williams 2003: 35). Such views reflect a research environment where the emphasis is on learning by doing, where supervisors themselves have no history of research training as a function of the point in time when they undertook their own postgraduate research, where students and staff work in a discipline that has no significant history of providing and discussing such training, and where — as both the English Subject Centre's report on this issue (Williams 2003) and the Arts and Humanities Research Board's Postgraduate Review (2002) indicate – notions of radical individualism in research, rather than research collaboration, prevail. To this day, and unlike research degrees in the Social Sciences, for instance, PhDs in English do not require, and in my experience virtually never have, a methodology section – something that is absolutely commonplace, not to say *de rigueur*, in other disciplines.

This situation has begun to shift dramatically since the turn of the century. In November 2002, as briefly indicated above, the English Subject Centre published a research report on *Postgraduate Training in Research Methods: Current Practice and Future Needs in English* (Williams 2003). The report was timely: it followed hot on the heels of the Arts and Humanities Research Board (AHRB) Postgraduate Review which had appeared in January 2002.[5] Given the vast range of postgraduate degree courses across the UK and the intense competition for resources to support them, the AHRB's review recognised the need 'to nurture research cultures' (AHRB 2002: 3), and 'to encourage best practice in research training' (ibid.: 3). In this it followed the already-existent research councils in the UK such as the Economic and Social Research Council (ESRC) which have well developed, if in some ways contested,[6] research training requirements that must be explicitly and mandatorily incorporated into postgraduate schemes in order for these to receive funded studentships.

The AHRB has recognised that historically it has not paid much attention to the issue of research training. Neither, it might be said, have some disciplines, especially in the arts and humanities. The AHRB's review includes details of what such training might look like and a recognition that beyond skills and knowledges, research methods need to be part of research training. Since 2004 the AHRB has required the provision of a 'Departmental Research Training' statement as part of every application for a funded studentship. In its application forms for research leave, research grant applications and so on it also explicitly requires applicants to discuss the research methods they will employ in the process of undertaking their research. One student, quoted in the English Subject Centre's report, said: 'It's important to have the discourse so that you can communicate knowledgeably in your own subject' (Williams

2003: 14). Such discourse includes a research methodological one: the demand to be explicit about one's research methods in grant applications and reports requires a meta-discourse on how we do what we do and why, and part of learning about research methods is about the acquisition of that meta-discourse.

Unlike other research councils, the AHRB has not become prescriptive in what content it requires from research training courses but it has produced a 'Joint Statement of the Research Councils'/AHRB's Skills Training Requirements for Research Students' which is intended to re-emphasise 'that training in research skills and techniques is the key element in the development of a research student' (2002: 41). [7] The statement lists an extended number of research skills, techniques and competencies which the AHRB considers necessary for the adequate training of research students. Thus, there is now a requirement to incorporate proper research training in all postgraduate provision.

RESPONSIVE VERSUS PROACTIVE MODELS OF RESEARCH TRAINING

The requirement for postgraduate research training has driven universities and individual disciplines to review their research training provision, and has led directly to the English Subject Centre's own report. That report is telling. Based on interviews with a range of English studies staff and research students, it indicates that conducting research in different periods requires different kinds of research skills – working with medieval manuscripts, producing a scholarly edition of an eighteenth-century text, writing a theoretical intervention in the area of postcolonial theory or on the history of metaphor plainly demand different research skills. In consequence, the report reproduces the repeatedly articulated views that 'there is a limit to what you can teach in a group way . . . the particular skills an individual needs are so specific' (Williams 2003: 18), and that 'It's artificial to see skills as being separable from the actual research work . . . A lot of those skills they learn on the job . . . That makes it hard to teach in a common way' (ibid.: 21).

Such comments chime with the AHRB's decision not to prescribe in detail what research training courses should deliver, its focus on individual training needs in line with the requirements of the specific proposed research topic, and its recognition that much humanities research in general, and English studies research in particular, is done by individual scholars on their own. However, these comments also deliver a particular view of research. It is a responsive model in that it focuses on the identification and response to individual needs as they arise from a specific research project; it assumes implicitly that the research methods relevant to that particular project are *the only ones* a research student needs to acquire, presumably because the kind of research conducted at postgraduate level is assumed to be the kind of research that a scholar will go on to (re)produce throughout the rest of her/his academic life. However, both disciplinary and research technological developments over time require changes in research practice – one need only think of the impact of the advance in computer technologies on textual editing to understand this (see Chapter 12 in this volume for further details). Few scholars will utilise for the rest of their professional lives only those research methods they acquired to complete their thesis. Research methods training beyond the needs of a particular project thus widens a researcher's research skills and knowledge base in anticipation, not least, of future needs.

In English studies it is common practice to assume that 'in the end it's about reading, about text. Provided you know your way around a library and how to find things out, it is a case of knowing your texts . . .' (Williams 2003: 14). Such a view admits only to the notion of text-based research and textual analysis as the proper domain of English studies research. But, as the 2001 Research Assessment Exercise panel's definition of its domain makes clear, English studies is, and can be, much more than textual analysis.[8] The failure to recognise this is a failure of the research imagination[9] which reduces the possibilities of conducting divergent and innovative research, and has led to a lack of engagement with large areas of potential enquiry such as the interaction between texts and readers, for instance, which is much theorised but rarely underpinned by any empirical evidence. In contrast to the notion that research students should only be taught those research methods that are directly relevant to their immediate project, I take the view that understanding research methods more broadly is about opening up the possibilities of the kinds of research one might conduct, and about providing researchers with more choices regarding what kinds of research they might do, both immediately and in the future. Knowing about a broad range of research methods enables researchers to think divergently about research.

This volume therefore aims to introduce readers to a range of research methods in order to suggest to them new and different, as well as tried and tested, ways of conducting research in English studies. Its purpose is to present readers with introductions to different research methods that might be employed in English studies, particularly for those working on materials from the nineteenth and twentieth centuries, and to suggest ways in which one might structure a research methods training programme for postgraduates in this field. The volume takes as its premise that research methods constitute not only a tool for research but also that they shape both the research and its outcomes. In consequence, it also assumes that knowledge of a range of research methods enables students to ask different research questions and to make informed choices about research methods rather than adopt a default position, and that this might generate divergent and innovative work. Additionally, it assumes that students benefit from familiarity with a range of research methods beyond what they might need for the immediate research project they are engaged in, on the basis that they may do different kinds of research at different points in their postgraduate and subsequent employment lives.

RESEARCH SKILLS, METHODS, AND METHODOLOGIES

A word about research methods, skills, and methodologies: the English Subject Centre's report uses the word 'skills' to describe what postgraduates need 'to undertake PhD work in English' (Williams 2003: 58). However, I would want to make a distinction between research skills, methods and methodologies, a differentiation that is common in many disciplines. **Research skills** are techniques for handling material. According to the English Subject Centre report which summarised views of staff about the skill set needed for postgraduate work in English, they include search skills in libraries, editorial skills, bibliographic skills, dissertation skills (such as how to structure a book-length piece of writing), IT skills, period-specific skills (such as learning to read secretary script, or how to record variants among different manuscripts), and professional skills such as how to present papers at a conference (Williams 2003: 58–9).

Such skills may be distinguished from **research methods** which are concerned with how you carry out your research. The choice of method will depend on the kind of research one wants to conduct. The comparison of manuscripts for authorship attribution purposes, for instance, requires different methods from understanding why listeners to a BBC programme vote for a particular poem or novelist as the best one. For the former one might use ICT methods, while for the latter one might conduct interviews or use a quantitative method such as a survey. Both are perfectly valid research projects within the field of English studies, a term deliberately used here to highlight the great range of activities which is subsumed under the heading 'English'.[10] Theses on television adaptations of 'great classics', of which there were quite a few during the 1980s and 1990s, require very different methods from theses that seek to understand how viewers of such television programmes understand them, relative to readers of such classics who have not seen the televisual adaptation. The analysis of texts originally written for a medical audience may require very different methods from those used to consider the aesthetic dimensions of a particular poem. Textual analyses will yield findings very different from those gathered by conducting interviews with a reading group.

Whilst research methods are concerned with how you conduct a given piece of research, **methodologies** are concerned with the perspectives you bring to bear on your work such as a feminist or a postcolonialist one, for example. The many different critical readings of diverse literary texts are possible not least because different people bring different perspectives to bear on their analyses of a given text. A feminist reading of Jane Austen's *Mansfield Park* might consider the ways in which space is differently assigned to women and men in the text, and remark upon the Austen novels' trait of confining women to house and garden (they tend to fall in every sense of that word if they leave that space), whilst a postcolonialist reading of *Mansfield Park* might focus on the role which Sir Bertram's ownership of plantations in Antigua plays in the novel's portrayal of male authority, distribution of power, the relationship between 'at home' and 'abroad', and the absence or presence of rulers.

This brief description of the differences between bringing a feminist or a postcolonial perspective to bear on a text indicates one important aspect of conducting a research project: selection. Deciding on a particular research project is to a significant extent about deciding on the specific research skills, methods and methodologies necessary and appropriate to conduct that research. When examiners read PhD theses, or panels assess research applications, they do it in part on how appropriate that selection is, and what it shows about a candidate's knowledge of the area they want to investigate, and their understanding of the skills and methods necessary to complete the task.

Such selection implies a narrowing-down of the vast array of skills, methods and methodologies available to a researcher. This should not, however, blind one to the fact that all research requires more than one research skill or method (though not usually methodology). For instance, if one decides to write a biography one might conduct archival research, textual and document analyses, interviews and discourse analysis, as well as employing visual methods and possibly even quantitative methods to arrive at the final product. Even quite conventional close readings of texts require a range of such methods and skills. Researchers, then, never employ just one research skill or method – usually they work with a combination of methods. This is evident in the traces of research made increasingly explicit by writers of historical novels, or of fictions that have a base in material history, for example. They tend to cite, either at the beginning of their texts or at the end, the (re)sources and archives they have drawn on. This is as true of Pat Barker's *Regeneration Trilogy* as it is of Margaret Atwood's *Alias Grace*. And, of course, the same applies to writers of auto/biography. Even Margaret Forster's 'Author's Note' on her family memoir *Hidden Lives* starts with the sentence: 'In one sense there was no real research, or what I would term research, needed for this book, since it relies so heavily on personal memory . . . but attempting to place these memories, many of them not mine, in some historical context did lead to a great deal of delving into the Cumbria County Council Archives . . .' Such disavowal, followed by an acknowledgement of a research process, is itself interesting, and research might be undertaken into how and why authors articulate the research process underpinning their writing.

The distinction between research skills, methods and methodologies is useful for understanding different aspects of the research process but it is also a distinction that is in some respects artificial since the three are interdependent, and are equally necessary to the successful completion of a research project. Without the skills to read medieval script, it is not possible to do any work on such scripts. A researcher may want to understand the theatre-going history of a particular group of people but without a proper understanding of how to conduct interviews may not get the data necessary for the project. The skills, methods and methodology employed will thus determine the focus and outcome of a research project.

INTRODUCING RESEARCH METHODS

This volume, as is common in writing on research methods, is divided into chapters, each focusing on a particular research method. They are intended to serve as an introduction to the issues involved in employing that particular method. They therefore offer reflections on the related skills, different ways of using a given method, methodological considerations underpinning the method in question, and some comments on the limitations of that method. Carolyn Steedman's chapter on 'Archival Methods' (Chapter 2) includes practical advice, such as the need for pencils in archives (do not come with just a biro – because you may not be allowed to use it) and the smallest handbag possible (likewise, bags are not usually allowed in). It also includes methodological reflections on the nature of archives, and on the fact that the agenda underlying their establishment will be different from the agendas of the researchers visiting them; and method-related reflections such as the incompleteness of any archive, and the search for the 'lost' object within these. All of these points influence the outcome of using archival methods to conduct research: for instance, understanding the incompleteness of archives impacts on what other archives or sources one decides to draw on to 'complete' (if this is ever possible) the information one has. Similarly, understanding the reason why an archive was established helps one to assess its contents: for example, the desire to preserve a particular memory of a specific person may lead to the destruction – not necessarily immediately evident to the researcher – of all materials (letters, diaries and so on) that detract from the particular memory the archive is intended to preserve.

Such incompleteness also haunts those who use auto/biographical research methods either to write an auto/biography or as part of their research on a particular person or text/s. Chapter 3, by Mary Evans, concentrates on auto/biographical research methods for the purpose of writing such auto/biographies.

It provides a brief historical overview of changes in auto/biographical writing from the nineteenth to the twentieth century, and focuses intensely on the methodological considerations that inform the idea of the subject (as individual, as part of a collective) in different kinds of auto/biographical writing. It further analyses the ways in which auto/biographical methods are underpinned by specific perspectives on those depicted, revealing the 'fantasies' of their authors both about themselves and about others. Evans discusses some of the many biographies of Sylvia Plath to reveal the particularities of their authors' position that emerge in these volumes, highlighting the way in which notions of auto/biography have shifted from an idea of presenting '*the* truth' about someone to portraying '*a* truth' – one of many possible readings.

This understanding of the partiality of research findings (which is not particular to the conduct of auto/biographical research but applies to all forms of research) has, in some disciplines, led to a discussion of what constitutes 'good' research. Auto/biographies, for instance, are often slated by critics – when they are criticised – for their incompleteness, for failures to include certain kinds of information or omissions of research (see the beginning of Chapter 10 in this volume for one such example). In the (hard/natural) sciences, criteria such as verifiability of data (can one independently produce the same results?), falsifiability (can the results be proved wrong?), reliability (can the results be independently reproduced time and again?), generalisibility (is what is found true of all texts/people belonging to the category for which claims are made?) have been invoked to establish whether or not something constitutes 'good' research. But the nature of much research in English studies, and, indeed, a changing climate in our understanding of what research can and cannot do or be, has increasingly led to the interrogation of the validity and appropriateness of those criteria (for example, Gergen and Gergen 2003; Peräkylä 1997; Phillips and Jørgensen 2002: 182–212) which are, in any event, clearly not equally applicable across all research and knowledge domains. Instead, writers on research methods increasingly invoke criteria such as plausibility (how persuasive are a set of findings to a given community of readers?), reflexivity (how much awareness of the particularities of the research process and its impacts on the findings are articulated by the author?), and comprehensiveness (how extensive and exhaustive was the research conducted?) to evaluate what constitutes 'good' research (for example, Hollway and Jefferson 2000; Smith and Deemer 2003).

These are useful criteria to bear in mind, not least in undertaking oral history projects, discussed in Chapter 4, where information provided by interviewees has to be triangulated with other evidence to understand the workings of personal memory. Penny Summerfield utilises her experience of such projects to show how the narratives of 'ordinary' people can modify public records of events – in this instance, of women's role during the Second World War in the Home Guard. Oral history is not a method much discussed in English studies but, as Summerfield's chapter demonstrates, such histories which engage with questions of memory, narrative, culture and transmission can facilitate our understanding of events and experiences – social, cultural, literary – within living memory. Summerfield's account of the imbrication of personal memory in the reproduction of cultural narratives (revealed in one of her interviewee's critical engagement, through the lens of her own experiences, with the popular television programme *Dad's Army*) suggests the possibilities for English studies of the use of oral history as a means of understanding the workings of, for example, literary and cultural phenomena in and on people's imagination.

Like oral history, visual methods are not much discussed in English studies although visual signs are, perhaps increasingly, part of our cultural world. As Gillian Rose suggests in Chapter 5, such signs – in the form of illuminations of manuscripts, graphic novels, the photographs that accompany W. G. Sebald's acclaimed novels and that invariably form part of auto/biographies, for instance – produce a rich visual world as an integral aspect of literature. Yet we tend either to ignore them or to treat them in a positivistic manner as if their meanings were self-evident and required no specific engagement. Rose details three different ways in which visual signs might be approached methodologically: namely via compositional interpretation, semiology and discourse analysis. She argues that these different approaches draw attention to diverse aspects of visual images such as the detail of the image itself and its context of production and/or reproduction, and thus suggest new avenues of research for English studies. She also, importantly, points out that visual images do not only accompany texts; frequently, the reverse is true: namely that texts accompany visual images, for instance as captions to photographs, explanations for exhibits in museums and galleries, or as accompaniments to images in books. Implicit in this is frequently a hierarchisation of sign systems within contemporary culture, where one sign system is privileged over another although their interplay operates to question that structure. Obvious examples of this are textual explanations in art galleries. Such sites privilege the visual image but viewers frequently bend first to read the caption, all the better to 'understand' the image. Similarly, when looking at photographs in auto/biographies, people read their captions to identify who is in the picture. That interplay between text and image, central to Rose's analysis of visual methods, is an area of research that deserves much more attention in English studies research.

In discussing discourse analysis as a method for exploring visual material, Rose draws on Michel Foucault's notion of discourse as a form of discipline that produces subjects. Visual images, such as signs in libraries telling us to turn off mobile phones and not to smoke, effect such disciplining, thus constructing us as particular subjects. Rose argues that discourse analysis can be used as a research method to show how images construct specific views of the world. The same is true of the use of discourse analysis for textual interpretations. Chapter 6 suggests that discourse analysis simultaneously references a theory of language, namely of language as *invested*, and a method for researching written and oral language as it is actually used. Discourse analysis, especially the variety known as critical discourse analysis, is centrally concerned with analysing patterns in language use in order to uncover the workings of ideology or investment within/through it, and thus to be able to resist it. As is the case with other research methods, discourse analysis entails selection of focus – we may, for instance, concentrate on the verb forms used in a given text in order to highlight how that text constructs agency. In this sense, the discourse analysis of any given text is never complete.

One way in which discourse analysis may be conducted is with the use of computer programs; Chapter 6 provides a brief introduction to the possibilities of discourse analysis with the help of relevant software, commenting both on its possibilities and its limitations. Computer-aided discourse analysis is carried out by an increasing number of researchers within English studies; it is part of the amazing IT revolution in English studies, explored in Chapter 12 in this volume, which is set to produce new, and change some of the existent, ways in which we conduct research in the discipline. It also requires a change in disposition among researchers – learning to use computer programs to conduct discourse analysis requires time and effort, something frequently not built into individuals' research plans. This, however, looks set to change with the requirements for much more explicit research training programmes for research students.

Where discourse analysis centres on language, ethnographic research methods extend that concern to cultural and social practices. In Chapter 7, Rachel Alsop offers a brief exposition of ethnographic methods and changes in understanding of those methods as a function of the recognition that ethnographic accounts constitute 'fictions' about an experience (and are thus, of course, amenable to the kinds of literary analyses to which we might subject other fictional accounts, regarding, for instance, narrative structure) and reflect particular dispositions *vis-à-vis* those written about. Alsop demonstrates that ethnographic methods inform a variety of writings that might be analysed in the context of English studies. In particular, she focuses on travel writing and the ways in which one of the key methods of ethnography – participant observation – plays a role in producing travel accounts. Alsop further engages with the recent rise in reading groups to discuss how these offer a site for ethnographic research in English studies. Audience research, too, in the theatre, cinema and at performance sites such as literature festivals, might be conducted utilising ethnographic methods to create what have become known as microethnographies. Alsop thus demonstrates the imbrication of ethnographic methods in writing that is already part of English studies, and the utility of these methods for emergent areas within the field.

Quite different opportunities are offered by the use of quantitative methods in the study of literature. In Chapter 8, Pat Hudson asks why scholars of literary texts have tended to ignore the numbers they encounter in such texts, for instance in the detailing of wealth in eighteenth-century novels, or in the use of dates in literary texts, and in connection with authors. She suggests that this is partly attributable to the different values we attach to words and numbers – crudely, viewing the former as subjective and the latter as objective. Hudson argues that this distinction is misguided, and she outlines how numbers may be used both as interpretive tools and as a means of conveying sets of information not readily producible in another form. In particular, she shows that computational methods for calculating the frequency with which certain words occur and the contexts in which they are set can act as a useful tool for interpreting the meaning of a text, and for the purposes of authorship attribution. This is especially so when one is dealing with a large body of text. Secondly, Hudson shows how statistical methods can be useful for displaying information about texts, audiences, the production and consumption of texts, and so on. Importantly, she highlights the ways in which numerical information – frequently treated by those who consider themselves numerately challenged as representing absolute values – needs to be understood as partial and as productive of very specific kinds of information. Hudson's chapter provides insights into how one might use quantitative methods in English studies and into the meaning of the information and interpretations thus produced.

Textual analysis, the focus of Catherine Belsey's chapter, is, of course, a staple of English studies research. Understanding 'textual analysis' to be about the close reading of cultural artefacts, Belsey chooses to base her empirical account of how one conducts textual analysis on a painting, Titian's *Tarquin and Lucretia*. Taking the reader through a close analysis of that work and thus laying bare her methods, Belsey highlights how textual analysis relies on other and additional research methods as well as a methodology or perspective (in this instance, a feminist and deconstructionist one) to give focus to, support and illuminate the reading one produces. Textual analysis has to be informed by background research into the context of the cultural artefact under scrutiny, the context of its production, its content and its consumption. Belsey emphasises the need for the researcher to consult original sources rather than rely on second-hand accounts in this process. She suggests that understanding meaning-making, differently understood in different historical periods and by different theoreticians, is key to undertaking textual analyses. She herself understands meaning-making as a relational process, between cultural artefact and consumer, but also between the consumer (viewer, reader) and those to whom consumers communicate the meanings they have established for a given artefact. This understanding relativises meaning; it reiterates the situatedness of knowledge, its partiality and specificity, also highlighted in other chapters in connection with other research methods.

That situatedness is equally prominent in the discussion of interviewing as a research method in Chapter 10. There I show how the representation of interviews with living authors, one of the more common kinds of interview conducted in English studies research, tends to obscure the interview process and the influences it exerts on the interview material, even as it is evident in that material. I argue that interviewing requires a series of practical skills, a clear understanding of the different kinds of interview one might conduct and their underlying assumptions, knowledge of the different ways in which interviews can be transcribed and how these constitute and influence interpretations of interview material. Interviewing as a research method often combines with, or is part of, other research methods including auto/biographical methods, ethnographic methods, oral history and, indeed, textual analysis or discourse analysis at the point where the interview material is interpreted. It thus forms a central plank of many research processes.

Whereas interviewing may be viewed as uncontentiously representing a research method, creative writing, the subject of Chapter 11, has only recently been considered in that light. The 2001 Research Assessment Exercise panel saw creative writing 'as an important element within English departments' which was 'assessed in accordance with the provision in Research Assessment Exercise 2/99, in so far as it represents "the invention and generation of ideas, images, performances where these lead to new or substantially improved insights"' (Barnard and Sherwood 2001: 1–2). Jon Cook engages with the issue of how to define creative writing as a research method *inter alia* in the light of public funding bodies' attempts to grapple with this particular issue. Across the creative arts, from creative writing to music, performance, dance, film, video and digital work, and fine art, debates are occurring about the assessment of creative work as research. In consequence, Edinburgh University Press intends to bring out a volume on this issue as part of its 'Research Methods for the Arts and Humanities' series.

To qualify as research, creative work is frequently required to be accompanied by a theoretical piece of writing, detailing the research dimension of that creative work. The articulation at meta-discursive level of how the research process underpinning creative work is embedded within it constitutes one way of establishing creative work as research. Cook takes another approach, focusing on the notion of creative writing as discovery and utilising essays by Seamus Heaney and Mark Schorer to explore the ways in which writing skills, or craft, and technique, as the means of materialising subject matter, can constitute a research method. He juxtaposes these positions with that of Denise Riley who regards writing not as active discovery but as a form of passivity before the assault of language that rushes at us from outside. A distinction emerges between the work of language and the work of the writer, resulting in creative writing as 'a mode of research into the nature of literary form and language'. Cook links this insight into the practice of re-writing as the process through which research into form takes place, (re)producing the process of discovery at every draft. He ends by relating this process to the need for reading as the activity which informs writing as discovery both of content and form. His assertion that these inter-related processes and activities can be documented and critically analysed – that is, a meta-narrative about the research process informing creative activity can be derived from these – is an important contribution to the question of how to understand creative writing as a research method.

Like Jon Cook, Harold Short and Marilyn Deegan tread on relatively new ground in their chapter on 'ICT as a Research Method' (Chapter 12). ICT methods in English studies are a relatively recent phenomenon, to date still mainly carried out by specialist researchers in particular fields of textual analysis and in linguistics. However, as Short and Deegan make clear, the advent of more and more computer software and hardware, which is also becoming easier to use, has greatly enhanced opportunities for researchers in literary studies to work on literary and other texts. Short and Deegan offer a brief history of textual computing, and then discuss the various ways in which ICT has been used to store and analyse literary texts. They discuss the issues involved in creating digital archives of manuscript sources, and provide information about some of the most interesting literature digitisation projects and what these involve. They analyse how computers as a medium change our relations to texts, and the implications that this has for literary criticism, for theories of the text and for interactions with texts, including interactions in the area of scholarly editions where new possibilities of conducting research have been opened up by digital media. Importantly, Chapter 12 highlights the implications of this for possibilities of collaborative research. Like all other contributors to this volume, Short and Deegan offer an extensive reading list for readers who want to pursue the issue of ICT as a research method.

Altogether then, this volume represents an attempt to engage research students, as well as researchers and research methods teachers in English studies, with a broad range of research methods relevant to and practised in the study of English, particularly of work from the nineteenth and twentieth centuries. Inevitably there are areas of research practice not covered in this volume. These include, for instance, textual editing, on which Edinburgh University Press intends to publish a separate volume as part of its 'Research Methods for the Arts and Humanities' series. However, as the explosion of volumes on research methods in the social sciences during the past fifteen years or so has shown, no single volume can do justice to all the possible research methods one might utilise in a given discipline, or all the ways in which these might be understood.

Indeed, in relation to that explosion of research methods texts in the social sciences, a point came up as a matter of debate in several conversations I had about this volume with scholars of English. Some expressed the view that the demand for explicit research methods training, inaugurated by the AHRB as part of becoming a research council, was a backdoor, and erroneous, form of scientisation of humanities subjects including literary studies since it relied on a social sciences model – derived from the ESRC's research training requirements – which was inappropriate for the humanities. I found this argument unconvincing since the 'cultural turn' in the social sciences, as any perusal of 'research methods' catalogues by publishers such as Sage or Blackwell will show, has led to an extensive appropriation within the social sciences of research methods entirely derived from the humanities, a fact that surprisingly has gone largely unremarked upon by the humanities community itself. Thus, instead of thinking of research methods as an alien graft upon humanities disciplines, we should proudly be reclaiming those methods, and making them more explicitly our own. We should also recognise that such reclamation will aid dialogue and collaboration across disciplines, and will encourage researchers to think divergently about the kinds of research they might engage in. It was in this spirit that I chose, for this volume, to work with a group of distinguished contributors, each one an authority in her or his field and subject, from across a range of disciplinary backgrounds, but all with a profound and research-explicit interest in culture and literature. Their contributions are intended to open up the debates we have yet to have within the field of English studies about the research methods we use and what these signify.

REFERENCES

Arts and Humanities Research Board (AHRB) (2002), *Postgraduate Review*, at http://www.ahrb.ac.uk/strategy/pgreview.htm

Barnard, John and Jane Sherwood (2001), *Overview Report of the RAE 2001 English Language and Literature Panel*, at http://www.hero.ac.uk/rae/overview/

Eliot, Simon and W. R. Owens (eds) (1998), *A Handbook to Literary Research*, London: Routledge.

Forster, Margaret (1995), *Hidden Lives: A Family Memoir*, London: Penguin.

Gergen, Mary M. and Kenneth J. Gergen (2003), 'Qualitative inquiry: tensions and transformations', in Norman K. Denzin and Yvonna S. Lincoln (eds), *The Landscape of Qualitative Research*, London: Sage, pp. 575–610.

Hollway, Wendy and Tony Jefferson (2000), *Doing Qualitative Research Differently*, London: Sage.

Peräkylä, Anssi (1997), 'Reliability and validity in research based on naturally occurring social interaction', in D. Silverman (ed.), *Qualitative Research: Theory, Method and Practice*, London: Sage, pp. 283–304.

Phillips, Louise and Marianne Jørgensen (eds) (2002), *Discourse Analysis as Theory and Method*, London: Sage.

Smith, John K. and Deborah K. Deemer (2003), 'The problem of criteria in the age of relativism', in Norman K. Denzin and Yvonna S. Lincoln (eds), *Collecting and Interpreting Qualitative Materials*, 2nd edn, Thousand Oaks: Sage, pp. 427–57.

Williams, Sadie (2003), *Postgraduate Training in Research Methods: Current Practice and Future Needs in English*, London: English Subject Centre, Royal Holloway College.

NOTES

1. Eliot and Owens' (1998) *Handbook to Literary Research*, designed to accompany the Open University's MA in Literature, is one of the very few books that has appeared on the subject.

2. It should be pointed out that the rapidly increasing sophistication of computer software and the introduction of programs such as Masterfile and Endnote, designed to enable the production of large documents such as theses and books with automatically generated lists of contents, indexes and so on on the one hand, and bibliographies on the other, means that both practising academics and research students need updating and training in the use of these advanced technologies. Many academics still tend to use their computers as a superior form of typewriter – a function of the moment when they entered the computer age. As someone whose first computer was the earliest Amstrad, onto which one had to load the software program every time one wanted to use the computer, and which had no footnote/endnote facilities, never mind anything like the sophisticated software now standard issue with all computers, I am keenly aware of the discrepancy between technologies available in the 1970s and 1980s and those available now to aid research.

3. See the English Subject Centre's report on *Postgraduate Training in Research Methods* (Williams 2003), para 4.1.1 on the rejection of that terminology.

4. According to the 2001 Research Assessment Exercise English panel's 'Overview Report' (Barnard and Sherwood), eighty-nine institutions submitted a total of 1,526 full-time equivalent numbers of staff to Unit 50.

5. The report is viewable on the AHRB's website www.ahrb.ac.uk

6. One of the frequent complaints about the ESRC research training requirements is that, at Masters level, they are so extensive that they leave little room for the substantive content of a given Masters course and that they are too heavily weighted in favour of quantitative methods which many social scientists do not routinely employ.

7. View at http://www.ahrb.ac.uk/strategy/pgreview.html

8. Thus, the 2001 RAE English panel's Criteria and Working Methods stated: '3.41.3 The Panel recognises that English includes a very broad range of approaches and is by its nature frequently interdisciplinary, and it will take a broad view of what constitutes English. Where appropriate to the assessment process it will consult with other relevant Panels when submissions span the boundary between two or more Units of Assessment' (see www.hefce.ac.uk).

9. It is also a function of long histories of disciplinisation which engage in active boundary patrols regarding their domains. When I recently submitted a research leave application centring entirely on the work of women playwrights to panel 7, 'Music and Performing Arts', Subject Drama and Theatre Studies, of the AHRB, I was advised to resubmit the proposal to panel 3, 'English Language and Literature', because my research was text- rather than performance-based, despite being focused entirely on contemporary theatre

work. Irrespective of the relative merit of my application, it is interesting to note that this advice constitutes research-method based policing of disciplinary boundaries where it is not so much what you work on, but how you work on it, which determines your categorisation for funding purposes.

10. This is evident both in publishers' catalogues on 'Literature' and in definitions of the discipline as they emerge in assessment criteria in exercises such as the Research Assessment Exercise (RAE) and the Teaching Quality Assurance exercise (TQA).

CHAPTER 2

Archival Methods

Carolyn Steedman, University of Warwick

INTRODUCTION

A rchives and 'the archive' now have a wider range of meanings and potential meanings attached to them than they have had at any point since the
inauguration of European and North American state archives in the early nineteenth century.[1] There is, for a start, Jacques Derrida's compelling philosophy
of the archive in *Mal d'archive* (1995) in which the *arke* of the Greek city state
is named as the place where things begin, where power originates, with power's
workings inextricably and for all time, bound up with the authority of beginnings, origins, starting points.[2] Those who make their way through Derrida's
Archive Fever will discover how much the modern allure of the archive is to do
with a Freudian romance, of finding all the lost things and names, whatever
they may be: things gone astray, mislaid, squandered, wasted. They will also
discover a great deal about what they are doing when they sit down with pencil
in hand (always, always a pencil, never a pen!) before the first folder of literary
papers called up to the British Library Manuscript Reading Room, or in the
uneasy graciousness of the space set aside for you in some country house, where
a box of letters and jottings for a novel, old newspaper clippings and a disap-
pointingly blank appointment diary may allow you some new access to the
writer you are pursuing.[3] This private collection will have been difficult to track
down, and its existence may be quite unknown to the National Register of
Archives.[4] If it is catalogued, that was perhaps done by the son of the house,
home from university during one long hot summer, eighty years ago, and is
obfuscating rather than helpful (he was certainly not interested in what you are
interested in now). The *politesses* required of the researcher working on private
papers, to which she as a citizen has absolutely no right of access at all, are as
draining of emotional and intellectual energy as anything in that box that might
have to be transcribed . . .

Meanwhile, far away from the philosophical shores of the archive, and even further from this entirely imaginary country house muniment room, the education system has extended the meaning of 'archive'. A class of eight-year-olds, set to do a local history project, will learn to call the tape-recordings of older people who used to work at the bottle factory, little bits and pieces of memorabilia, postcards and photocopies of a ration book, and their own drawing of how they imagine the bottle factory to have been in 1955, an archive. A bundle of your own love letters, a record sleeve and the bus ticket that took you to the first, momentous encounter all make up your own, personal archive.

The allure of the archive for the novelist,[5] however, has not been in that informal sense, established (in the UK at least) through the school curriculum in history and creative writing. José Saramago, in *All the Names* (1997), and Ismail Kadere, in *The Palace of Dreams* (1981), have explored the more sinister implications of the historical proposition, that public archives were a first building block of the modern nation state and national identity.[6] Their interest is in registration, naming, cataloguing and archivisation as an aspect of totalitarianism. Both of them describe the character of an archivist – made through authority, rigid job specification, personal timidity – and the tragedy of believing that an archive contains everything there is to know or that might be knowable. Martha Cooley's *The Archivist* (1998) has as its hero the 'grey-mustached warden of the obscure Mason Room', the papers he presides over 'housed in a guest wing of the main (university) library'.[7] His archive and its 'objects of desire' (particularly for graduate students of literature) is 'among the finest anywhere' says Matthias Lane, 'and I am its guardian'. Being North American, and the hero of an archival romance quite different from the Freudian one (this is, in fact, a Romance in the Archive), we should not expect him to express political principle or political analysis, as Saramago's and Kadere's archivists do; but the self-characterisation as 'the unavoidable keeper of countless objects of desire' is interesting for those who have worked on literary papers (the object of desire in this case is a collection of T. S. Eliot's letters) in special collections rooms of university libraries on both sides of the Atlantic. Régine Robert has discussed this literary fascination with archives and archivists as a function of modern memory, in *La Mémoire saturée* (2003).[8] And behind all this contemporary interest in archives and their gate-keepers, probably lies Michel Foucault's poetics of these places and spaces and regimes: his suggestion of their magical quality. The magic is the way in which archives reflect, 'show us quite simply, and in shadow, what all those in the foreground are looking at'.[9]

None of this is very much help with archival method – how you go about things in different kinds of archive, what you do with what you take away – even though these novelists and philosophers offer a fine prolegomenon to, and a form of preparation for, visiting the archive for the first time. Historians like myself believe the archive to be our very own place, and there are important professional rites of passage attached to our first trip to the Public Record Office, one of the West Yorkshire Archive Service offices, or to the private records of Arsenal Football Club. But although we believe it to be our very own place, there is, in the pragmatic, pseudo-positivist way of the profession, an extreme reluctance to talk about what we do there as a method, or possessing a methodology. A framework for what follows here is that – of course! – we do possess a methodology, and that there might be something to learn from the historian's habitual way of going about things. A second framework must be the acknowledgement that most of the readers of this chapter will belong to disciplines other than history, and to the field of literary studies in particular. Other disciplines in the human and social sciences have contemplated the use of archives by non-historians, and they are a good starting place for those intending to base their research in one. There are two articles, both called 'Historical Research', in collections addressed to social work students and researchers, for example.[10] In both pieces, students of social policy are told about the purpose of history and its importance: that there was a past and that it was important for the phenomenon under their scrutiny; they are told that they can find traces of that past (and very correctly, about the fragmentary, incomplete nature of those traces) in various kinds of repositories and archives. They must go to them with a series of questions, and there they must collect information, either by note-taking, transcription or photocopying. Then they must analyse. This is all very sensible and important advice. The oddness for the historian reading this comes from finding something so obvious called a method/ology. Historians have this feeling every time they apply to the Economic and Social Research Council (ESRC) for funding, and have to call checking train times and opening hours, the sleepless nights in cheap hotels, and the boredom of evenings in an English county town . . . calling all of that something as elevated as a 'method/ology'. And you also feel edgy perhaps, because of the unquestioned connection of historical practice with archival work. As I point out at the beginning of *Dust*, many – perhaps most – historians simply do not use the classic archive that is figured in these instructions, which do not mention oral history, film, the novel, newspaper sources, nor all sorts of visual representation, as archive material. Most historians (if you put them together and measure them by the yard, on a universal scale) never set foot in a state archive, nor a local record office.[11] But anyone visiting an archive for the first time needs all the advice that a historian would give to her MA students and first-year PhD students, about asking questions to do with the origins and purposes of the documents they are consulting (Who collected them, and why? What are they doing there?). We can give good advice about how to survey and manage a large file, about how you manage your time (for time is money in the archive: the sooner you leave the county town you have had to visit in order to do your research, the sooner you can stop spending it); about how you take notes, and why you might decide to transcribe rather than photocopy. Many of these questions are to do with how to read and write in an archive, and they are discussed below under the headings 'Romance and Ritual' and 'Reality'. In these observations, I appear to be designing a graduate course, open to all comers in the social, human and literary sciences, to be called 'Archival Methods'! That is the best way of reading what follows.

ROMANCE AND RITUAL

My book *Dust* was about the historian's archival romance. I mean romance in the general sense, and as an aspect – a long-enduring one – of European Romanticism. Jules Michelet, whose extraordinary accounts of communing with the dead, making them live again, in the Archives Nationales and in the lonely nights in which he wrote his histories of France, was the first historian-child of the Romantic movement, though there were many others whose accounts of archival practice in the nineteenth century would be worth reading.[12] What Michelet wrote about breathing in the dust of the dead and making them live as they had never really done before through such an act of incorporation, is the focal point of my book. He also provided its title. Knowing about Michelet, and understanding what it was he did, gives direct access to the assumptions of resurrectionist historians, all the way through to E. P. Thompson and beyond. It was by reading Michelet that I first understood history-writing in generic terms, as a form of magical realism, with the historian's contribution not the mountains that move, the girls that fly, the rivers that run backwards, but the everyday and prosaic act of making the dead walk and talk. Seeing the very particular things that historians have taken away from archives, and the particular kinds of narrative forms they have produced from their material, may be a way of understanding all the other things that might be done, and that might be written, out of the archive.

Then there is romance in another meaning, in an earlier sense, as in chivalric romance, as in the sense of the quest: endurance of all kinds of trial and tribulation in pursuit of some goal or grail. Bonnie Smith has written well and engagingly about nineteenth-century historians, each of them seeing the documents they were pursuing as so many sleeping princesses, waiting for the historian/knight to awaken and release them.[13] *The Gender of History* also forces its readers to confront the idea that there may be differences between men's and women's archival romance, and in this way makes the historian more aware of what kind of social and psychological practice going to the archives actually is. If I were running a seminar on or designing a graduate course on Archives and Archival Method (which is what I seem to be doing in this chapter), then

Michelet and Smith would be required reading. And I would add the work of the modern historian who has written more explicitly about these questions than anybody else: Natalie Davis's *Fiction in the Archives* and her several versions of the Martin Guerre story.[14] Then I would ask students to find traces of the romance of endurance and quest in the Prefaces and Introductions of the most purblind of modern empiricist historians (though I would not make them pause too long over them). The *form* the romance takes in these works will be in the number of archivists thanked, the number of remote and obscure repositories visited, the length and detail of entries under the Primary Sources heading in the Bibliography, the hint of difficult journeys, uncomfortable beds, terrible food, loneliness . . . which I will come to when I get to reality.

I would ask all who were to use any kind of archive to think hard about the idea of *finding things*: about loss, the search for what has been lost, the dream of finding it, and of plenitude. This powerfully informing idea of Western modernity is connected to nostalgia, and to the idea of 'the might-have-been', a structure of feeling and cognition that has been most tellingly explored in film and literary studies. As a way of getting to grips with this large topic, I would suggest they read Jean Laplanche's *Life and Death in Psychoanalysis*, or at least the sections that deal with the task of psychoanalysis in finding that which cannot be found (what cannot be found?: something that happened, is now gone, and is no more).[15] It cannot be found partly because the very search for it alters it as an object. Laplanche has commented on the search, revealed in psychoanalytic practice, for the lost object. He discusses the way in which, through the processes of displacement and repression, the object sought is bound to be 'not the lost [one], but a substitute'. Students could read some Freud, perhaps a relatively straightforward account of the unconscious (the *Dreams* book might be the best here); or maybe, 'A Fragment of an Analysis of a Case of Hysteria', where Freud (analyst, narrator, historian of Dora's deeply unattractive family and social circle) makes the inchoate fragments of a story into something that may – with luck (but then Dora did not have luck) – last a while. And that is not, cannot possibly be, 'true'.[16] In *Strange Dislocations*, I discussed psychoanalysis, modern academic history and childhood (the idea of childhood) as emerging together in the long nineteenth century as cognate ways of thinking and feeling.[17] So I might even make students read some of that book. I would certainly be interested in having them read Donald Winnicott. He wrote within the long European tradition, perhaps inaugurated by Friedrich von Schiller, of trying to understand those situations in which people are free, in a kind of suspension between the constraints of external and interior dictates and compulsions. What twentieth-century theorists like Winnicott did was to locate the genesis of this cultural form in childhood, but it was conceptualised as a way of being in the world long before the 1950s.

Play has long been understood not just as something children do, but as a form of cultural experience that is to do with the capacity to be alone. As Winnicott so movingly described it, this aloneness is paradoxically dependent on the presence of someone else. When he attempted a theoretical statement of his many discussions of this point he made it in developmental terms and wrote about the child reaching 'the stage of being alone in the presence of someone . . .' This someone is 'reliable', is available and continues to be available when remembered after being forgotten. This person is felt to 'reflect back what happens in playing'. Then a 'near-withdrawal state' can be achieved by children, 'akin to the *concentration* of adults'. It is useful then, he claimed, 'to think of a third area of human living, one neither inside the individual nor outside in the world of shared reality. This intermediate living can be thought of as occupying a potential space, negating the idea of space and separation'.[18] Winnicott called this *potential space* the place of 'cultural experience'. He had his anxieties about the term 'culture' and his inability to define it much beyond saying it was 'the inherited tradition . . . something in the common pool of humanity, into which individuals and groups of people may contribute, and from which we may all draw *if we have somewhere to put what we find*'. In the archive, in the silence that we can make speak, many historians have discovered that they do have somewhere to put what they find. I am interested above all in understanding the cultural activity of historical research (and to a lesser extent) historical writing, as formative of this way of thinking and feeling. And outside its walls, has history not become the place where, quite ordinarily and by remembering, we can find the things where we have, in fact, already put them?

In this way, and through this reading, my hypothetical graduate students would thus, I hope, develop a greater awareness of what *they* believe the past is: what kind of thing it is, in their imagination, a thing gone and irretrievable, and yet of course existing, with absence – or gone-ness – as its very condition. We might then formalise this individual, visceral sense of pastness, by paying some attention to Paul Ricoeur's *Time and Narrative*, and his philosophic attention to the ways in which historians have narrativised absence into presence, and into time.[19]

My students may acquire nothing from all of this, except a phenomenology of the archive, and a series of sociologically interesting insights into what some historians do in archives and what they believe they are doing (though this phenomenology may help them acquire an understanding of what it is *they* do, when they finally get there). On this point, and as a bridging text from romance to reality, is W. H. Auden's 'Homage to Clio'.[20] The poet writes about the Muse of History as a blank-faced girl, present when anything happens, anything at all, at any time, but with absolutely nothing to say: after being 'brought face to face' with Clio's silence, 'nothing is easy.' I would find this the easiest way of establishing what 'history' is . . . a narrative form, unique to modernity, a form of thinking and a form of feeling . . . that which gets done *after the archive*, where there is nothing but fragments, traces, little bits of flotsam; where the past does not live. It lives only in the head of the historian.

I would approach the practical questions of how you read and write in the archive via a more metaphysical question, about the kind of writing that gets produced – by historians at least – when you have left the archive. I would like to establish that the formal, modern, academic history (a PhD thesis, the latest account of the Siege of Stalingrad; an account of T. S. Eliot's relationship with his wife and thus – *pace* Martha Cooley – his poetry) makes reference to . . . Everything. It seems probable that history cannot work as either cognition or narrative without the assumption, on the part of the writer and the reader, that somewhere there is the great story, that contains everything there is and ever has been – 'visits home, heartbeats, a first kiss, the jump of an electron from one orbital position to another', as well as the desolate battlefield, the ruined village – from which the smaller story, the one before your eyes now, has simply been extracted.[21] Robert Berkhoffer called this 'the Great Story'.[22] He remarks that

> Although historians may be wary of Great Stories . . . it seems they cannot do without them. Their histories need the larger and largest contexts that Great Stories provide, especially if the Great Past is conceived of as the Great(est) Context of all stories, small and Great.

REALITY

This observation marks my move from romance – or metaphysics – to reality, but I would start here with something like a novel. I would have us all read V. S. Naipaul's *A Way in the World*, which so elegantly introduces the first question you ask of an archive, long before you get to it. What is it? Who made it? And for what purpose? In his odd and moving autobiography (which is also a history of the southern Caribbean and of the first South American Revolution), Naipaul describes his first job, the one he took between leaving school and leaving Trinidad, in Register House in Port of Spain: the tedious clerkdom of a state servant making lists, filling in registers, recording what a census enumerator has collected, the way in which so many archives were brought into being.[23] Later, he describes actually using this archive, as a non-historian, part of that vast majority of archive users, seeking a replacement birth certificate (or, a century and a half ago, a duplicate bill of sale for a slave). This kind of question (How was it formed? How is it funded?) is a fundamental one; Naipaul's book helps you to make this point (and moreover the book has interesting things to say about the function of recording and registration in postcolonial identity and the accounts that are written of this).

There are no novels – none that I know – that deliver the hard practical advice that graduate students need before they set off. The advice is to do with reading and writing; with planning and organisation: to phone or email ahead of time, to discover the particularities of the archive such as its times of opening and closing, what you can take in with you (only the tiniest bag will be allowed in most of them); with wearing clothes you do not care about, for most record offices are filthy places.[24] Archives are also the coldest places you will ever sit in: atmospheric conditions most suitable for the preservation of paper and parchment are rather cold for human beings, and something warm needs to be packed.[25] More advice is needed: about where to stay, and about *what to do when the archive shuts* at 5.00. The long, dreary evenings of a provincial town . . . I advise the movies (but there may not be a cinema closer than the multiplex out on a bypass or motorway, for which you need a car) and a stack of novels. I think these considerations are possibly more pressing for women, who may not feel an evening brooding over a pint in the Dog and Duck is the option for them.

In the archive, what and how do you read? There is a practical and a romantic answer to that one. The important thing is not to be overwhelmed by the huge, unmapped contents of a large file. I tell students that once they have called a file up from the stack (and, yes, I forgot the advice about your rhythm of sending for documents, always filling in another call slip as you return something, so that you have the maximum number you are allowed on the go). Once you have something huge on the table before you, do not read: survey the thing; work your way through with some rapidity, noting what you will come back to and read. Give yourself a deadline for doing this. Take a little break by exploring the vagaries of the card catalogue and the hand-lists. Be creative in your keywords: there may be something there that you did not know about, if you look for 'diaries' under 'accounts' or 'domestic servants' under 'labour'.

The metaphysical answer to the question 'how do I read in the archive' is, for me, to do with the epistolary: the theory of the epistolary, as it has been developed by literary scholars over the last thirty years or so. Contrast the letter (the purloined letter, the letter lost, the letter gone astray, the letter read by someone who is not its addressee) with the novel.[26] In the paradigmatic literary form of modernity, you are the intended reader. Samuel Richardson may not have known about me personally; but in *Pamela* (1740) he wrote words intended to be read by someone like me. But the historian is always the reader of an unintended, purloined letter. The archive *forces* a practice of reading that may be called epistolary. When you read in an archive, you nearly always read something not intended for your eyes: you are the reader impossible-to-be imagined by the writer from two centuries ago, making her notes and jottings, or by the seventeenth-century schoolboy parsing his Corderius in a commonplace book. The vestryman recording an allowance of 6d a week in bread to a poor woman, the merchant manufacturer's wife listing the payments-in-kind to her serving maid (silk ribbons, a pair of stays, a hat-box) in Haworth in 1794 had no one like you in mind at all.[27] Productive and extraordinary as is Derrida's concept of the *carte-postale* (the idea of the relationship between language and truth that 'La Carte-postale' explores), as messages gone astray, messages not sent in the first place, or unread because you cannot see them for looking at them, as in Poe's 'Purloined Letter', none of it gives insight (indeed, it was not meant to give insight) into the message that was never a message to start with, never sent, and never sent to the scholar now, this minute, reading entries in a ledger, names on a list.[28] The gentry wife who pushed a recipe for Banbury cheese that she had just acquired from her so-called footman into her commonplace book, the justice's clerk wearily transcribing yet another life story told as settlement examination, had nothing like you in mind at all. Moreover, there in the archive, you are reading for what is *not there*, as well as what is. You – whatever your field or topic actually is – will become, just for a moment, a social historian, attentive to the silences and absences of the documents. Jacques Rancière claims that it was Jules Michelet who first formulated the proper subject of history, and the subject of this kind of reading: all the numberless, unnoticed *miserabiles personae* who had lived and died, as mute in the grave as they had been in life.[29]

If the scholar in the archive is reading some kind of purloined letter, no matter what is actually on the table before them, there is much work to demonstrate that the activity is an erotic one as well. Links between the epistolary and the erotic, which have been made since classical antiquity, certainly add another dimension to the historian's archival romance. The purloined letter stands in for anything that you might be reading; the letter – so intimately connected to the body, so easily opened by the wrong hand, misread, misplaced, torn, lost.[30] Certainly, the ways of reading that you are forced into in archives have something to do with the same dislocations of time that the epistolary stands in for. José Saramago suggests this well in *All the Names*, where an official report rather than a letter is the subject of the plot. The humble clerk who has laboured a lifetime in the state archive that holds the vast records of all the living and all the dead is compelled by a chance encounter with one random, insignificant record card, to pursue one Unknown Woman, not at first through the paper catacombs of the dead, but out in the streets, shops and schools of the capital city. He breaks into the Unknown Woman's former school to find details that the Central Registry does not hold, falling severely ill in the process. The suspicious Chief Registrar orders the Registry nurse to visit him, and curiously it is this relative outsider – not an archivist, not a labourer in the archive – who tells what happens to time in the documents stored in the archive (perhaps what happens to all writing that gets filed away and thus becomes a record). The nurse is contemplating the official report he will have to write about Senhor José's knee, damaged in the midnight clamber up the school wall:

What report, Mine, I can't see a few simple grazes can be significant enough to be mentioned in a report. Even the simplest graze is significant, Once mine have healed they'll leave nothing but a few small scars that will disappear in time, Ah, yes, wounds heal over on the body, but in the report they always stay open, they neither close up nor disappear.[31]

What you read in the archive is in that eternal, open moment.

And the writing you do in archives? I always recommend transcription, knowing full well that I really do not ever read properly the photocopies I take away; and I like the amount of thinking I get done, when letting someone else's words move through my head and hand and onto my own bit of paper, or my own computer screen. That is how I commune with the dead. It is advice that goes against all I have to say about saving time and money in the archive, but there you are. The advice about a method of recording, the organisation of notes and the classification of them *as you go along* and always, always making a full reference (so you do not have to go back, to check that it was PT 23/1b and not PT 23/1c) is less contradictory. And all reading and writing in the archive has to be done with the knowledge of what is not there – that these are tiny pieces of flotsam, floating on the great dark limitless river of Everything. For an extremely illuminating example of a novelist learning how to read an archive and how to tame the information it contains, there is nothing better, it seems to me, than Gabriel García Márquez's postscript to *The General in His Labyrinth*, his novel about Símon Bolivar's last and terrible journey to the Caribbean coast of Nueva Granada in 1830.[32] The novelist describes the information overload he experienced in the course of his research for the book. You wade through a swamp of historical facts that swarm and sting and itch, above and below the water line. They itch and sting because they have no meaning yet assigned to them; they are blind and deaf in their assault on your person, and they make you numb with panic, too. García Márquez had the advantage of a 'literary audacity' that determined him to 'recount a tyrannically documented life without renouncing the extravagant prerogatives of the novel', and only the last few weeks of that life, to boot; he also had friendly historians at the end of a telephone line to give him 'a first inkling of a method for investigating and ordering facts' (the brilliantly simple stalwart of the file card system); I hope that some of his professional informants also told him how unlucky he was, to have so very, very much.

At the end of it all, after these reams of advice about going to the archive (which historians are happy to hand out at the drop of a hat and over the telephone; it is, after all, our own, very special place) you have to discuss loneliness, which is what I think I have been doing all along. There is the loneliness already mentioned, pacing the deserted streets of the county town, until you can go and eke out time in Pizza Express. But there is also this most moving and peculiar way of being in the world, which is all I have been describing. One early reviewer of the historian Richard Cobb compared his 'arriving in the small French provincial town, looking round the cafés before proceeding to the archives, to Maigret putting his nose to the wind and getting the feel of the place'. And then: 'It is deeply moving to find him [Cobb] quoting Georges Lefebvre's feeling that the supreme satisfaction was that of untying the string on the bundles of archives in the attic of the village *mairie*'.[33] Those who have known that very deep pleasure will want others to know it too. The pleasure is the extraordinary kind of aloneness that emerges in the archive. In his *Second Identity*, Cobb pondered the historical subject who was most interesting to him:

> the individual unrelated to any group, the man, the girl, or the old
> woman alone in the city, the person who eats alone, though in company,
> who lives in a furnished room, who receives no mail, who has no visible
> occupation, and who spends much time wandering the streets.[34]

And then he made the act of identification that we know is there to be made, saying that the historian's main problem 'is that of loneliness, especially loneliness in the urban context'. He then went on to discuss in some detail his fondness for the *chronique judiciaire* of *Le Monde*, which provided him with modern examples of the desperation, madness and aloneness that mark his favourite historical subjects and he, himself, the historian. Aloneness, and the company of the dead we should note, is the very great privilege of the archive researcher.

This chapter has done several things: told something of what scholars and researchers do, and can do, in archives, and of that strange practice of modernity, perhaps inaugurated by historians, and how it is extended to scholars in other fields of enquiry. For myself, I have begun to design a course, called 'Archives and Archival Practice'. Together, they may constitute something like 'Archival Methods'.

NOTES

1. For the inauguration of European state archives, see Jacques Le Goff (1992), *History and Memory*, New York: Columbia University Press, pp. 87–9; Jules Michelet [1835] (1971), 'Rapport au Ministre de l'Instruction Publique sur les Bibliothèques et Archives des Départements du Sud-Ouest de la France', in *Oeuvres Complètes*, volume IV, Paris: Flammarion, pp. 536–63; K. Pomian (1992), 'Les archives', in Pierre Nora, *Les Lieux de mémoire, sous la direction de Pierre Nora*, volume III, *Les France. 3. De l'archive à l'emblème*, Paris: Gallimard, pp. 163–233; Philippa Levine (1986), *The Amateur and the Professional. Antiquaries, Historians and Archeologists in Victorian Britain, 1838–1886*, Cambridge: Cambridge University Press, pp. 100–19.

2. Jacques Derrida (1995), 'Archive Fever. A Freudian Impression', *Diacritics*, 25: 2, pp. 9–63; Jacques Derrida (1995), *Mal d'archive: Une impression freudienne*, Paris: Editions Galilée; Jacques Derrida (1996), *Archive Fever: A Freudian Impression*, trans. Eric Prenowitz, Chicago: University of Chicago Press. For a not-entirely-serious account of 'real' Archive Fever, see Carolyn Steedman (1992), *Dust*, Manchester: Manchester University Press, pp. 17–37.

3. Pencils not pens; and usually, now, laptop computers, though scholars will need to check beforehand if their use is allowed, and crucially, if there is anywhere to plug one in.

4. www.hmc.gov.uk/nra is a first port of call for scholars pursuing literary or any other kind of manuscripts. A brilliantly simple website, it allows you to search by name, place and organisation. It is only as comprehensive as you would expect any register to be, where entry is voluntary. It is, however, a rather profound expression of the citizen's right of access to (national) archives, first expressed during the Revolutionary years in France. See Le Goff, *History and Memory*, pp. 87–9.

5. See Suzanne Keen (2004), *Romances of the Archive in Contemporary British Fiction*, Toronto: Toronto University Press.

6. José Saramago [1997] (1999), *All the Names*, trans. Margaret Jill Costa, London: Harvill; Ismail Kadere [1981] (1990), *The Palace of Dreams*, a novel written in Albanian and translated from the French of Joseph Vironi by Barbara Bray, London: Harvill.

7. Martha Cooley (1998), *The Archivist: A Novel*, London: Abacus, pp. 5–6. The novel might be thought of as a guide to this kind of archive. See alternate chapters which describe the archivist's work, and in particular pp. 5–9, 23–6, 30–32, 256–7.

8. Régine Robert (2003), *La Mémoire saturée*, Paris: Stock. See in particular pp. 102–4 for 'L'archiviste dans le roman', in the section 'Le Sédiment de l'Archive'.

9. Antoinette Burton (2001) discusses Foucault's *The Order of Things* in 'Thinking beyond the boundaries: empire, feminism and the dominions of history', *Social History* 26: 1, pp. 60–71. See Michel Foucault [1966] (1973), *The Order of Things: An Archaeology of the Human Sciences*, New York: Vintage, p. 15.

10. Richard M. Grinnell (1988), *Social Work Research and Evaluation*, Ithaca, Illinois: F. Peacock; Bruce A. Thyer (2001), *The Handbook of Social Work Research Methods*, London: Sage.

11. Steedman, *Dust*, pp. ix–xi.

12. Jules Michelet [1869] (1974) 'Préface de l'Histoire de France', *Oeuvres Complètes, volume IV*, Paris: Flammarion, pp. 11–127. See Steedman, *Dust*, pp. 66–88.

13. Bonnie Smith (1998), *The Gender of History: Men, Women and Archival Practice*, Cambridge MA: Harvard University Press, pp. 118–21.

14. Natalie Davis (1987), *Fiction in the Archives: Pardon Tales and their Tellers in Sixteenth-century France*, Oxford: Polity; Natalie Davis (1985), *The Return of Martin Guerre*, Harmondsworth: Penguin. See also *Retour de Martin Guerre* (dir. Daniel Vigne, 1982).

15. Jean Laplanche (1976), *Life and Death in Psychoanalysis*, Baltimore: Johns Hopkins University Press, pp. 19–20.

16. Sigmund Freud [1900] (1991), 'The interpretation of dreams', *The Pelican Freud Library, Volume 4*, Harmondsworth: Penguin; Sigmund Freud [1905] (1977), 'Fragment of an analysis of a case of hysteria', *The Pelican Freud Library, Volume 8. Case Histories I*, Harmondsworth: Penguin, pp. 27–164.

17. Carolyn Steedman (1998), *Strange Dislocations: Childhood and the Idea of Human Interiority*, Cambridge, MA: Harvard University Press.

18. D. W. Winnicott (1971), 'Playing: A theoretical statement', 'The location of cultural experience', and 'The place where we live', in *Playing and Reality*, Harmondsworth: Penguin, pp. 44–61, 112–21, 122–9.

19. Paul Ricoeur (1983), *Time and Narrative*, Chicago: University of Chicago Press, pp. xi, 154–5.
20. W. H. Auden (1960), 'Homage to Clio', *Homage to Clio*, London: Faber and Faber, pp. 15–17.
21. P. A. Roth (1988), 'Narrative explanation: The case of history', *History and Theory*, 27, pp. 1–13.
22. Robert Berkhofer (1995), *Beyond the Great Story: History as Text and Discourse*, Cambridge, MA: Harvard University Press, p. 44.
23. V. S. Naipaul (2001) *A Way in the World: A Sequence*, London: Vintage, 'History: A smell of fish glue', pp. 11–41.
24. This advice has to be tempered by the knowledge that archives are almost always visually dreary places, inhabited for the main part by the greyly and badly dressed. You might well like to wear something that pleases you, and that looks good, as a prophylactic against depression.
25. They are cold when they are not boiling hot. An airless search room in an English country record office on a hot summer's day allows historians in Britain to boast of feats of endurance comparable to those experienced by their colleagues who work on Latin America, or Antique China. But boasting about hard times in the archives has been the historian's way, since the century before last. Joking aside, however, heat and cold are real factors that need to be planned for.
26. For the historian as reader – always this kind of reader – of the unintended, purloined letter, see Carolyn Steedman (1999), 'A woman writing a letter', in Rebecca Earle (ed.), *Epistolary Selves: Letters and Letter-Writers, 1600–1945*, Aldershot: Ashgate, pp. 111–33.
27. See the vagaries and silences of the archives from which these examples are taken in Carolyn Steedman (forthcoming), *Pregnant Phoebe: Love and Labour in West Yorkshire, 1780–1820*.
28. Jacques Derrida [1980] (1987), *The Post Card: From Socrates to Freud and Beyond*, trans. Alan Bass, Chicago: University of Chicago Press.
29. Jacques Rancière [1992] (1994), *The Names of History: On the Poetics of Knowledge*, Minneapolis: University of Minneapolis Press. And see Hayden White's comments on these points, in his Introduction to this work, pp. xiv–xviii.
30. For reading and the erotic, see Terry Eagleton (1982), *The Rape of Clarissa: Writing, Sexuality and Class Struggle in Samuel Richardson*, Oxford: Blackwell, pp. 54–5; and Steedman, *Dust*, pp. 85–6, notes 24, 25.
31. Saramago, *All the Names*, p. 113.
32. Gabriel García Márquez [1990] (1991), *The General in His Labyrinth*, London: Jonathan Cape, pp. 271–4.
33. Douglas Johnson (1969), 'The historian as Frenchman', *New Society*, 7 August, pp. 223–9; Georges Lefebvre (1963), *Etudes sur la Revolution Française*, Paris: Presses Universitaires de France.
34. Richard Cobb (1969) *A Second Identity: Essays on French History*, Oxford: Oxford University Press, pp. 17, 19.

CHAPTER 3

Auto/biography as a Research Method

Mary Evans, University of Kent

The first question that should engage our attention is that of why we wish to do research. The issue is in no sense straightforward, since 'doing research' is a common mantra of academic life, and is, of course, an activity in which we are all expected to partake. *Not* 'doing research' is nowadays an unacceptable position for academics; to be described as 'not research active' implies (and indeed invokes) isolation in the distant steppes of the academic world, in which the only possible redemptive activity is teaching undergraduates. So let us not assume that 'doing research' is always, and simply, the chosen pursuit of an academic or a scholar. We do research for all kinds of reasons, and those reasons now include the imperatives of employment.

This essay begins by making the point that research is not always an entirely voluntary activity because it is an important part of the world of those who research into the lives of others. The modern world, or at least the modern West, has made much of the centrality of education and knowledge to the lives of modern citizens, and so our modern student of auto/biography is acting within a discourse that emphasises the importance of information and claims openness about it as a civic virtue. The individuals who are the subjects of auto/biography live in the same way as the researcher, within a world where the boundaries of the public and the private are increasingly fluid. Moreover, those boundaries are often re-written by the subjects of auto/biography themselves, so that what once appeared as a search for information (on the part of the researcher) about a subject is now made meaningless by the self-disclosure of the subject. This raises the question of whether or not auto/biography can actually survive in the twenty-first century, given that aspects of Western culture apparently compel individuals towards increasingly radical self-revelation. Just as researchers are now invited to disclose their 'standpoint' and make transparent their own sexuality, ethnicity and value system, so the potential subjects of auto/biography often remain anything other than closed books.

In this culture of revelation, the researcher – compelled by the imperatives of her professional life – has to attempt to establish a way of reading the lives of others, that does not become simply a collection of information. In the history of the writing of English auto/biography, the crucial watershed in the transformation of the genre was 1967 and the publication, in that year, of Michael Holroyd's life of Lytton Strachey.[1] Holroyd made it clear in his biography that Strachey was gay; moreover, not only was Strachey gay but the sexuality of his friends and associates was often complex and distinct from prevailing social mores. The permissive society of the 1960s assumed that it was now possible to write about the sexuality of named individuals; the following years would see an extension of this idea to the public creation of identity through sexuality. Paradoxically, greater disclosure has arguably led to the return to the need for more interpretation in auto/biography. Faced with a culture that assumes there are no necessary secrets or private spaces within a life, the researcher is increasingly under pressure to interpret the life, quite as much as to document it.

In this change, we can perhaps see the search in auto/biography transformed from a search for the person to a search for a convincing reading. Where once the search was for greater information about the person, now it has shifted to a search for an interpretation of how the individual could be located within a particular *zeitgeist*. The paradox of contemporary auto/biography, and research about it, is that in large part the individual life becomes almost less important. That is, the individual characteristics of a person become precisely that, whereas the important question becomes one that is outside the person, namely the puzzle of how a particular individual emerged in particular times. The researcher in auto/biography, versed in the necessities of reflexivity and standpoint theory,[2] confronts an individual who is now studied in terms of their own dialogue with their circumstances. Endless exchanges, literary conversations, begin between subject and researcher, in which both parties bring to the named subject long histories and often unspoken imperatives.

The 'new' auto/biography (essentially the auto/biography written in the period after Holroyd on Strachey) has had, in common with 'old' auto/biography, a number of failings as well as a number of strengths. Those failings are threefold: partiality and exclusion in an account of a life, with both partiality and exclusion (for example, in Roy Harrod's biography of John Maynard Keynes) sometimes reaching almost parodic heights.[3] Second, there is the often uneasy relationship between the context in which an auto/biography is written, and the emphasis in interpretation and range of material. Here, an example is the biography of Evelyn Waugh by Christopher Sykes, a biography deeply sensitive to Roman Catholic mores, but because of that a biography unable to grasp Waugh's dialogue between modernism (and the modern) and Roman Catholicism.[4] This kind of partiality can obscure much about a life, as

Sykes did, but more than that it flouts the major rule of the writing of history in the second half of the twentieth century: the acknowledgement and recognition of diverse constructs of knowledge in any one culture. The third and final flaw of auto/biography is that, by definition, it focuses on one individual; the very nature of the genre is its greatest source of weakness, and more particularly so for anyone who regards the individual self as a complex mix of the personal and the public. This last issue raises questions about whether or not auto/biography can ever be of use as a tool of social research, be it in the humanities or the social sciences. Reviewing Sarah Churchwell's recent account of the life of Marilyn Monroe,[5] Andrew O'Hagan writes:

> The journey towards who a famous dead person wasn't is a tricky kind of exploration, and much welcomed at this desk. But what happens as time goes by and new lies appear? Can you always be sure that a person isn't who you think she isn't? Some people just happen to have been very good at appearing not as they are, which may be one of the reasons Marilyn Monroe became such a saint of modern culture in the first place. But maybe – just to run with the hare and the hounds for a second – we are asked to be more interested in the story of the story than in the story itself for simple reasons. Maybe it's just what Damon Runyon would call a new angle. Because once everything's been said about a subject what is left for new writers but the pleasure of unsaying it all?[6]

O'Hagan asks us to consider the status of the 'fact' in auto/biography. He concludes that 'afterlives are not more interesting than lives; they are just more ongoing' and asks if a person actually *has* a life before that life is interpreted. In that sense, of course, we give up ownership of our own lives (and what we think we are doing in them) and pass the ownership of our lives to others.

Marilyn Monroe, in the same way as Princess Diana (or Evelyn Waugh or John Maynard Keynes in a less populist mode) became the object of mass, as well as individualised, fantasy. The novel interpretation of the lives of these famous people which the late twentieth and early twenty-first centuries have given us is that these women and men, in common with all of us, were acting out their own fantasies about themselves. The explicit recognition in contemporary culture of emotional life as a determined player in a social world has allowed us all, in all our lives, to recognise the ways in which we construct ourselves. Arguably, however, it has made us rather less aware (about ourselves and about others) of the structural constraints that underpin our lives. The belief in the level playing field of existence, with its partner of limitless individual entitlement, is part of the contemporary Western ethic, and one that other cultures find both alien and suspect. If we wish to find out about Marilyn Monroe (or Princess Diana), we have to recognise that there are certain 'facts' which we, as a public, can never know. Equally, we have to acknowledge that wanting to know, as much as endorsing the fantasies that allowed Monroe and Diana to become global icons, is part of a particular cultural response to the modern world.

The many problems with auto/biography as a research tool are most acute when we fail to recognise our fantasies, both about the subject of auto/biography and those of the author. It is evident that many writers of autobiography are motivated by nothing except self-justification, an emotion that may reveal itself in either greater or lesser simplicity. Barbara Windsor on Barbara Windsor acknowledges the lure of the greasepaint and the roar of the crowd, whilst Lorna Sage was prepared to move towards the parodic for a vivid account of her early life.[7] In both cases the authors wished to explain themselves, in both cases the 'others' in their lives had little choice about their representation. Nevertheless, both authors demonstrate the first great strength of auto/biography, the ability of the genre to show that out of generalities, differences emerge. Auto/biography is, in a sense, the most individual of literary genres; its very existence is premised on the belief in the particularity of the individual. For disciplines such as sociology and social anthropology, which are primarily concerned with the patterns and similarities of social life, auto/biography is an important reminder of the deep faultlines of social life. Auto/biography makes plain the limitations of those subjects which too easily assume the inevitability of the links between, for example, gender or race and social exclusion. In the way in which auto/biography documents the individual's progress through the social world, we see human agency at work. If we can take the time to read and note auto/biography, we have before us the means of recognising the dynamics of the choices which human beings make.

One of the more visible features of the genre of auto/biography is its greater popularity in Protestant societies and cultures. Protestantism arguably made individuals more generally anxious about the world: without the reassurance of confession, prayer to saints and the possibility of securing the forgiveness of sins through acts of penitence, Protestants were left with the prospect of intense self-regulation and self-examination. As Max Weber described it:

> In its extreme inhumanity this doctrine must above all have had one
> consequence for the life of the generation which surrendered to its
> magnificent consistency. That was a feeling of unprecedented inner
> loneliness of the single individual in what was for the man of the age of
> the Reformation the most important thing in life, his eternal salvation,
> he was forced to follow his path alone to meet a destiny which had been
> decreed for him from eternity. No one could help him.[8]

It is the bleakness of that last sentence which should attract our attention, since it suggests so much about the culture in which we live and in which we have lived since the sixteenth century. Contemporary sociologists have argued that we now live in what Frank Furedi has described as a 'culture of fear', and although he acknowledges (as do other writers on the same subject such as Iain Wilkinson) Weber's contribution to the literature on anxiety, there is seldom a recognition that the cultural history of the West of the past 300 years is littered with examples of individuals trying to reassure themselves, and others, about the meaning of their existence.[9] Zygmunt Bauman has written thus of these fears:

> Thus men and women have been left alone with their fears; they are told by philosophers that the void is here to stay, and by politicians that coping with it is their own duty and worry.
> Postmodernity has not allayed the fears which modernity injected into humanity once it had left it to its own resources; postmodernity only *privatised* these fears . . . the privatisation of fears may not bring peace of mind, but it just may take away some of the reasons for the wars of classes, nations or races.[10]

Bauman thus draws attention to those fears and anxieties which the Protestant ethic bequeaths to us; at the same time, his remarks implicitly suggest much that is useful for an understanding of auto/biography.

As remarked above, Bauman emphasises, as Weber before him had done, the psychic reality of Western life. Individuals are both on their own in a religious sense, and on their own within a social ethic, that of capitalism, which stresses individual achievement and responsibility. The social consequences of the individualism of the West have been discussed by both historians and social scientists for some time; most recently, Robert Putnam has used the term 'bowling alone' to describe the erosion of community ties in the United States.[11] Individualism, the ethic that sustains capitalism, is by the same token the ethic that undermines it. Richard Sennett and Robert Bellah are two examples of writers who review the emergence of ideas about self-realisation and conclude that this attitude to the world brings with it, or can bring with it, nothing except instrumentalism.[12] In his comments on Bellah – in a work which in part valorises modern ideas about the self – Charles Taylor wrote: 'What is more, the primacy of self-fulfilment reproduces and reinforces some of the same negative consequences as instrumentalism. Community filiations, the solidarities of birth, of marriage, of the family, of the polis, all take second place.'[13] The ground which Taylor covers is shared with Sennet, Putnam et al.: their concerns are with the social impact of individualism. Here, the concerns are with literature, specifically auto/biography; the question is the extent to which the genre is a consequence of individualism and how, if at all, those consequences impact upon auto/biography.

The most obvious way in which individualism structures auto/biography is in the motive. Part of the psychic restlessness of individualism is to discover the self; it is not an ethic which is content to see the work, the external manifestation of the inner self, but, rather, it wishes to see and know the internal self. It is in this sense that contemporary auto/biography becomes something akin to a detective story. We want to find out why we – and others – act because through this knowledge we might be better achievers in the remorseless achievement culture of the Western twenty-first century. As Bauman and others have pointed out, the world of the contemporary West is one in which there is increasingly little surveillance of individual moral behaviour (in that sense, sex, drugs and rock and roll have won the day) and in the words of Elizabeth Wilson 'we are all bohemian now'.[14] But once we emerge from our private pluralism, we face a world in which the measurement of achievement is a significant part of our daily lives. Our minds, and indeed our bodies, may follow their own private paths in a private place but in public they are expected to fulfil the normative order of late capitalism.

The part which auto/biography has to fulfil in this culture is that of offering insight less into a particular individual than into the extent to which a particular individual can be understood, and evaluated, in terms of achievement. Herein lies part of the paradox of contemporary auto/biography: as the genre becomes more popular, so it becomes, arguably, less about the person and more about the relationship between the individual and the organising ethic of the twentieth and twenty-first century. When James Boswell wrote about Samuel Johnson he did so with a sense of the definitive peculiarity of his subject; when Lorna Sage wrote about her early life she did so with a powerful sense of the peculiarity of her circumstances and her social world. What is different here is that Sage is writing in the light of an internalised sense of the normal. Her account of her early life is premised on the sense of difference about her world. Again, we encounter a paradox here: Sage (and in much the same way, Carolyn Steedman) wish to ensure an understanding of the very different ways in which people do live.[15] Nevertheless, what they achieve in doing this is in part a re-affirmation of apparent morality and the conventional. Lorna Sage's mother is only deviant if we accept that there is such a person as a 'normal' mother.

One of the important strengths of great detective fiction is that in the course of its narrative it exposes the many cracks and fissures in the conventional landscape. From Agatha Christie to Ian Rankin, detective fiction involves the gradual revelation of layers of guilt; there is always the absolute villain or murderer, but on the way to her or his unmasking there is a gradual demonstration of other degrees of guilt. Detective fiction emerged in the early nineteenth century and came to maturity in the early years of the twentieth; given the number of distinguished women writers who adopted the genre, it might be interpreted as women's reaction (and resistance) to the moral stances of modernity. At about the same time as Margery Allingham, Dorothy Sayers and Agatha Christie were polishing their art, Lytton Strachey was offering the world his view of the great and the good. The man whose sexuality was to constitute a major focus of the 'new' autobiography was also the man who suggested that the great figures of conventional Victorian moral codes were riddled with contradiction and, in certain cases, a history of abuse of others. The parallel theme of Strachey and Allingham et al. is that of the demonstration of the impossibility of achieving absolute virtue. The monolithic figures who were the butt of Strachey's pen were similar to the apparently 'respectable' villains who peopled detective fiction. Indeed, the great detective figures created by Allingham and her colleagues were either in some way vulnerable themselves (as was Dorothy Sayer's Lord Peter Wimsey) or from the slightly eccentric fringes of the culture (as was Christie's Miss Marple).

The common thread between auto/biography and detective fiction is thus the setting out of the complexities of moral choice and moral action. For women, those choices and that action have often been given as passive or defensive. Women have historically been allowed less moral agency than men: our place has been that of the 'angel in the house', and the right to act outside the house has long been contested by feminists. Much feminist scholarship of the 'second wave' of feminism has been concerned with the documentation of the difficulties which women have had in achieving particular goals, and gaining access to forms of experience conventionally allowed to men. This rich source of auto/biography has emphasised the point made by Foncault: history is not a linear progression but the resolution of competing ideas.

The detection and the unmasking of the past is, therefore, an important part of place that auto/biography occupies as a research tool for both the social sciences and the humanities. As noted above, auto/biography has shifted radically in its relationship to its subject in the past forty years, but all auto/biography demonstrates the way in which individuals are perceived and judged both within a culture and by those with more distance from it. To read different accounts of the same life reveals the essential instability of cultural judgements, as well as bringing into sharp relief those certainties of the nineteenth century which modernism made a determined effort to disturb. The feminist 'project' of using auto/biography to uncover the hidden lives of women is just one example of the use to which genre can be put.

At the same time as the library shelves have been filled with accounts of the lives of women, it has become important to distinguish – as in detective fiction – between the motives responsible for different kinds of auto/biography. The commonplace remark about the act of murder is that it is motivated by either sex or money. We can enlarge both those terms to encompass jealousy, inheritance

and the fear of loss of person or property but essentially the motivational structure purposed for murder is simple. It is difficult to make the same epigrammatic
comment about the writing of auto/biography. Its gestation can be accounted
for by political motives – for example, the wish to reclaim the history of women
– but at the same time it may be important to distinguish between the various
kinds of auto/biography in order to ask if common motives inform them all.
Auto/biography can be – and often is – about an individual, but as well as being
either by or about an individual, it can also be about a collective subject. What
counts as 'evidence' for all these forms may differ: a diary written for publication might be accorded less status than the views of close associates. Biographies
of collective subjects (for example, of the Suffragettes or the Lake Poets) are
inevitably less able to deal with aspects of individual psychology but what these
works can do is to demonstrate the impact of shared experience on particular
people. Writing about the Bloomsbury group, Leon Edel remarked that: 'They
performed the acts of life with an intensity and unself-consciousness that
derived partly from their comparative security. There was among them a mutual
feeling of love and affection rare in such diverse and temperamental talents.'[16]
At the same time, Edel went on, 'they had no sense of their collective power.'

This comment is extremely interesting in its implications for the study of
auto/biography, collective or otherwise. It is that the missing element in most
(if not all) auto/biography is a sense of the part that culture, and collective
experience, play in our lives. Equally, just as our culture encourages us to minimise our collective experiences, and to see ourselves as products of a highly
particular set of circumstances, we find it difficult to entertain the idea – as Edel
argues members of Bloomsbury did – that we act as people who have experienced social life as much as personal life. When individuals write autobiographies, they often locate themselves as people who have had a battle against a
particular culture. Simone de Beauvoir's *Memoirs of a Dutiful Daughter* is an
example of an autobiography written about escape from a certain social milieu:
omnipresent in that work is the sense of emergence into the 'light' of intellectual life; entirely absent is any sense that this milieu is just as much part of the
social world as the one left behind.

If we are to use auto/biography as a research method, in both the humanities and the social sciences, we should perhaps consider the problems of using
a method that, for all its strengths, can pathologise the subject beyond general
relevance. The very real, the very salutary importance of auto/biography is
that it acts as a bulwark against the over-socialised account of human beings.
Once we simply define individuals as members of classes, genders or races we
obscure, I would argue, not merely individual difference but also much of the
dynamic of social life. If the social world was made up of groups of people who
did not constantly re-affirm and question their social identity, then little cultural or intellectual life would emerge. But at the same time, whilst the cen-

trality of auto/biography to an understanding of any culture and any society can be demonstrated, so there is equally a case to be made for the recognition of the social, the general, in the lives of individual. One telling example of the way in which culture and the social world can be left out of accounts of individual lives is in the various biographies of Sylvia Plath.

In Janet Malcolm's *The Silent Woman* a powerful argument is made to persuade us to recognise the partiality of the various accounts of Sylvia Plath's life.[17] Essentially, Malcolm's book is about the way in which biographers can project onto their subjects their own fears, disappointments and values, and in order to make her own case about the veracity of the various biographies of Sylvia Plath, Malcolm embarks upon a subtle form of character assassination. As one reviewer said of Malcolm's book,

> Malcolm never tells us that Hughes is believable and the others are not, but instead carefully crafts vignettes that force readers to draw that conclusion themselves. She appears to present both sides with open-mindedness and healthy ambivalence but in fact she makes only one alternative plausible/morally right and intellectually compelling.[18]

In Malcolm's account of the various worlds of the biographers of Sylvia Plath, Anne Stevenson becomes the drab and over-anxious hostess just as Jacqueline Rose becomes the knowing mistress of the interview in her dealings with Malcolm. The various individuals become parodies of themselves in Malcolm's various vignettes, just as – by implication – we are strongly advised to read their accounts of Plath as projections of themselves. The worried and nervous Stevenson defines Plath in terms of her own uncertainties, just as Rose annexes Plath for her own theoretical satisfaction. The poet is swallowed by the theory in Rose's account, is the argument Malcolm dangles before us.

The thesis of *The Silent Woman* is, as suggested, projection. The origins of that thesis lie in psychoanalysis. But what is remarkable about *The Silent Woman* is that it includes as part of its thesis an account of Britain, and British culture, which is fascinating in terms of what is not recognised. Throughout *The Silent Woman* Janet Malcolm comments on the cold in Britain: the streets are not cleared of ice, the restaurants are chilly and public transport is delayed by snow. The country is deeply inhospitable and apparently unnourishing (Janet Malcolm's book was published in 1993 and not, we should remember, in an age before central heating). The meals which Malcolm eats with her interviewees are either flawed or served in cold surroundings (at Clarissa Roche's house the small dining room 'had a fireplace in which, English style, a few flames wanly flickered').[19] As readers we are given a sense of England as an unwelcoming, domestically backward country, beset with exactly the same kind of dirt and inefficiency that upset Sylvia Plath herself. But another way of

reading Malcolm's account of Britain, and the people she meets, is that this is
a particularly North American account: a reading of a foreign culture by a
person from a culture of entitlement and plenty. The dynamics of Plath's relationship to the English social world, and English cultural expectations, is
seldom emphasised in accounts of her life, with the exception of the deeply
critical account of Plath by Dido Merwin in Anne Stevenson's biography. Dido
Merwin clearly did not care for Sylvia Plath, but she did not care for her in part
because of what she saw as her 'American' values.

Those 'American' values were values which Plath set herself against, and
here that sense of our negotiations with the cultures in which we live should be
an issue for all biographers. Towards the end of her life, Plath was asked by her
mother to return to live in the United States. Plath replied that she could not;
it was one of the instances where her enthusiasm for Britain is greater than her
nostalgia for the United States. Yet her views on both countries swing from
approval to disapproval. After the birth of her daughter, she writes to her
mother: 'Well I've never been so happy in my life. The Whole American rig-
amorale of hospitals, doctors' bills, cuts and stitches, anaesthesia etc seems a
nightmare left behind.'[20] But on a trip to Whitby she notes:

> There is something depressingly mucky about English sea resorts. Of
> course, the weather is hardly ever sheer fair, so most people are in
> woollen suits and coats and tinted plastic raincoats. The sand is muddy
> and dirty. The working class is also dirty, strewing candy papers, gum
> and cigarettes wrappers.[21]

Plath's account of England, and of life in Cambridge, London and the Devon
countryside, is replete with a transcultural enthusiasm about the natural world
which becomes distinct after her meeting with Ted Hughes. Her largely autobiographical novel *The Bell Jar* has little to say about her relationship with
nature – or England – but it has everything to say about her relationship with
gender and the cultural politics of the United States in the Eisenhower years.[22]
Sylvia Plath/Esther Greenwood finds it difficult (indeed problematic to the
point of attempted suicide) to locate herself within the social world of the
United States. The modern world offers Sylvia/Esther few possibilities and
the Sylvia/Esther who emerges at the conclusion of *The Bell Jar* is a person
who has agreed to *play* a social role. That compromise with the social world was
one that Ted Hughes apparently wished his wife to abandon: he wrote in
Birthday Letters of his wife's 'strange dummy stiffness' in the clothes she had
chosen to wear when teaching at Smith College.[23] Indeed, throughout *Birthday
Letters* Hughes keeps up an attack on Plath's internalised values: her version of
Paris was 'American', and when ill in Spain she longed for America and 'its
medicine cupboard'.[24] Hughes' own jealousies and prejudices speak loudly

throughout *Birthday Letters*; he claims himself proudly as the 'postwar, utility son-in-law' and issues a warning to all ambitious women:[25] 'Fame cannot be avoided./ And when it comes/You will have paid for it with your happiness,/Your husband and your life.'[26] Bad luck then to any women who aspire to any personal agency; the values we can detect here are values about what women are allowed to do. Janet Malcolm and Ted Hughes – in their different ways – embrace a theory about the hierarchy of the social world in which authority in the auto/biographical world belongs to them. Sylvia Plath can be read in numerous ways but in her later poetry and in *The Bell Jar*, she attempted to position women within modernity, within a culture that was apparently free, yet as she discovered still riven with the same structures of traditional, often misogynist controls. The point then is not that we should endlessly re-interpret Plath's individual pathology but that we should interpret the meaning of the events of Plath's life within the culture she knew and grew up in. Plath, like all subjects of auto/biography, did not live in a historical void, she lived in a particular moment of the modern world, a world that increasingly, and explicitly, emphasised personal and sexual fulfilment, yet offered few structural supports, in particular for women, for the enjoyment of these possibilities. Hughes clearly recognised the sense of entitlement in American culture: he emphasises 'your mother's ambition' in *Birthday Letters* and comes extremely close to locating Mrs Aurelia Plath as the cultural source of all those values of ambition and professional engagement which he questions in his wife.

It is this fusion of the cultural and the personal that we can see in the poetry and prose that emerged from the Plath/Hughes marriage. Yet while the relationship between the couple has been commented on extensively, relatively little has been said about the contribution to that dynamic of the difference between postwar Britain and postwar United States. The dialectic of scarcity/plenty, individualism/communitarianism and social democracy and political democracy are rarely part of the Plath literature. Janet Malcolm's experience of the 'cold' in Britain is akin to an extended (if acknowledged) metaphor about the refusal of Britain to welcome either her or psychoanalysis, and yet much of the narrative of *The Silent Woman* is about the impossibility of engaging with British culture: the natives are either too confused or too theoretically sophisticated to admit outsiders. This sense of culture as active is seldom noted in literature on auto/biography: we all know that circumstances matter to individuals, but we are less inclined to recognise ourselves as agents and products of culture. Giddens' plea for reflexivity appears in many sociological contexts, as yet less so in that of auto/biography.[27] The social world is less fully acknowledged in auto/biography than is often its due; the paradox here is that a research method (and a hugely rich source of social data) is used, often effectively, to illuminate the limitations of over-generalised accounts of the world, and yet the hidden theme within auto/biography is often the dynamic of the social world.

The example of the literature on Sylvia Plath provides us with material from which it is possible to make some comments about the actual process of researching auto/biography. We might note initially that Plath provides an excellent case of a subject being 'discovered' by a shift in a culture or a politics. Immediately after Plath's death in 1963, relatively little was written about her; she died at the age of thirty but in doing so claimed her place with those other great romantic poets who died early. Plath's *oeuvre*, and specifically her later work, was troubled; bourgeois culture has long expected that troubled souls do not live out their allotted three-score-and-ten years, and Plath was no exception. Thus, in 1963 Plath could be assigned to an existing category – the troubled soul category – and little further needed to be said. However, by 1963 the times were definitely beginning to change in terms of our evaluation of women's relationship to the social world and the assumption that Plath belonged to a general rather than a specific category was questioned by second-wave feminism.

From this we should note that one of the most important aspects of researching for an auto/biography is the establishment of the relationship between author, subject and culture. Such an understanding is, of course, part of that self-consciousness about ourselves as authors (or investigators) which Sandra Harding and others have developed. We are not simply observers of a society, or collectors of information about another person, we carry some of the values and the ideas of some parts of the society we inhabit. Once we recognise this, the author of auto/biography becomes the 'hidden subject' (as I would describe it) of the study. Here we have, however, to recognise that some authors are more transparent than others. To return to Sylvia Plath: Anne Stevenson's account of Plath's life is an outstanding example of an author with a richly developed point of view. For example, in the following passage Stevenson writes categorically of Plath's understanding:

> Alfred Kazin, who taught her at Smith, once remarked that the world for Sylvia Plath existed only for her to write about. That may have been unfair, but her inward fears did restrict a wider acceptance of that world to which she aspired. No doubt against her better judgement, she was imaginatively confined to her own approved, heavily defended areas of achievement: marriage, parenthood, and the ideal of a well-managed 'home' . . . It was more than misunderstanding that isolated her in that glass cage; it was something like a blindness or incompleteness of the imagination.[28]

This passage is so riddled by judgemental assertions that it is impossible to single out any one line or comment for attention. What is revealed here (and similar passages are to be found on almost every page of the Stevenson biography) is an explicit view of the world and its values, a view of the world which judges Sylvia Plath harshly and, to use a term which is less weighted with its own baggage of censure, subjectively. Subjectivity, we have been taught in the twentieth century, is perfectly acceptable provided we acknowledge it; Anne Stevenson does not acknowledge her own values and in failing to do so lays herself open to the charge that she becomes not the rational, objective chronicler of Plath's life, but an embattled participant in it. One of the most interesting aspects of Stevenson on Plath is that she speaks for Ted Hughes and she attempts to defend him against the very imaginative possibilities of relations between the sexes that Plath raised in her later poetry.

In Stevenson on Plath there are, therefore, not just two hidden subjects (Stevenson and Hughes) but also collective hidden subjects, in this case feminism, patriarchy and Anglo–American understanding. Any student of auto/biography, or anyone attempting to research auto/biography, would do well to read Stevenson on Plath and note the presence of 'the others' (be they individual or collective) in the work. Moreover, as writers of auto/biography (or, again, as students of it) we also owe it to our subjects to think through the possible boundaries of our objectivity and subjectivity. Many biographers (and most often those who have written about the great and the good) have not had to examine their own relationship to their subject; they take on the mantle of their subject's worldly standing. But in doing this they obscure part of the crucial ingredient of any person's life: her or his relationship to the culture that produced them and (emphatically) the culture within which the auto/biography is being written. These cultural definitions and revelations should be part of the method of auto/biography since they provide a crucial ingredient of the final work.

'Hidden subjects' need, therefore, to be made plain in work on, and works of, auto/biography. A second feature of the 'method' of auto/biography is closely aligned: the recognition of the boundaries of the work. The question of the many 'silences' within auto/biography is raised here: what is not said, what cannot be said, and what we can never know. In Stevenson on Plath there is, remarkably in the case of any human being, no instance of 'bad' behaviour on the part of Ted Hughes. This is astonishing in the case of anyone, but it does show how authors of auto/biography can easily cast either themselves or their subjects into the rigid roles of hero/heroine and villain. Once these identities are set, it is difficult for individuals to escape them. But this rigidity of characterisation (Plath the neurotic, obsessive American against Hughes the good-natured, easy-going Brit) also raises questions, and issues, about the tyranny of the 'fact' in auto/biography and the internalised need, on the part of authors, to produce 'evidence' about their subject.

The history of science, and indeed the philosophy of the social sciences, has taught us that we should regard 'facts' with some scepticism. Yet in auto/biography there is often evidence of a relatively simplistic attitude to, and use of, facts. Biographers collect 'facts' about their subject, authors remember 'facts'

about themselves, and what is forgotten is that these 'facts' arose out of particular circumstances and particular exchanges. We might, for example, question
the 'fact' that Sylvia Plath was, as Stevenson suggests, 'obsessive'. What might
be dedication, or determination or concentration can very easily become
'obsession' if we do not admire a person or their works. In just the same way
that we learnt that what conservative historians deem 'the mob' is a group of
politically aware citizens to more radical historians, so we have to learn that
subjects of auto/biography can be both friends and enemies.

When Emily Brontë allowed Catherine, the heroine of *Wuthering Heights*, to
say 'I am Heathcliff', she opened up an important space in both literature and
auto/biography in modern Europe. Brontë suggested that the young Catherine
had chosen an identity outside herself, and although she had no expectation of
'becoming' Heathcliff, his presence and his being informed her sense of self. So
it is with many individuals, and an important recognition that we are not, as
people, ever final or secure in our identities. Inevitably, we occupy 'facts' about
age, gender and ethnicity, but as postmodernism has informed us, those 'facts' are
often themselves negotiable. Indeed, if auto/biography was re-conceptualised in
terms of accounts of negotiation rather than definitive histories, then perhaps
clearer understandings of individuals might emerge. To do this we have to recognise the complexity of cultures and their relationships with other cultures: when
Stevenson attacks Plath for her 'American' aspirations and expectations, we have
to recognise both political hostility to the United States and yet at the same time
the unspoken envy of a country which did appear to be both richer and more
accommodating than those of Europe. In choosing her husband's country as her
place of residence, Sylvia Plath made an entirely traditional choice in her marriage; reading about this choice in the early twenty-first century may not provoke
attention for we are told we live in a global age. Yet in the 1950s the choice may
well have had different implications and different meaning. The meaning of language, the very resonance of culture, is not always easily conveyed on this printed
page, yet this geography of experience has to be recognised by any writer of
auto/biography. When Sylvia Plath sat freezing cold in her room at Newnham
College, she may well have wondered why a great imperial power could not heat
its domestic space. As *Birthday Letters* makes clear, Hughes recognised the dialogue of expectations between himself and Plath: that kind of awareness is precisely the kind of awareness that writers of auto/biography need to claim. Above
all, finally, writers (and students) of auto/biography need to recognise the porous
boundaries between fact and fiction. We 'are' individuals' in a factual sense but
we are also individuals who construct ourselves, and others, in terms of imagined
possibilities.

The West does not encourage us, as individuals, to think of ourselves as
social actors. There may well be collective impulses in many societies, but
maintaining a sense of self, as Charles Taylor and others have pointed out, is

about maintaining an individual self. Detection of the social, admitting the social to our individual lives, can take the form of the extreme trauma experienced by Sylvia Plath/Esther Greenwood when she realised that for all her *individual* achievements (high scholastic grades and precocious literary talent) she was also, in the eyes of much of the world, a *collective* subject. The shattering impact on her sense of self of the realisation that she belonged to a gender quite as much as a high scholastic caste undermined and challenged an individual with personal demons of her own. We do not all experience those same demons and losses (indeed, many people know circumstances that are even more disadvantaged) but we all have to confront that dynamic between ourselves and the culture. Auto/biography provides rich evidence of the worlds we, as individuals, know. In reading auto/biography as part of an exercise in the detection of the social world, we are also able, on occasions, to establish those faultlines of our culture that enable change and creativity.

NOTES

1. Michael Holroyd (1967), *Lytton Strachey*, Harmondsworth: Penguin.
2. See Nancy C. M. Hartsock (1998), *The Feminist Standpoint Revisited*, Boulder, Co: Westview.
3. Roy Harrod (1951), *The Life of John Maynard Keynes*, London: Macmillan.
4. Christopher Sykes (1977), *Evelyn Waugh*, Harmondsworth: Penguin.
5. Sarah Churchwell (2004), *The Many Lives of Marilyn Monroe*, London: Granta.
6. Andrew O'Hagan (2004), 'Short cuts', *London Review of Books*, 8 July, p. 20.
7. Lorna Sage (2000), *Bad Blood*, London: Fourth Estate.
8. Max Weber (1976), *The Protestant Ethic and the Spirit of Capitalism*, London: George Allen and Unwin, p. 104.
9. Frank Furedi (2002), *The Culture of Fear*, London: Continuum Books; Iain Wilkinson (2001), *Anxiety in a Risk Society*, London: Routledge.
10. Zygmunt Bauman (1993), *Intimations of Postmodernity*, London: Routledge, p. xviii.
11. Robert Putnam (2000), *Bowling Alone*, New York: Touchstone.
12. Richard Sennett (1986), *The Fall of Public Man*, London: Faber; Robert Bellah et al. (1985), *Habits of the Heart*, Berkeley: University of California Press.
13. Charles Taylor (1994), *Sources of the Self*, Cambridge: Cambridge University Press, p. 507.
14. Elizabeth Wilson (1998), 'Bohemian love', *Theory, Culture and Society*, vol. 15(3–4), pp. 111–17.
15. Carolyn Steedman (1986), *Landscape for a Good Woman*, London: Virago.
16. Leon Edel (1979), *Bloomsburg: A House of Lions*, Philadelphia: J. B. Lippincott, p. 253.
17. Janet Malcolm (1993), *The Silent Woman*, London: Picador.
18. Robin Tolmach Lakoff, and Mandy Aftel (1996), 'In the Malcolm Archives', *The Nation*, 16 December, pp. 32–5.
19. Malcolm, *The Silent Woman*, p. 149.
20. Aurelia S. Plath (ed.) (1975), *Letters Home by Sylvia Plath*, New York: Harper and Row, p. 374.
21. Plath, *Letters Home by Sylvia Plath*, p. 391.

22. Sylvia Plath (1963), *The Bell Jar*, London: Faber and Faber.
23. Ted Hughes (1998), *Birthday Letters*, London: Faber and Faber, p. 67.
24. Hughes, *Birthday Letters*, p. 36.
25. Hughes, *Birthday Letters*, p. 34.
26. Hughes, *Birthday Letters*, p. 56.
27. Anthony Giddens (1991), *Modernity and Self-Identity*, Cambridge: Polity.
28. Anne Stevenson (1989), *Bitter Fame: A Life of Sylvia Plath*, Boston: Houghton Mifflin, p. 187.

CHAPTER 4

Oral History as a Research Method

Penny Summerfield, University of Manchester

Oral history has a salience and familiarity at the beginning of the twenty-first century that is both popular and academic. The oral telling of public and personal histories is an everyday event on radio, television and in film, and it also occupies a recognised place within the scholarly practices of numerous academic disciplines, including anthropology, education, history, geography, political science and sociology.[1] Oral history offers several benefits to the discipline of English. Interviews with literary authors, as well as recordings of personal experiences of cultural phenomena such as theatre-going and reading, are available for study in collections in, for example, the National Sound Archive.[2] More generally, oral history enables the study of subjective constructions of the self and others through spoken narratives.

This chapter focuses on some key aspects of the theory and method of oral history. The first part addresses the idea of oral history as 'recovery history'. It demonstrates the sense in which oral history can contribute to the recovery of histories that would otherwise remain hidden, and also addresses issues of memory and validity raised by critics of oral history. Then the chapter engages with the psycho-dynamics of an oral history interview – notably life review and the 'composure' of the subject – and discusses the significance of the narrative form used by the interviewee for the meanings produced in the interview. Next it addresses the popular-memory approach to oral history, exploring the relationship of the personal account to popular beliefs and public culture through the concept of the 'cultural circuit'. Finally the chapter discusses the ethics and protocols of oral history interviewing. It draws for illustration on a recent research project in which the methodology of oral history was extensively deployed, and it uses as a case study one of the thirty oral history interviews undertaken as part of the research. The project, involving myself and a research associate, was on women, men and home defence in Britain in the Second World War.[3] The case study, an interview with a woman we shall call

Kaitlin Wells, was selected because it exemplified numerous oral history interviews in respect of both the research process and the creation of knowledge.

RECOVERY HISTORY

Oral history in Britain and the USA became distinct from the collection of folk-
lore and ethnography – the oral tradition – in the 1960s. The main influence
was the radical social history movement which challenged the focus of mainstream history on political elites and economic trends and demanded an end to
the neglect of the ordinary person.[4] At the same time that pioneers in literary
studies such as Richard Hoggart and Raymond Williams were revaluing 'the
masses' as sources and subjects of literature,[5] historians turned their attention
to the history of working-class people, participants in the labour movement and
members of sub-cultures. Aided by the advent of cheaper and smaller-sized
recording technology, the advocates of oral history insisted that where records
did not exist they could be created. Oral historians could ask new questions
about social and cultural life which policy documents and social statistics could
not answer, recovering histories that would otherwise be lost. The key advocate
of this new wave of oral history was Paul Thompson, whose book *The Voice of
the Past*, first published in 1978, was re-issued in both 1988 and 2000.[6] The
'recovery' approach was enthusiastically taken up by historians of women and
feminist historians, such as Elizabeth Roberts[7] and Jill Liddington[8] as a way of
putting an end to the hidden-from-history status of women, especially
working-class women. It was also used in the 1980s and 1990s by historians of
ethnic minorities.[9] The radical intention was to give a voice to the voiceless, to
raise consciousness, and to empower those who now found a place in history.

Because of the intellectual stable from which this initiative came, namely
social history and sociology, the methods used in this early phase of oral history
were informed by social science practices. Survey methodologies were
favoured, involving large-scale structured sampling to achieve representativeness, and standardisation of questionnaires to aid the comparison of 'data' to
be subjected to statistical analysis and tests of validity. The recovery motif in
the oral history of the 1960s to the 1980s was informed by these methodological requirements, and I shall return to these shortly.

The desire to recover a missing history inspired the project about home
defence in the Second World War, for which our case-study interview was
undertaken. The particular home defence organisation under scrutiny was the
Home Guard, a military force in which members gave part-time service. The
Home Guard was established in May 1940 to protect British homes and local-
ities against invasion. Fragments of evidence in existing publications indicated
that women were excluded from it, and initial archival research showed that

they campaigned to join, led by the Labour MP Edith Summerskill who, as part of the campaign, set up an organisation called the Women's Home Defence League (WHD). The WHD not only organised women as a defence force but trained them to shoot and to use a variety of weapons. Despite the fact that it was never officially recognised and was, strictly speaking, illegal, it recruited some 20,000 women. Categorical bans on members of the Home Guard recruiting women as unofficial Home Guards and training them to use weapons were repeatedly issued by the War Office.[10] In April 1943 a compromise was finally reached between Summerskill and the government: a limited number of women over forty-five-years-old were to be allowed to assist the Home Guard as Women Home Guard Auxiliaries, doing typing, cooking and driving, but without uniforms and emphatically without weapons training.

This much history came from research in wartime newspapers, Hansard (the parliamentary record), and the official War Office files in the Public Record Office, even though it had been all but omitted from the historiography of the Home Guard.[11] But such documentation revealed little about women's experiences and relationships, including, for example, what motivated women to join the WHD or the Home Guard, what happened when they did, and how the wartime context impacted upon their participation. The capacity of oral history to recover such otherwise unrecorded aspects of the past suggested that it was a methodology that would enable the hidden history of women's participation in the Home Guard to be addressed.

How does an oral historian find suitable people to interview? Survey research methods involve the identification of a 'sampling frame', that is a list of all members of the 'population' on which the research focuses, and the selection from it of a group of manageable size, representative of the whole. Oral historians have aspired to such precision but their quest has been hampered by a number of factors that can be summarised under the headings 'specificity', 'survival' and 'consent'. Our project needed to find women who had participated in the past in a specific activity: home defence. Documentary sources quoted 32,000 as the approximate number of women involved in the Home Guard in 1944.[12] Even though this figure almost certainly omitted some groups (for example, women who were members of the WHD), it suggested the involvement of a relatively small proportion of the fourteen million adult women in the Second World War.[13] There were, to our knowledge, no surviving lists of female members of either the Home Guard or the WHD. Thus, we were not in a position to identify the complete population we wished to research and to select a representative sample from it. Secondly, even if we had found lists of members and it had been possible to trace them more than fifty years after the lists were compiled, we would have confronted the problem of survival. Many of the women would have been dead or too old or sick to be interviewed. Thirdly, oral historians need the consent of those they wish to interview. The same is true of survey researchers, but oral historians make more extensive personal demands upon their interviewees. Oral historians, as we shall go on to discuss, have found that reminiscence produces material that is more valuable for historical recovery than answers to structured question-naires. They record individuals' interpretative accounts of their personal remembered pasts rather than brief statements of fact or opinion. However, not everyone wants or is able to reminisce; nor is everyone willing to do so in the company of a researcher.[14]

Most oral history projects use a sample that has been gathered opportunisti-cally, that is via personal contacts and through publicity of various sorts. The Home Defence research was no exception. The first interviewee, Jeanne Gale Sharp, was discovered by a friend who noticed a piece Jeanne had placed in the personal columns of *Saga* magazine seeking other women Home Guards to share memories and to campaign with her for a place in the Remembrance Day parades. Jeanne Gale Sharp not only agreed to be interviewed but contacted on my behalf seven other women who had written to her. This development was significant. It demonstrated the practical possibility of finding women to interview and hence the viability of planning to use oral history more extensively in the project.

Local and national popular publications are appropriate places to announce a quest for interviewees. We chose *Woman's Weekly* for its wide circulation, its appeal to the over-sixties, and an editorial policy sympathetic to requests for memories. The notice about the project appeared in the magazine on 14 December 1999 under the general headline 'Lovely to Hear from You':

> Memories wanted
> We're seeking men and women with memories of working in, or
> assisting, the Home Guard and Women's Home Defence in the Second
> World War. Please write or e-mail me with your memories: [name,
> address, email address].

Altogether, twenty-four former women Home Guards contacted us, a tiny pro-portion of the estimated 32,000 wartime members, but in view of the hidden history of their wartime experiences, a very precious one. We aimed to meet them all, but inevitably some were unable or unwilling to participate, so we finally interviewed seventeen.[15]

Kaitlin Wells was one of those who responded to the *Woman's Weekly* announcement, writing on the day the issue appeared, 'I was a member of Women's Home Guard at Workington – about twelve or fifteen of us, doing typing, filing, general office duties, acting as messengers and drivers'. Her letter referred to rifle training, a badge, the toughness and keenness of the men of the Home Guard, shooting contests with a rival 'Ladies' Unit', driving and other aspects of the work.[16]

Kaitlin's interview, recorded on a small cassette recorder and lasting about two and a half hours, took place at her home near Newcastle-upon-Tyne on 19 May 2000. The recording was copied (for security) and transcribed by an experienced audio-typist using appropriate technology (headphones and a tape player operated by a foot pedal). Transcription is a laborious process but oral historians in general prefer to work with the written text of interviews.[17] Some critics have warned of the danger of losing the interviewee's 'voice' in the transcript, and the Italian oral historian Alessandro Portelli points out the importance for the meanings communicated, of the tone, volume range and rhythm, the emphases and the pauses, of the recorded word: the transcript and recording need to be used together, when analysing an interview.[18] In addition to transcribing the interview, we used software for qualitative data analysis to add reference numbers to the 'text units' (that is, the paragraphs) of the transcript, and to enable us to index and cross-reference under some basic categories, such as 'family', 'Home Guard' and 'Women's Home Defence', as well as more abstract ones, such as 'constructions of the self' and 'gender consciousness'. We had fifty-five such index headings. The objective was to aid retrieval of interview material concerning topics important to the project.

What did we 'recover' for the history of women and the Home Guard, and women in the Second World War more generally, from Kaitlin's interview, once it had been recorded, transcribed and indexed? There were three main findings. Firstly, Kaitlin was recruited by her father, a local bank manager and a lieutenant colonel in the 5th Battalion Border Regiment Home Guard. In other words, she was not part of the WHD campaign but was recruited directly into the Home Guard. She explained that her father wanted typists, and so called on her both to join and to bring in other young women. She remembered the date as 1940 to 1941. This was surprising, since it was the period of the official ban on women members. Secondly, Kaitlin was taught to shoot, both by her father in their back garden and by the chief postmaster on the floor of the Workington sorting office. Again, this is startling, both in itself and in view of the explicit ban on weapons training. Thirdly, Kaitlin evidently made a seamless transition to becoming a Women's Home Guard Auxiliary after the compromise in April 1943. She had no memory of any alteration to her status but recalled receiving a certificate issued to Women's Home Guard Auxiliaries at the end of the war.

MEMORY ISSUES

One of the criticisms of using oral history to recover evidence from the past concerns memory. The distinguished radical historian Eric Hobsbawm is on record as decrying oral history because of the slipperiness of memory.[19] Defenders of oral history, such as Trevor Lummis, have argued in response that while short-term memory declines with age, so that it becomes difficult to remember what happened yesterday, long-term memory is not impaired and may even improve.[20] Others have added that the reliability of memory varies with the types of things remembered: specific things like dates are hard to remember; often-repeated routines and particular incidents are recalled even at a vast distance in time.

Kaitlin, like many interviewees, was apologetic about her memory. She had difficulties with dates. Like other oral history interviewees, she looked for land-marks that might help her remember. So, as to when she joined the Home Guard, she asked the interviewer 'When was Dunkirk?', then said 'must have been 1940 to 41', then recalled that she was not in the Local Defence Volunteers (the name by which the Home Guard was known from May to July 1940) but joined after that 'when they got organised'.[21] She struggled to remember details, notably by which letters of the alphabet the eight Home Guard companies in Workington were known. Thus, she referred uncertainly to the town's company as 'whatever company, B company, or whatever it was that trained at the Hippodrome Cinema', and said that 'C company' was at Clifton Colliery. She also tentatively remembered the name of a woman in the 'Steel Works' company, 'Sister, Short was it?', with whom she recalled intense rivalry. But she spoke unambiguously about joining up and what she did in the Home Guard. She also spoke in detail about other aspects of the Second World War such as coping with shortages of cosmetics and clothing, the operation of the black market, and her regular job.

VALIDITY AND REPRESENTATIVENESS

We noted earlier that the social science approach to oral history demands that the validity of evidence be tested. This is often done through 'triangulation', that is seeking other sources, either similar – such as other oral interviewees – or different – such as documentary evidence – to corroborate testimonies. We did not find other interviewees from Workington but we found another specific account of the Workington Home Guard on a website called 'The Real "Dad's Army"', by an enthusiast, R. W. Barnes. This confirmed much of Kaitlin's account and threw light on details with which she had struggled, stating that there were women in 'A Company' at the Steel Works from 1942 led by 'Sister Short' and in 'Headquarters Company' (to which Kaitlin belonged) from 1941. It confirmed that Kaitlin was right about the Town Company being 'B Company' but wrong about 'C Company' which was attached to the railway. The miners of Clifton were in 'D Company'. Our other oral-history interviews corroborated her account in a more general way. Out of the seventeen women we interviewed, nine (including Kaitlin) joined the Home Guard directly, later becoming Women Home Guard Auxiliaries, and four of them were trained to use rifles.[22] Thus, we learned that this was not something that happened only to Kaitlin, or only in Workington. Documentary sources, including a set of papers deposited at the Birkenhead Library by a Women's Home Defence organiser in Wallasey, and evidence collected and published by Charles Graves, the first historian of the organisation, confirmed that the Home Guard worked with women in the period of the ban and trained them to shoot. This triangulation indicated that, notwithstanding Kaitlin's small lapses of memory, there was no reason to consider her evidence unreliable.

Our interviews enabled us to recover a lost aspect of women's role in the Second World War, and to ask historiographical and theoretical questions about why that element had been lost. The project demonstrated that oral history as recovery history is valuable and important. However, it also indicated some of the limitations of the social-science methodology, on which the recovery approach has been based. Most fundamentally, there are difficulties about representing oral-history findings statistically, for two major reasons. Firstly, there is the problem of obtaining representative samples: of people who have survived long enough (since the Second World War), who have experienced the specific things the oral historian is interested in (the Home Guard), and, crucially, who are contactable and willing to be interviewed. Secondly, oral history interviews work against the production of data that can be statistically represented: they are typically semi-structured dialogues conducted very differently from the structured questionnaire of, say, the market researcher. Interviewers ask follow-up questions, prompting their interviewees to elaborate and explain what they mean; they do not tick boxes. The conversation thus pursues areas unanticipated by the researcher and as a result not all interviewees are asked the same questions. Interviewees understand the same questions in different ways, and answers vary in length, complexity and ambiguity. A heuristic encounter occurs in an oral-history dialogue. The interests of the interviewer in a particular subject about which they know something and wish to find out more are constantly modified by the preoccupations of the interviewee with other aspects of a past unknown to the interviewer, and which the dialogue can enable the interviewee to rediscover.

There is a tension in oral-history writing such as that of Thompson and Roberts between the science-based preference for reliable generalisations about what was typical in the past, and the desire to select a small number of cases for their striking revelations and powerful language. The 'scientific' approach, in short, undersells the 'richness' of oral history evidence, derived less from the so-called objective evidence of what happened in the past (although this otherwise-unrecoverable evidence is important), than from the subjectivity expressed in and constructed through the language of the interchange. Acknowledging that oral history is about subjectivity suggests that its practitioners need to address at least two other issues: the dynamics of the interview, and the relationship of culture to memory.

INTERVIEW DYNAMICS

Gerontologists argue that reminiscence in old age is affected by life review, the process of looking back questioningly over a life to gauge its value. Life review typically involves comparisons with other individuals, reappraisal of the morality and integrity of particular relationships and incidents, and the search for self-affirmation.[23] Kaitlin's interview contained some such reflections. She referred repeatedly to her father and at one point compared herself directly with him. She explained that he had been a soldier in India in the First World War, became a bank manager, and was a public figure in West Cumberland (chair of the West Cumberland Health Authority and Deputy Lord Lieutenant of the county). He was also a leading Freemason, that is a member of a secret all-male fraternity that offered mutual assistance, and he was a commanding officer in the Home Guard. At one point Kaitlin said reflectively: 'he worked very hard and his family were very important to him. I hope I'm like him in some ways. I hope so.'[24]

In what sense, exactly, did Kaitlin hope she was like him? Asked if her father had passed on his values to her, she answered in the affirmative, relating this to the way her father 'always treated everybody exactly the same way' whatever 'walk of life' they were from, and saying that like him 'I accept people as they are'.[25] But in other respects it seems that she was not like him. She did not appear to seek or achieve public prominence, for example, she worked as a bank clerk, then as a member of the Women's Royal Naval Service from 1947 to 1949, and later as a secretary. Her family history was different, too, in that she married twice and had no children. Instead, she may have been referring to her father's rectitude. She was emphatic that he was a model of propriety, although her account was not without contradiction: she resented his prohibition of the use of the wartime black market to obtain clothing and food, and his disapproval of her use of make-up and nail varnish; she also remembered occasions when his upright stand had been compromised, for example when the family had kept a salmon thrown into their garden by a fleeing poacher and when he had been reprimanded by the authorities for teaching her to shoot.[26] Further analysis might reveal more about the life review that was clearly occurring in the interview, for example the precise sense in which Kaitlin's father was a benchmark for her and the meaning of her relative silence about her mother.

A related aspect of the dynamics of the interview is 'composure'. This term has been used by Graham Dawson, Al Thomson, and others, to indicate a dual process at work in an interview.[27] It refers to both the composition of the story that the interviewee tells, and to the achievement of personal composure or psychic equilibrium through the process of telling. Regarding the composition of the narrative, some oral historians, especially those from a socio-linguistic background such as Marie-Françoise Chanfrault-Duchet, consider the narrative style and form used by the interviewee as significant for the meanings conveyed about the subject and their historical world.[28] Thus, the choice of the fairy-tale form, where fate determines outcomes and benign and malign influences are clearly polarised, suggests a particular type of relationship between the individual and society. The choice of the epic form, on the other hand, where individuals set themselves an objective for which they strive against obstacles, overcoming setbacks including their own weaknesses until they ultimately triumph, suggests a different construction of the self in history. There are obviously other narrative forms, such as the confession, the conversion narrative and the escape story.

Oral history interviewees frequently combine several different narrative forms depending on what aspect of their lives they are talking about. Like many narrators, Kaitlin specialised in an anecdotal style, in which short snapshots, complete in themselves and often with a punchline or final reflection emphasising the intended meaning, were strung together to form an account.[29] An example comes from the first half hour of the interview. Kaitlin told a vivid story of learning to shoot her father's First World War revolver in the back garden, to which the interviewer responded, 'Do you think you could have defended yourself if the Germans had invaded then?' whereupon Kaitlin started to reflect on what we now know about Hitler's intentions as far as Britain was concerned. The interviewer adeptly returned the conversation to 'what you knew at the time', since it was Kaitlin's reconstruction of her wartime self that was relevant to the project. Kaitlin then produced a lengthy and fluent account consisting of a series of six anecdotes. Four addressed defence, one addressed invasion, and one addressed bombing. The themes of heroism, stoicism and incompetence permeated them.

The first anecdote focused on Kaitlin's (heroic and competent) father who told her after the war that he had been recruited to help organise a secret government resistance organisation linked to the Home Guard. 'It was about ten years after the end of the war that, that he told me about that.'[30] The next anecdote concerned the Home Guard units under her father's command and the incompetence manifest in some of them. The anecdote focused on B Company's use of the ballroom under the cinema for their meetings and an occasion on which a Home Guard member had forgotten to clear the bullet from his rifle and let it off by mistake: 'the bullet went straight up to the ceiling, straight through a poor woman's foot, in the cinema. Well, you can imagine absolute pandemonium in the cinema, the sound of gunfire and screaming you know!'[31] The third anecdote was about the Clifton Home Guard company, to which the local miners belonged. There was a ridiculous side to these Home Guards, although they were not as incompetent as the 'idiot' who let off his rifle under the cinema. Kaitlin told how, when performing mock battles as training exercises, the miners frequently refused to be 'dead'. She brought this vividly to life by mimicking the interchanges of the miners, but the concluding sentence of the anecdote indicated that she nevertheless regarded them as serious defenders: 'They were very tough. I wouldn't like to have been any German that had got into their hands.'[32]

The fourth anecdote substantiated this final point: it was a story of German prisoners of war, much favoured by the local farmers as a cheap source of farm labour, who occasionally tried to escape. When they did so, they were rounded up by the Clifton Home Guard: 'their blood was up, you know, hunting down these er these chaps'.[33]

The fifth anecdote was a dénouement to the preceding stories, bringing attention back from events remembered through stories her father had told her, to Kaitlin herself. It concerned her memories of the fear of the invasion and its imagined outcomes:

> we honestly thought that the Germans would invade us and it would be
> like another Dunkirk, you know, that they would just come and they
> would sweep through everything, and if we weren't shot we'd be taken
> off to, er, detention camps . . . and of course I had, I had long ash
> blonde hair, and I was terrified that I'd be carried off with some
> German, you know! To some, you know, they had these baby factories
> to make a pure Aryan race.[34]

The final anecdote concerned what did in fact happen: not an invasion that called forth everyone's heroism, but prolonged, though intermittent, bombing that demanded stoic endurance. Kaitlin evoked the noise of the German planes going to Glasgow to the north and Silloth to the West 'yurimmmm, yurimmmm', the 'glow in the sky' that was Glasgow on fire, and the dropping of no more than 'occasional random sticks of bombs' on Workington. The actual experience of war was different from the drama and sexual threat of the invasion of her imagination: 'I suppose we were quite lucky really but er, it was the dreariness of everything, really. The blackout and the dreariness, and the rationing you know. It um, it wasn't a very easy time at all.'[35]

Narrative style, as well as narrative content, communicates messages about the subjectivity under construction. Kaitlin's succession of anecdotes, mostly about others than herself, established her as an observer, able to draw lessons from events and characters of the time. They tell us that she did not feel herself to have been a direct participant who could produce a coherent narrative focused on herself. The personal and historical meanings of the form and content of her narrative are that the heroic aspects of the war were lodged in her father's world of defence secrets rather than her own world of stoic coping; that the heroic defence intended by the Home Guard was precariously close to incompetent and ridiculous defence; and that what linked her to this world and led her to train to use weapons and join the Home Guard were apprehensions that ultimately proved groundless (although she could not have known this at the time).

Kaitlin's composition of her memories was effective and evidently satisfying to her. The second meaning of the term 'composure', used in relation to oral history, refers to these personal gains. Her reconstruction of her past in a dialogue with her interviewer evidently facilitated her personal composure and resulted in mutual enjoyment of her narrative. Coleman has observed that a particular type of reminiscence that some elderly people engage in involves the repetition of stories that produce a feel-good factor conducive to self-affirmation.[36] Kaitlin had written several of her stories to us in the letter that she sent in response to the original announcement of the project, so they had some of this quality.

However, the uncertainties and discoveries of life review were also present in the interchange, and intermittently put Kaitlin's composure at risk. While some interviewees experience interviews as an enjoyable 'trip down memory lane' through which they can reclaim their past, Kaitlin was preoccupied with the dangers of losing hers. She said of the Second World War in general: 'a lot of it's all forgotten now. I think it's such a pity, because it is all part of our heritage and history.' More specifically, she agonised over the loss of the receipt and key for a bank box in which she had stored mementos of the past (specifically, in this context, her Women's Home Guard Auxiliary certificate).[37]

My previous research revealed that women commonly encountered disbelief or dismissal when they spoke of their wartime jobs and roles in the family or community.[38] Kaitlin was no exception. She spoke of her consequent habitual silence about her membership of the Women's Home Guard Auxiliary. About halfway through the interview, she asked: 'What are you going to do with all this information that you're gathering?' and was told that it would be presented at conferences and published 'because we find especially women's contribution to the Home Guard tends not to be even known about.' She replied to this: 'I don't think it is. You know, I mean I keep quiet about it because I, I think people would just laugh, you know, and say, "What was the Home Guard?"'[39]

The interview gave Kaitlin the opportunity to break this self-enforced silence about her wartime experiences, and hence to overcome the tragedy of losing her past. But Kaitlin's hold on her sense of herself in the past was not strong. In contrast to the integration gained from telling life stories to which Charlotte Linde refers as a common outcome,[40] Kaitlin expressed a strong sense of discontinuity. She stressed the difference between the person whose life story she was composing, and the person she felt herself to be in the present. 'When I look back on it, it all seems so long ago you know, as though it never really happened, as though it probably happened to somebody else really, more than me.'[41] Life review was not giving her a comfortable sense of coherent identity but of disjuncture conducive to discomposure.[42]

Recall is frequently accompanied by nostalgia, or wistful longing for the past. Kaitlin's memories did not produce a longing to return to the past or the type of nostalgia, common in reminiscence, which works as a critique of the present.[43] Kaitlin's recall produced a certain alienation: during the interview she composed a part for herself in history and, having done so, she found her past self almost unrecognisable. Understanding the relationship of interviewees to their past selves requires exploration of their present circumstances. For Kaitlin, the significant present-day factors apparent in the interview were her state of health and the state of her marriage. On the first, she referred to various health problems that made it hard for her to go out as she used to, and in addition the interviewer found out (off tape) that Kaitlin had been suffering from leukaemia for the past twenty years. On the second, Kaitlin talked about her second husband's rages and sulks, the assertive way in which she would like to have dealt with them (but of which she felt incapable), his undemonstrative personality similar to that of her first husband, and her anxiety about his health.[44]

In the light of an approach to oral history informed by the concept of composure, the expectations of the empowerment of the subject who, through an oral-history interview, discovers her place in history, seem rather glib. Composure or integration is likely to be the objective of the teller of the life story, but discomposure is a possible and even probable outcome. It raises issues unresolved among oral historians, about the proximity of the interview to a therapeutic session as well as about the nature of the skills required in consequence by an interviewer.

POPULAR MEMORY ISSUES

A criticism made of recovery history is that oral historians often rather naïvely regard what their interviewees say as a window on the past. They establish the reliability of the witness through triangulation, but then treat the account of experiences as unmediated and authentic. There are clearly problems with this. Memory interacts with experience and with ideological and cultural representations of both the present and the past, so that accounts of the past are never 'pure recall' of life as it was. As poststructuralists have observed, accounts of experience cannot give direct access to 'reality' because it is impossible to compose them outside the language and discourses in which we make sense of our lives.[45] What are oral historians to do with these insights? An attempt to scrape off the influence of cultural constructs to get at the underlying truths would clearly not work. Should one relinquish the mission of oral history – to place personal experience at the heart of history – and study only the discourses that shape consciousness and behaviour? Or should one concentrate on what memories tell us about the present, through a study of the 'way in which popular memories are constructed and reconstructed as part of a contemporary consciousness'?[46] Both are possibilities, but both take the focus away from the individual's relationship to history.

Another possibility is to accept that oral history taps mediated memory, and that the mediation is as much a part of the history one is studying as the memory. Education, religion, politics, local and family traditions and public culture all influence the way the past is remembered and interpreted. These are historical phenomena and the oral historian can study their interrelation with memory and recall. Italian oral historians such as Luisa Passerini and Alessandro Portelli stress the role of ideology and collective memory within personal accounts. Al Thomson and other oral historians, including myself, have stressed the relationship between popular culture and personal memory.[47]

The idea of the cultural circuit is important to the study of the interactions of culture and memory. According to this concept, developed by Dawson and Thomson, locally-told, individual life stories are picked up, developed and portrayed in a generalised form in popular culture, including, for example, film, television, fiction and newspapers. As a result, the meaning of experiences of, say, the Second World War becomes crystallised in such popular and general accounts. Local and personal versions subsequently use elements of this generalised form in recalling the personal past. It becomes difficult to speak outside it.

For the Home Guard in Britain in the Second World War, there is an easily identifiable cultural construction in the television series *Dad's Army*. This was an immensely popular situation comedy first broadcast in eighty episodes from 1968 to 1977, about a seaside Home Guard unit led by the local bank manager and containing a number of other distinctive characters. The Walmington-on-Sea Home Guard was not very competent, its members were mostly old and unfit, and when they triumphed in their endeavours it was more by luck than good management. They never had to fight, but they were in earnest, and their patriotic leader took the enterprise seriously. This sitcom, which has been repeated many times since 1977, achieved undoubted dominance as a cultural representation of the Home Guard. Our interviews revealed how salient it was to personal memories.

Kaitlin herself spontaneously made a number of references to *Dad's Army*. These were of two types: one concerned what it omitted mistakenly, and the other what it included wrongly. The first related to the idea that it provided a model for recalling the Home Guard. Kaitlin suggested that the series should have had women in it. Having said she always watched it, she volunteered, 'I'm surprised that he never had any women's Home Guard section because it could have been developed into quite a useful er, offshoot of his er comedy show you know. But they never mentioned it at all.'[48] In fact, one of the eighty episodes did refer to women joining the Home Guard, but did so not to explore, humorously, women's participation, so much as to develop the romantic side of Captain Mainwaring. Kaitlin's point remains valid: in seventy-nine of the eighty episodes there are no women in the Home Guard, and the message of the single episode that did include them is that women had no place there. Kaitlin argued that the inclusion of women throughout the series would have been suitable given the nature of the comedy. She referred to the male Home Guards she knew as 'so ham-handed with their er, trying to use the typewriter and things like that,' and she mimicked her father insisting that she find some women to join. The inclusion of women would also have removed the silence within contemporary collective memory over women's participation in the Home Guard, from which she felt she suffered.

Kaitlin's second reference to *Dad's Army*, concerning what the programme included wrongly, related to the incompetence of the Home Guard. Kaitlin argued that in fact the Home Guard changed over time and became a well-equipped, well-disciplined and efficient adjunct of the army, a dimension never portrayed in the programme. She was aware of the demands of television humour: 'well of course that is a comedy programme'.[49] She struggled with the issue of typicality: *Dad's Army* both was and was not typical of the people who joined the Home Guard and their activities.

> I think it was er, it was very typical of what went on, you know. The, all sorts of people involved in it you know. The opportunist and the patriotic. I think, er, I think it, it – I don't know, it was reasonably true to life I think. Although we never had anything like that happening.[50]

The contradiction in this statement (it was true to life, but nothing like that happened), suggests that *Dad's Army* established its own typicality, drawn from Home Guard experience and mediated by sitcom conventions. It was inevitably not a direct and accurate representation of the Home Guard but it nevertheless became a touchstone for memory; it shaped the imaginative possibilities open to individuals to recall and recount Home Guard experiences. Kaitlin followed the statement quoted above with a recapitulation of two anecdotes of Home Guard incompetence and unintended humour. It was not that Kaitlin invented these accounts as a result of the influence of *Dad's Army*, but her reiteration of them in the context of the discussion of the television programme suggests that she consciously or unconsciously identified them as suitable 'Home Guard stories' because they conformed in a general sense to the content of *Dad's Army* episodes. *Dad's Army* also, of course, communicates a wider set of meanings and values concerning Britain in the Second World War imbricated with personal memory and interpretation.

ETHICS AND PROTOCOLS

This last section addresses briefly the procedures governing oral history interviews. There is not an agreed code of practice, although the ethics of oral history interviewing have been debated (for example, by Minister) and some practitioners, including Thompson, offer useful lists of 'dos and don'ts' about the use of equipment, keeping records, interview technique, accepting hospitality and so on.[51]

I shall focus here on issues of ownership. It is common to secure the interviewee's written consent to the release of the material on the tape of the interview. This is because in law the copyright of the spoken word belongs to the person who said it. Thus, if an interviewee signs a release agreement (see Annex 1), the oral historian is entitled to quote it without having to request permission each time they want to do so. Oral historians vary in how much control they give interviewees over this, and there are at least three approaches. In one, the oral historian returns a written transcript with the release form, enabling interviewees to exclude from public use as much as they want. However, the transcript, a literal record of the spoken interchange, may be alienating to interviewees because textualised conversation offends literary rules of phrasing, grammatical construction and so on. In addition, the written form of a conversation that has ranged over much more than the specific focus of the interview may suggest to interviewees that they should censor what they regard as extraneous material. These two problems may lead interviewees to restrict the interviewer's opportunities to make use of the collected material. The second approach is to return a copy of the tape recording to interviewees with the release form. This has the advantage of giving back to interviewees a facsimile of what they actually did and said during the interview. Interviewees can still identify material they wish to restrict, but it is not presented to them in the altered form of a text. The third approach is to ask interviewees to sign the release form immediately after the interview. The advantage is that interviewees do so in the context of the relationship they have built up with the interviewer and in a situation where they can talk about the kinds of uses to be made of it. The disadvantage is that interviewees may have a hazy memory of what they have just said and that this approach leaves little time for reflection. In all three cases, interviewees can be offered anonymity as one of the conditions on which they release the material of the interview.

It is very common to offer interviewees a pseudonym. Kaitlin took up this offer. She did not say why she wanted one, but she and her interviewer agreed on the spot the name by which she was to be known. She joked that 'Kaitlin Wells' sounded like a tourist site. What are the issues relating to this type of anonymity? Firstly, it cannot guarantee literal anonymity, unless all the details are changed (place, occupation, and so on), which would defeat the specificity integral to the enquiry. Nevertheless a pseudonym makes the interviewee's identity less obvious. Secondly, however, a pseudonym contradicts the objective of giving the subject a place in history in her own right, as an identified historical actor. On the other hand, the experiences recorded and the person to whom they happened become part of the historical account, even if not by name.

A third, rather different, issue is that interviewers may want to protect interviewees from the academic analysis to which they subject the testimony. Kaitlin asked her interviewer what was going to happen to the 'information' collected, and the interviewer answered in terms of recovery history. But the modes of analysis of oral-history material discussed above are not focused on 'information' alone. Analysis also includes attention to the underlying intersubjective processes at work in the interview, such as life review, composure and discomposure. Interviewees are unlikely to have been aware of these dimensions, and might feel personally exposed by their public discussion. 'Triangulating' interviewees' accounts could seem to imply that their 'evidence' is suspect. Contextualising it in relation to popular culture and exploring it in relation to a 'cultural circuit' could suggest that their memory is indeed felt to be contaminated or that interviewees are being accused of speaking from a script. Any of these could cause offence or distress.

Oral historians have a number of choices about the protocol to follow in relation to pseudonyms. They can allow interviewees to decide, even though they do not and cannot know the extent and type of the interview's subsequent interpretation. If interviewees decline pseudonyms, oral historians can make a decision on their behalf. The difficulty with this, of course, is that they might thereby rob interviewees of their much sought-after place in history. This is an unresolved issue still troubling oral historians.

CONCLUSION

I have reviewed the original mission of oral history to recover lost histories and thereby to give ordinary individuals a place in history. I have emphasised the enduring importance of recovery history, at the same time as drawing attention to the problems of expecting a social science methodology to be suitable for it. The dynamics of the oral history interview, notably the life review and search for composure, constitute an important part of the meanings generated. The same is true of the narrative form that is used. Far from amounting to 'contaminations' that need to be eradicated, ideology and discourse – borne, for instance, by popular culture – are integral to memory, and their relationship to it needs to be analysed. All this complicates the ethical issues associated with oral history, but should not discourage its use. On the contrary, it is an exciting and developing methodology which has a vital role to play not only in recovering lost histories but in enlarging our understanding of the past.

ACKNOWLEDGEMENTS

I should like to thank the Feminist Research Seminar at the University of Hull for stimulating discussion of an earlier version of this paper; Dr Corinna Peniston-Bird who worked with me on the Home Defence project as a research associate; and all the women who agreed to be interviewed, especially Kaitlin Wells.

ANNEX 4.1: ORAL HISTORY RELEASE AGREEMENT

[Address]

COPYRIGHT AGREEMENT

[Title of project]

This is to certify that I give permission for the transcript of my interview to be quoted and for copies of my photographs and documents to be published and used for teaching purposes.

I understand that the material will most probably be used by [the researchers] as part of their research, and that it may be archived in a [named] library, where other researchers will have access to it.

I accept the above arrangement.

I do/do not wish my name to be used in any publication arising from the research. (Please delete as applicable).

Signed: ....

             (interviewee)   (interviewer)

Date: ....

NOTES

1. See, for example, Shulamit Reinharz (1992), *Feminist Methods in Social Research*, Oxford: Oxford University Press; ch. 7; Graham Hitchcock and David Hughes (1989), *Research and the Teacher: A Qualitative Introduction to School-Based Research*, London: Routledge, ch. 5.
2. http://www.bl.uk/collections/sound-archive/nsa.html
3. Leverhulme Trust, Research Project F/185/AK, 'The gendering of British National Defence 1939–1945: The case of the Home Guard', June 1999 – August 2000', University of Lancaster; henceforth referred to as 'GBND Project'.
4. A key text was, and is, E. P. Thompson [1963] (1968), *The Making of the English Working Class*, Harmondsworth: Penguin.
5. Richard Hoggart (1957), *The Uses of Literacy: Aspects of Working-class Life*, London: Chatto and Windus; Raymond Williams (1958), *Culture and Society 1780–1950*, London: Chatto and Windus.
6. Paul Thompson [1978] (2000), *The Voice of the Past: Oral History*, 3rd edn, Oxford: Oxford University Press.
7. Elizabeth Roberts (1984), *A Woman's Place: An Oral History of Working-Class Women 1890–1940*, Oxford: Basil Blackwell.
8. Jill Liddington and Jill Norris (1978), *One Hand Tied Behind Us: The Rise of the Women's Suffrage Movement*, London: Virago.
9. B. Bryan, S. Dadzie and S. Scafe (1985), *The Heart of the Race: Black Women's Lives in Britain*, London: Virago; Ben Bousquet and Colin Douglas (1991), *West Indian Women at War: British Racism in World War II*, London: Lawrence and Wishart.
10. For instance, *The Times*, 12 November 1941.
11. For a historical analysis based on such sources, see Penny Summerfield (2000), ' "She wants a gun not a dishcloth!": Gender, service and citizenship in Britain in the Second World War', in G. J. DeGroot and C. Peniston-Bird, *A Soldier and a Woman: Sexual Integration in the Military*, Harlow: Pearson Education, pp. 119–34. The most recent history of the Home Guard is S. P. MacKenzie (1995), *The Home Guard, A Military and Political History*, Oxford, Oxford University Press.
12. Central Statistical Office (1995), *Fighting with Figures: A Statistical Digest of the Second World War*, London: HMSO, Table 3.9.
13. Women aged twenty to sixty, 1939, calculated from ibid., Table 1.4.
14. See Peter Coleman (1999), 'Creating a life story: The task of reconciliation', *The Gerontologist* 39/2, pp. 133–9.
15. We sent a page of questions to all the women who contacted us, asking for open-ended answers. This included 'Would you be prepared to be interviewed?' We also found eleven interviews with former women Home Guards in the Imperial War Museum Sound Archive, and eight documentary accounts (diaries, memoirs) in the Imperial War Museum Documents Department.
16. GBND Project, Correspondence, 14 December 1999.
17. It takes many hours to word-process one hour of tape. A careful written summary of a long interview, used with the recording, can save time and expense.
18. Alessandro Portelli (1998), 'What makes oral history different', in R. Perks and A. Thomson (eds), *The Oral History Reader*, London: Routledge, pp. 64–6.
19. Eric Hobsbawm (1997), *On History*, London: Weidenfeld and Nicolson, p. 206.
20. Trevor Lummis (1987), *Listening to History: The Authenticity of Oral Evidence*, London: Hutchinson, Ch. 11.

21. GBND Project, Wells Interview, 106–10.
22. The other eight women either joined the WHD or the Women's Home Guard Auxiliary.
23. Coleman, 'Creating a life story'.
24. GBND Project, Wells Interview, 17.
25. Ibid., 23.
26. Ibid., 51–4, 59.
27. Graham Dawson (1994), *Soldier Heroes: British Adventure, Empire and the Imagining of Masculinities*, London: Routledge; Al Thomson (1994), *Anzac Memories: Living with the Legend*, Melbourne: Oxford University Press, Australia.
28. Marie-Françoise Chanfrault-Duchet (2000), 'Textualisation of the self and gender identity in the life story', in T. Cosslett, C. Lury and P. Summerfield (eds), *Feminism and Autobiography: Texts, Theories, Methods*, London: Routledge.
29. See T. G. Ashplant (1998), 'Anecdotes as narrative resource in working-class life stories: parody, dramatization and sequence', in M. Chamberlain and P. Thompson (eds), *Narrative and Genre*, London: Routledge, pp. 99–113.
30. GBND Project, Wells Interview, 69–73.
31. Ibid., 75.
32. Ibid.
33. Ibid.
34. Ibid.
35. Ibid.
36. Peter Coleman (1991), 'Ageing and life history: the meaning of reminiscence in late life', in S. Dex (ed.), *Life and Work History Analyses: Qualitative and Quantitative Developments*, London: Routledge, pp. 120–43.
37. GBND Project, Wells Interview, 78, 130.
38. See Penny Summerfield (2004), 'Culture and composure: creating narratives of the gendered self in oral history interviews', *Cultural and Social History*, 1, pp. 65–93.
39. GBND Project, Wells Interview, 176–7.
40. Charlotte Linde (1993), *Life Stories: The Creation of Coherence*, Oxford: Oxford University Press.
41. GBND Project, Wells Interview, 360.
42. See Penny Summerfield (2000), 'Dis/Composing the subject: intersubjectivities in oral history', in T. Cosslett et al. (eds), *Feminism and Autobiography: Texts, Theories, Methods*, London: Routledge, pp. 91–106.
43. See Jeffrey Richards (1997), ' "Dad's Army" and the politics of nostalgia', in J. Richards, *Films and British National Identity: From Dickens to 'Dad's Army'*, Manchester: Manchester University Press, pp. 351–66.
44. GBND Project, Wells Interview, 383–91, 213–15. I have also drawn on the project research diary here. Both researchers wrote brief accounts of each interview as it happened, and shared them, so that we would both have knowledge of the context in which interviews took place, as well as access to off-tape additions to interviewees' life stories.
45. See, for example, Joan W. Scott (1992), 'Experience', in J. Butler and J. W. Scott (eds), *Feminists Theorize the Political*, London: Routledge, p. 34.
46. Richard Johnson et al. (eds) (1982), *Making Histories: Studies in History-writing and Politics*, Hutchinson, London, p. 219.
47. See, for example, Luisa Passerini's 'Introduction' in L. Passerini (ed.) (1992), *Memory and Totalitarianism*, Oxford: Oxford University Press; Alessandro Portelli (1991), *The Death of Luigi Trastulli and Other Stories: Form and Meaning in Oral History*, Albany: SUNY Press;

Penny Summerfield (1998), *Reconstructing Women's Wartime Lives: Discourse and Subjectivity in Oral Histories of the Second World War*, Manchester: Manchester University Press, especially ch. 1; Thomson, *Anzac Memories*, especially Introduction and Appendix 1.

48. GBND Project, Wells Interview, 179.
49. Ibid., 278, 326.
50. Ibid., 326.
51. K. Minister (1981) 'A feminist frame for the oral history interview', in S. B. Gluck and D. Patai (eds), *Women's Words. The Feminist Practice of Oral History*, London: Routledge; Thompson, *The Voice of the Past*, ch. 7.

CHAPTER 5

Visual Methodologies

Gillian Rose, Open University

Visual images have been the object of study for a variety of disciplines for as long as those disciplines have existed. They include art history in the humanities, most obviously, but also, within the social sciences, the sub-disciplines of visual anthropology and visual sociology. Geography has long understood maps and photographs as central to its project (Harley 1992; Cosgrove 1998; Matless 1996), and clearly many natural sciences use images as evidence for their claims. More recently, however, certain kinds of images, and some discipline-specific modes of approaching them, have started to cross those disciplinary boundaries, with interesting results. Part of the intrigue of the much acclaimed texts by W. G. Sebald, such as *The Emigrants*, rests on the inclusion of images, the meaning of which is never explained. Similarly, Roddy Doyle's (2002) *Rory and Ita* contains photos devoid of captions, activating the reader into interrogative mode. In a different manner, certain kinds of art history are now being read by geographers, among others (for an early example, see Cosgrove and Daniels 1988). Anthropological approaches to documentary photography are deployed by those on the border between science and science studies (Latour 1999), while some art historians are studying scientific illus-trations (Stafford 1984). This cross-border traffic in images and analytics is beginning to congeal into a new field of study called visual culture.

'Visual culture' is by no means an uncontested term. It was hotly debated in the journal *October* in 1996, and again in the first volume of the *Journal of Visual Culture* in 2002. While some argue that visual culture is an object of study, based on the assumption that modern societies make meaning through visual imagery more now than ever before – the claim has even been made that 'modern life takes place onscreen' (Mirzoeff 1999: 1) – others regard visual culture as an approach to understanding specific instances of vision and visu-ality (Foster 1988). This latter approach has focused on an enormous range of images as they have been deployed in different places at different times.

Given these academic developments – and perhaps also a shift in the wider cultural context within which Western academics work – it seems more and more likely that researchers in the field of English will notice and be intrigued by the visual images that also proliferate in and around their traditional object of study, the book. Many books have images as covers, illustrations or photographs, as part of their associated publicity, or through film adaptation. Conversely, it is hard to think of a visual image that is not accompanied by language in some form. Paintings in galleries have captions, catalogues and sometimes price tags; most advertisements have their meaning anchored by text; painted altarpieces in churches are viewed with a guidebook in hand, or a guide's voice explaining them; films are watched through the filter of written reviews and interviews with their stars; maps have their keys; family photographs have stories spun around them.

Images and written or spoken words seem, then, to live in an intimate relation. But by and large, the critical apparatuses brought to bear upon them seem intent on keeping them apart, or rather, seeing one as subsidiary to the other or failing to discuss the ways in which meaning cannot be self-evidently read from these images. English studies, except in discussions of illuminated manuscripts, rarely pays attention to the imagery that accompanies the written text. And while the way in which visual images are scrutinised for their meaning very often depends on broader contextual accounts that rely on a wide and scholarly reading of contemporary texts of many kinds, it is still unusual to find a detailed concern with the texts found in close actual proximity to the image in question.

For me, coming from a discipline deeply concerned with the construction of closeness and distance, this refusal to place visual images – and indeed literary texts – in their material setting seems not only strange but troubling. Why split things apart when they are almost always found in spatial proximity? Yet this splitting is deeply established. In his book on 'the nature of seeing', James Elkins (1996) describes precisely this erasure of the context of visual imagery or objects as 'the primary scene' upon which visual criticism depends. The primary scene, for Elkins, is the fundamental scene for such criticism, and it is one 'where one observer encounters what appears to be one object' (1996: 39). Face to face with their object of study, in Elkins' account, the critic simply ignores any kind of grounding of that object in particular places, and with specific people. Elkins describes these site-specific inflections to visual images as 'sources of confusion' (1996: 39). Well, yes, they might be confusing and challenging to understand, but that is surely no reason to ignore them.

Indeed, some of these so-called 'sources of confusion' make a greater engagement with visual materials by those interested in literary texts exciting. Those sources of complexity may be many and various, and other chapters in this volume address some of them in relation to written texts in ways that are just as valid in relation to visual images: the sites and practices of reading, the intersection of texts and rituals, the diversity of audiences. But one source of complexity that more recent literature on visual culture has paid remarkably little attention to is the particular relationship between the images and the texts that so very often accompany images. Rare, for instance, is a discussion of the captions that help museum visitors make sense of the objects on display (but see Bal 1996); and rare is any discussion of the publicity that attends the openings of big art shows (but see Bolton 1989).

This lack of attention is odd on another ground, too: two of the most influential and pervasive methodologies for approaching visualisations both have firm roots in the study of language. These are the second and third methods I will discuss in this chapter: semiology and discourse analysis (the first is what I call 'compositional interpretation', which has its roots in a certain kind of art history practice). While some critics continue to doubt whether these methods can be easily transferred onto visual materials, many others seem quite happy to make that move. Yet the imagery discussed is then most often treated in isolation from its written companions.

In turning to methods that might enable a more careful engagement between the visual materials that infiltrate and inflect literary texts and the texts themselves, it will become clear that the decision to use these methods cannot be based solely on a judgement concerning how apposite they are for visual as well as written materials. I have chosen to discuss semiology and discourse analysis as two useful methods for approaching visual imagery with a further consideration in mind: that is, to encourage a critical approach to visual imagery (see Rose 2001). Images are important not simply because, for some people in some places, they are pervasive, but because they have effects. In particular, they have effects in relation to the construction of social differentiation. Different identities, different subject positions are reiterated in highly complex ways by visual images. And since such differences are riven by power relations, Fyfe and Law's comments remain apposite:

> a depiction is never just an illustration . . . it is the site for the
> construction and depiction of social difference . . . To understand a
> visualisation is thus to enquire into its provenance and into the social
> work that it does. It is to note its principles of inclusion and exclusion,
> to detect the roles that it makes available, to understand the way in
> which they are distributed, and to decode the hierarchies and
> differences that it naturalises. (Fyfe and Law 1988: 1)

Critical approaches to visual images are necessary because visualisations do work: they have effects, in depicting and reinforcing social differences and hierarchies. Hence my discussion of methods that follows is not only descriptive but evaluative. Not only will I describe, albeit briefly, three methods for interpreting visual imagery, but I will also assess what they produce as evidence in relation to their utility for critical understanding.

COMPOSITIONAL INTERPRETATION

This is a term I have coined for a way of proceeding in relation to images that is particularly common in art history. Compositional interpretation is a method that offers a way of looking very carefully at the content and form of images. In my experience, as an outsider to art history, it is a method that seems second nature to all art historians; what distinguishes between the different kinds of art history eventually produced is what is then done with the evidence thus constructed. All art historians, however, are trained to scrutinise the image itself carefully, to produce what one might describe as a close reading of the image.

Exactly what this entails is not very often made explicit, and in fact, although I am going to offer some guidelines that do make compositional interpretation an explicit method, I will also suggest that this method depends on a certain element of intuition, a certain sensibility. For those not trained in art history, however, making this procedure a little more transparent is necessary, not least because the successful deployment of the other methods discussed in this chapter – methods that I think are more appropriate for a critical visual methodology – also relies, initially, on detailed scrutiny of the image itself.

'Composition' refers to the structure of an image: how all its elements combine together (which might or might not make some sort of whole). Although the aim of compositional interpretation is indeed to describe the image as attentively and as fully as possible, the notion of composition can nonetheless be broken down into a number of component parts (and here I draw on Taylor (1957) and Acton (1997)).

Firstly, then, there is the content of an image. What exactly is it showing? This may be very obvious for some images, but less so for others, particularly those made in periods when certain kinds of symbolism were routinely deployed to make meaning through images. Then there are the colours of an image. The colours themselves can be described in terms of their hue (the colour itself), its saturation (how intense a version of that colour it is), and its value (how light or dark it is). But there is also the question of how these colours work together. Are they harmonious or not? What is highlighted by the use of what colours? Are connections made between certain parts of an image by the repeated use of one colour? Do certain colours mean something (Gage (1993) has written at length on the symbolism of colour)? How does the light in the image play into this? Where is the light source, what kind of light is it, what effects does it have?

These questions merge into another set of questions, about how the image is organised internally. Does it have figures and a background? Where are its volumes, and do they balance or not? What movement or rhythm is there in the image between its volumes? Is there a depth indicated by some kind of perspective, or a flatness? Importantly, this internal organisation of an image often offers a particular viewing position to its spectator. So, how does the image position you? Are you expected or invited to occupy a certain location in order to see it? Or does it baffle your look, dispersing you across its surface? Finally – and this is the moment where something more intuitive happens – what is the overall effect that these various elements produce? This is an invitation to describe the feel or the tone of an image, to say something about its particular qualities, to evoke its character.

Compositional interpretation thus offers a series of questions that should lead to the careful description of the content, colour, spatial organisation, light and expressive content of a still image (for an equally detailed vocabulary for describing moving images, see Monaco 2000). This is very useful as a first stage of getting to grips with an image. In its concern for the spatial organisation of an image, moreover, compositional interpretation may also begin to say something about an image's possible effects on a spectator; and I have suggested that this is particularly important for methodologies concerned with imagery's effects. However, as a method for developing a critical account of a visual image, compositional interpretation on its own has various shortcomings. Its greatest limitation, perhaps, is its resolute descriptiveness. It focuses almost entirely on the image itself and is therefore highly formalist in its approach; it has nothing to say about the inter-relations between an image and its companion writing, and I opened this chapter by arguing precisely for the importance of those inter-relations. It also has little means to address how an image might be used and interpreted by specific viewers. Because of this unproblematised concern for visual images 'as they are', compositional interpretation needs to be combined with other methodologies in order to address these other pressing issues.

SEMIOLOGY AND DISCOURSE ANALYSIS

Semiology and discourse analysis are, I would argue, the most common methodologies now deployed by those interested in visual culture. In fact, that literature is also rather coy methodologically – it is fairly unusual to find someone actually describing what methods they used to work towards their account of the visual image in question. This reluctance to discuss methods has various effects, including a certain mystery which seems to shroud the process of visual criticism. Another effect, however, is a slippage between semiology and discourse analysis, so that an amalgam of both seems to be the dominant method deployed in visual culture studies at the moment. Yet semiology and discourse analysis emerge from very different traditions. The genealogy of semiology as it is used in visual criticism is often placed firmly with the structuralist tradition of thought and critique. Judith Williamson, whose *Decoding Advertisements* (1978) still repays careful scrutiny, cites most of the founding fathers of twentieth-century structuralism in her bibliography: Althusser, Barthes, Benjamin, Berger, Brecht, Freud, Gramsci, Lacan, Lévi-Strauss, Marx and Saussure (she also cites Foucault, although his influence was barely perceptible to this reader at least). Discourse analysis, on the other hand – or at least the variants most fully taken on board in the social sciences – owes much of its conceptual apparatus to Foucault and his reluctance not to seek structural causes for discursive formations. My sense is that, currently, the use of 'discourse' as an analytical category is so loose as to blur this distinction. Methodologically, however, as well as philosophically, the distinction between structuralist epistemologies and ontologies, and poststructuralist ones is fundamental. I will therefore discuss semiology and discourse analysis separately.

SEMIOLOGY

The most important tool for semiological analysis is the 'sign': semiology means 'the study of signs'. As Mieke Bal and Norman Bryson (1991: 174) say in their defence of semiology, 'human culture is made up of signs, each of which stands for something other than itself, and the people inhabiting culture busy themselves making sense of those signs'. Semiology has an elaborate analytical vocabulary for describing how signs make sense, and this is one of its major strengths. A semiological analysis entails the deployment of a highly refined set of concepts which produce detailed accounts claiming to describe the exact ways in which the meanings of an image are produced through that image.

Semiological understanding of the sign rests in part on Ferdinand de Saussure's *Course in General Linguistics* (1916). Saussure wanted to develop a systematic understanding of how language works, and he argued that the sign was the basic unit of language. The sign consists of two parts, which are only distinguishable at the analytical level; in practice, they are always integrated into each other. The first part of the sign is the signified. The signified is a concept or an object, for instance 'a very young human unable to walk or talk'. The second part of the sign is the signifier. The signifier is a sound or an image that is attached to a signified; in this case, the word 'baby'. The point that Saussure made with this distinction between signifier and signified, and the point that semiological analysis depends upon, is that there is no necessary relationship between a particular signifier and its signified. We can see this if we think of the way in which different languages use different words for the same signified: 'baby' in English is 'bimbo' or 'bimba' in Italian, for example. Moreover, the same signifier can have different meanings; 'baby' can also be a term of endearment between adults, for example, and in English 'bimbo' does not refer to babies at all but is rather a term that stereotypes certain kinds of adult women. Whatever stability attaches to a particular relationship between a signifier and signified does not depend on an inherent connection between them. Instead, Saussure argued that it depends upon the difference between that particular sign and many others.

There are limits to the usefulness of Saussure's work in relation to visual images. As Iversen (1986: 85) points out:

> Linguistic signs are arbitrary in the sense that there is no relation between the sound of a word and its meaning other than convention, a 'contract' or rule. It is clear that visual signs are not arbitrary, but 'motivated' – there is some rationale for the choice of signifier. The word 'dog' and a picture of one do not signify in the same way, so it is safe to assume that a theory of semiotics based on linguistics will fall far short of offering a complete account of visual signification.

Many semiologists, therefore, acknowledge the importance of Saussure's discussion of the sign, but prefer to turn to the work of the American philosopher Charles Sanders Pierce. Pierce suggested that there were three kinds of signs – iconic, indexical and symbolic – differentiated by the way in which the relation between the signifier and signified is understood. In iconic signs, the signifier represents the signified by apparently having a likeness to it. This type of sign is very important in visual images, especially photographic ones. Thus, a photograph of a baby is an iconic sign of that baby. Diagrams are also iconic signs, since they show the relations between the parts of their object. Indexical signs, on the other hand, have an inherent relationship between the signified and signifier. 'Inherent' is often culturally specific, so a current example familiar to Western readers might be the way that a schematic picture of a baby soother is often used to denote a room in public places where there are baby-changing facilities. Finally, symbolic signs have a conventionalised but clearly arbitrary relation between signifier and signified. Thus, pictures of babies are often used to represent notions of 'the future'.

The distinction between signifier and signified is crucial to semiology because it means that the relation between meanings (signifieds) and signifiers can be problematised. Since 'a sign is always thing-plus-meaning' (Williamson 1978: 17), the connection between a certain signifier and a certain signified can be questioned, and the relations between signs can also be explored. The elaborate technical vocabulary of semiology is aimed at clarifying the different ways in which signifiers and signifieds are attached to (and detached from) each other. The first stage of a semiological analysis, then, is to identify the basic building blocks of an image: its signs. Bal and Bryson (1991: 193–4) point out that it is often quite difficult to differentiate between visual signs, because often there are no clear boundaries between different parts of an image. However, once certain elements of an image have been at least tentatively identified as its signs, their meanings can be explored. One of the most productive aspects of Williamson's (1978) analysis of advertising images, for example, is precisely the way in which she shows how advertisements work by shifting signifieds from one signifier to another. Indeed, she suggests that this is crucial to how advertisements work. Thus, in an ad showing a famous tennis player wearing a certain brand of watch, for example, the qualities attached to that sports star – the signifieds attached to his or her images, such as fitness, wealth, glamour, professional dedication – are shifted onto the watch and its brand, and hence, the argument goes, consumers will want to buy that watch in order to acquire some of those qualities themselves.

Signs are complex, however. Any one sign may have several different meanings and can be doing several things at once, so in analysis the same sign might have to be described using several of these terms. That complexity also often requires the use of written text to specify which of the many possible meanings a particular image might have. Barthes (1977: 38–41) called such a use of text 'anchorage'. Text in advertisements often works as anchorage. In other media, however, (television is an example) the text is much more important in relation to the image; they are complementary, and in such cases Barthes (1977: 38–41) described the written or spoken text as having a 'relay-function'.

The slipperiness and arbitrariness of signs are also stabilised, to greater or lesser degrees, by the wider systems of meaning that give sense to them. These 'wider systems' can be characterised in a number of ways. They have been called 'codes' by Stuart Hall (1980), 'referent systems' by Williamson (1978), and 'mythologies' by Barthes (1973). Each of these terms means something rather different, and each has somewhat different methodological implications. A 'code', for example, as used by Hall (1980), is a set of conventionalised ways of making meaning that are specific to particular groups of people. In the context of making television news programmes, for example, Hall (1980: 136) comments on what he calls the 'professional code' that is mobilised in the work of producers, editors, lighting and camera technicians, newscasters and so on. This professional code guides such things as 'the particular choice of presentational occasions and formats, the selection of personnel, the choice of images, the staging of debates'. It has a 'techno-practical nature', according to Hall, because it operates with 'such apparently neutral-technical questions as visual quality, news and presentational values, televisual quality, "professionalism" and so on' (Hall 1980: 136). Advertisements depend on a professional code too, but also on other codes, crucially those codes held by the particular group of consumers their makers want to sell their product to. Thus, in the tennis star example above, an audience who did not recognise the star would not 'get' the advertisement. Moreover, codes also refer to more profound knowledges in a culture. As Hall (1980) makes clear, codes allow the semiologist access to the wider ideologies at work in a society. 'We must refer, *through* the codes, to the orders of social life, of economic and political power and of ideology', because codes 'contract relations for the sign with the wider universe of ideologies in a society' (Hall 1980: 134). Hall (1980) describes such ideologies as 'metacodes' or 'dominant codes'.

Williamson (1978) describes the underlying structures of meaning patterning the advertising she studied as 'referent systems'. She says that there are three major referent systems on which the signs of advertisements depend: Nature, Magic and Time. Referent systems, like dominant codes, are knowledges that pre-exist advertising and that structure not only advertisements but many other cultural and social forms too. Thus, of the referent system Nature she writes, 'Nature is the primary referent of a culture' (1978: 103). However, Williamson characterises referent systems in a more rigid way than Hall does dominant codes. Following the work of the structuralist anthropologist Claude Lévi-Strauss, Williamson argues that referent systems are organised in binary terms. Hodge and Kress (1988: 30) refer to this structure as 'an abstract elemental binary principle, with infinite particular forms produced by this principle applied repeatedly to the material basis of the code'. Hence the referent system of Nature, as it is used in advertising, depends on a binary distinction between raw and cooked, according to Williamson.

Using Willamson's notion of referent systems depends on a broader understanding of the cultural that is more likely to come from social theory than from empirical investigation. Indeed, Leiss, Kline and Jhally (1986: 165) find Williamson's referent systems too huge to shed much light on advertisements specifically. Barthes' notion of mythology is different again. Barthes (1973: 117) argues that 'myth is not defined by the object of its message, but by the way in which it utters this message: there are formal limits to myth, there are no "substantial" ones'. That is, whereas Williamson's referent systems are substantive – her discussion of Nature, for example, is about how Nature is pictured in advertisements – Barthes instead argues that mythology is defined by its form, not its content. Myth, he suggests, is a 'second-order semiological system' (1973: 123), which builds upon a first level of meaning. 'In meaning', Barthes (1973: 127) writes, 'the meaning is already complete, it postulates a kind of knowledge, a past, a memory, a comparative order of facts, ideas, decisions'. Barthes elaborates what he means by this with an example: 'I am at the barber's, and a copy of *Paris-Match* is offered to me. On the cover, a young Negro in a French uniform is saluting, with his eyes uplifted, probably fixed on the fold of the tricolour' (Barthes 1973: 125). This is the meaning of the image, and he suggests that the image contains a kind of richness at this level (his claim that the photograph carries its referent with it in ways other forms of visual imagery do not); the black boy 'appears as a rich, fully experience, spontaneous, *indisputable* image' (Barthes 1973: 128). When this meaning becomes form at a second level, however, this richness is almost lost. The meaning is put at a distance, and what fills the gap is signification. In this case, signification produces the implication that:

> France is a great Empire, that all her sons, without any colour
> discrimination, faithfully serve under her flag, and that there is no better
> answer to the detractors of an alleged colonialism than the zeal shown by
> this Negro in serving his so-called oppressors. (Barthes 1973: 125)

The contingency and the history of the meaning becomes remote, and instead a myth inserts itself as a non-historical truth. Myth makes us forget that things were and are made; instead, it naturalises the way things are. Myth is thus a form of ideology. French imperialism is the drive behind this myth, says Barthes, and this image presents it as natural. But the myth is believable precisely because form does not entirely replace meaning. 'The meaning will be for the form like an instantaneous reserve of history, a tamed richness, which it is possible to call and dismiss in a sort of rapid alternation' (Barthes 1973: 127); the meaning both hides and sustains the form.

Despite the doubts voiced by some about the appropriateness of using semiology to interpret visual images, it seems that semiology can nonetheless be a very productive way of thinking about visual meaning. Semiology demands detailed analysis of images, and its reliance on case studies, and its elaborate analytical terminology, create careful and precise accounts of how the meanings of particular images are made. Moreover, semiology is centrally concerned with the construction of social difference through signs. Its focus on ideology, ideological complexes and dominant codes, and its recognition of resistance to those, means that it cannot avoid considering the social effects of meaning.

> Sign-events occur in specific circumstances and according to a finite
> number of culturally valid, conventional, yet not unalterable rules . . .
> The selection of those rules and their combination leads to specific
> interpretive behaviour. That behaviour is socially framed, and any
> semiotic view that is to be socially relevant will have to deal with this
> framing, precisely on the grounds of the fundamental polysemy of
> meaning and the subsequent possibility of dissemination. In the end,
> there is no way around considerations of power, inside and outside the
> academy. (Bal and Bryson 1991: 208)

As Bal and Bryson's last sentence indicates, semiology can also imply the need for academic accounts of signs to reflect on their own meaning-making tactics. What kinds of meanings, what kinds of truth does an interpretation of a visual image claim? Whose views are not being acknowledged in that interpretation?

Thus, it would seem that semiology fulfils many of the criteria for a critical visual methodology. It takes images seriously, providing a number of tools for understanding exactly how a particular image is structured. It considers the social conditions and effects of images, both in terms of how an image itself may have its own effects and how the wider social context shapes its production and reception. And it is able to acknowledge that semiologists are themselves working with signs, codes and referent systems and are thus imbricated in nothing more – though certainly nothing less – than another series of transfers of meaning in which a particular image participates. This allows a certain reflexivity.

However, semiology also has some methodological drawbacks. Firstly, its preference for detailed readings of individual images raises questions about the representativeness and replicability of its analyses. This is a doubt Leiss, Kline and Jhally (1986: 165) have about Williamson's work. They are unclear about how or why Williamson chose the advertisements she works with. Are they representative of advertisements in general? And would someone else using those same advertisements have come to the same conclusions about them? Williamson would presumably respond that these questions are not important since she was using the advertisements to construct a general theory that could critique how advertisements work; she was not trying to offer empirical generalisations about what they are. And certainly her book's illustrations are there to forward her argument about particular processes of meaning-making, not to exemplify particular types of advertisements.

Another issue to consider when deploying semiology is that, while its practioners are very ready to admit to polysemy and to the contestation as well as to the transfer and circulation of meaning in theory, there are in fact very few semiological studies that really get to grips with diverse ways of seeing. Bal and Bryson, for example, argue strongly that semiology is centrally concerned with the reception of images by audiences: 'semiotic analysis of visual art does not set out in the first place to produce interpretations of works of art, but rather to investigate how works of art are intelligible to those who view them, the processes by which viewers make sense of what they see' (Bal and Bryson 1991: 184). Yet semiology is a method that focuses in great detail on images and not on their audiences. Don Slater (1983) has addressed this absence and suggests that it is not a coincidence: semiology is simply not concerned with the social practices, institutions and relations within which visual images are produced and interpreted. He blames this on the structuralist tradition within which much semiology was situated when he was writing, and he argues that this 'takes as assumed, as given, precisely what needs to be explained: the relations and practices within which discourses are formed and operated' (Slater 1983: 258). This is certainly the case with Williamson's work. She does not explain how she decided that there were only three referent systems underpinning advertisements, for example, nor how she decided that Nature, Magic and Time were the three; nor does she explore the extent to which audiences other than herself sensed these systems at work.

DISCOURSE ANALYSES

Semiology is a rich and diverse field, and there are many variations on the themes that I have just discussed. However, its roots in various kinds of structuralist thought have meant that in recent years, as the cultural turn has taken hold, the particular analytical framework that Williamson deployed, for example, has been found less and less often. While current approaches to visual images remain heavily indebted to notions of signs and their decoding, the understanding of the wider systems of meaning within which particular signs work has undergone, for many critics, a fundamental shift. Instead of referent systems and mythologies, 'discourse' is now most often the site of meaning production. (There have been other moves, too, towards emphasising some of those things to which structuralist accounts also rarely gave attention: reflexivity, audiences, the vulnerability of semiological interpretations themselves to reinterpretation.) Foucault's methodological programme is perhaps spelled out most clearly in *The Archaeology of Knowledge* (1972). Foucault refused the premise that forms the basis of structuralist semiology, which is that analysis needs somehow to delve behind the surface appearance of things in order to discover their real meaning. Foucault rejected such 'penetrative' models of interpretation at the level of method, but also at the level of explanation, since he also wanted to avoid explanatory accounts of *why* power works in the way it does. He explicitly rejected the Marxist claim that meaning was determined by the system of production, for example; he was always vague about how discourses connected to other, non-discursive processes such as economic change; and while he acknowledged that power has aims and effects, he never explained these by turning to notions of human or institutional agency. Michele Barrett (1991: 131) argues that his notion of causality and dependency was 'polymorphous'. Both methodologically and theoretically, then, Foucault rejected approaches that look behind or underneath things and practices for other processes that would explain them.

Foucault was centrally concerned with how meaning is made, and the enormous recent impact of his work has led to a rather general use of the notion of 'discourse' across both the humanities and the social sciences, so that it sometimes seems to refer to little more than 'meanings' (see also Chapter 6 in this volume). Yet Foucault meant more by 'discourse' than just a rather vague indication that knowledges were structured in particular ways. He specified and deployed the term 'discourse' carefully, and I believe that its implications are rather different from those of semiology. In particular, his sense of the productivity and diversity of discourses, and how they are practised in all sorts of everyday ways, could lead to a much richer approach to visual images, more grounded in their contexts and in their audiencing. The fact that it has not so far produced much work that focuses on the latter concern is perhaps explained by that lingering hold of semiological analysis and its radically internal analysis of images and their meanings, as well as the grip of Elkins' 'primary scene' on the practice of criticism.

However that may be, Foucault took care to specify 'discourse' quite carefully, and it might be useful to remind ourselves of his discussion. 'Discourse' refers to groups of statements that structure the way a thing is thought, and to the way we act on the basis of that thinking. In other words, discourse is a particular knowledge about the world which shapes how the world is understood and how things are done in it. Lynda Nead (1988: 4) defines it as 'a particular form of language with its own rules and conventions and the institutions within which the discourse is produced and circulated', and suggests that 'art', for example, can also be understood as a discourse, as a specialised form of knowledge. She says that 'the discourse of art in the nineteenth century [consisted of] the concatenation of visual images, the language and structures of criticism, cultural institutions, publics for art and the values and knowledges made possible within and through high culture' (Nead 1988: 4). Discourse also produces subjects, such as 'artists', 'critics', and 'curators'. On this understanding, 'art' becomes not certain kinds of visual images but the knowledges, institutions, subjects and practices that work to define certain images as art and others as not art.

Discourses are articulated through all sorts of visual and verbal images and texts, and also through the practices that those languages permit. The diversity of forms through which a discourse can be articulated means that intertextuality is important to understanding discourse. Intertextuality refers to the way that the meanings of any one discursive image or text depend not only on that one text or image, but also on the meanings carried by other images and texts. Hence, again, the importance of written texts for visual images; one example of intertextuality is the catalogue essays that accompany art exhibitions and that are read by visitors to these exhibitions in order to make sense of the images.

Foucault was quite clear that discourse was a form of discipline. This leads us to his concern with power. Discourse, he maintained, is powerful, but it is powerful in a particular way. It is powerful because it is productive. Discourse disciplines subjects into certain ways of thinking and acting, but this is not simply repressive: it does not impose rules for thought and behaviour on a pre-existing human agent. Instead, human subjects are produced through discourses. Our sense of our self is made through the operation of discourse. So too are objects, relations, places, scenes: discourse produces the world as it understands it. An important implication of Foucault's account of power is that power is not something imposed from the top of society down onto its oppressed bottom layers. Power is everywhere, since discourse too is everywhere. And there are many discourses, some of which clearly contest the terms of others. Foucault (1979: 95) claimed that 'where there is power, there is resistance . . . a multiplicity of points of resistance', and by this he meant that there are many discourses that jostle and compete in their effects. But certain discourses are nonetheless dominant, and Foucault was particularly concerned in his own work with the emergence of institutions and technologies that were structured through specific, even if complex and contested, discourses. And he suggested that the dominance of certain discourses occurred not only because they were located in socially powerful institutions – those given coercive powers by the state, for example, such as the police, prisons and workhouses – but also because their discourses claimed absolute truth. The construction of claims to truth lies at the heart of the intersection of power/knowledge. Foucault insisted that knowledge and power are imbricated one in the other, not only because all knowledge is discursive and all discourse is saturated with power, but because the most powerful discourses, in terms of the productiveness of their social effects, depend on assumptions and claims that their knowledge is true. The particular grounds on which truth is claimed – and these shift historically – constitute what Foucault called a regime of truth.

As Barrett (1991) makes clear in her account of his work, Foucault focused on this problematic about *how* power worked. How does it do what it does, how did it do what it did? In exploring how critics drawing on Foucault's work have set about answering those questions in relation to visual materials, I would argue that Foucault's work has produced two somewhat different methodological emphases, which I call discourse analysis I and discourse analysis II. Discourse analysis I tends to pay rather more attention to the notion of discourse as articulated through various kinds of visual images and verbal texts than it does to the practices entailed by specific discourses. As Gill (1996: 141) writes, it uses 'discourse' to 'refer to all forms of talk and texts'. It also has an explicit methodology. Discourse analysis II, on the other hand, tends to pay more attention to the practices of institutions than it does to the visual images and verbal texts. Its methodology is usually left implicit. It tends to be more strongly concerned with issues of power, regimes of truth, institutions and technologies. This distinction is not clear-cut, of course. It is not difficult to find work that examines visual images, verbal texts, institutions and social practices together (see Green 1990 for example). However, it does seem to me that there is a case to be made for discussing these two methodological emphases separately, since they do produce rather different kinds of research work.

Discourse analysis I

This first type of discourse analysis is centrally concerned with language. But, as Fran Tonkiss emphasises:

> language is viewed as the topic of research . . . Rather than gathering accounts or texts so as to gain access to people's views and attitudes, or to find out what happened at a particular event, the discourse analyst is interested in how people use language to construct their accounts of the social world. (Tonkiss 1998: 247–8)

Discourse analysis can also be used to explore how images construct specific views of the social world, in which case, to paraphrase Tonkiss, visuality is viewed as the topic of research, and the discourse analyst is interested in how images construct accounts of the social world. This type of discourse analysis therefore pays careful attention to images themselves (as well as to other sorts of evidence). Since discourses are seen as socially produced rather than created by individuals, this type of discourse analysis is especially concerned with how specific views or accounts are constructed as real or truthful or natural through particular regimes of truth. As Gill (1996: 143) writes, 'all discourse is organised to make itself persuasive', and discourse analysis focuses on those strategies of persuasion. It also pays attention to the more socially-constituted forms of discursive power, looking at the social construction of difference and authority, for example. Discourse analysis is thus concerned too with the social production and effects of discourses.

Since discourse analysis I depends heavily on the notion of intertextuality, its first step is to collect a wide range of texts that are relevant in some way to the research question in hand. The precise ways this collecting happens usually relies on some understanding that the texts to be interpreted are or were significant and productive, in the Foucauldian sense. These texts are then read carefully, repeatedly. Efforts are made to read them for their assumptions (and this may mean trying to be aware of, and problematising, your own assumptions of what is true as you read). It is suggested that you should immerse yourself in your sources, becoming so familiar with them that their assumptions and their themes become more obvious to you. There is a concern that accounts of discourse should acknowledge their complexity and their contradictions, too, and that what is excluded or made invisible may be crucial to the effects of what is included and visible.

Hence discourse analysis depends on reading with great care for detail. It assumes that the efficacy of discourse often resides in the assumptions it makes about what is true, real or natural, in the contradictions that allow it interpretive flexibility, and in what is not said. None of these is accessible to superficial reading or viewing. Hence Gill's (1996: 144) emphasis on the scholarship entailed in discourse analysis: 'the analysis of discourse and rhetoric requires the careful reading and interpretation of texts, rigorous scholarship rather than adherence to formal procedures'.

Finally, as well as this close attention to the productive power of a range of texts, this kind of discourse analysis also pays attention to the institutional location of a discourse. Foucault, for all his reluctance to ascribe unidirectional causality, insisted on the need to locate the social site from which particular statements are made, and to position the speaker of a statement in terms of their social authority (Foucault 1972: 50–2). Thus, a statement coming from a source endowed with authority (and just how that authority is established may be an important issue to address) is likely to be more productive than one coming from a marginalised social position. Thus, the social location of a discourse's production is important to consider in relation to its effects.

This type of discourse analysis has clear strengths. It pays careful attention to images themselves, and to the web of intertextuality in which any individual image is embedded. It is centrally concerned with the production of social difference through visual imagery. It addresses questions of power as they are articulated through visual images themselves. There are also some difficulties in the method, however. One of these is knowing where to stop in making intertextual connections, and another, related one is the grounding of those connections empirically. Gilman's (1990) essay on the 'Jack the Ripper' murders in late nineteenth-century London illustrates the dangers (to me at least) of making so many connections that some start to seem rather tenuous. In order to understand why the murderer was seen by many contemporaries as Jewish, Gilman cites a huge range of contemporary sources, including London newspapers, Wedekind's play and Berg's opera *Lulu*, Freud and Fliess, Hogarth, medical texts, Bram Stoker's novel *Dracula*, Hood's poetry, paintings, engravings and posters, Hahnemann (the founder of homeopathy), 'Jack's' notes, criminologists Lombroso and Lacassagne, contemporary pornography, *Daniel Deronda*, contemporary tracts, and Proust and Zola. The breadth of scholarship is extraordinary, but I do wonder how many of those sources could really be said to have produced, however indirectly, the London newspapers' and police's description of the Ripper as Jewish. Some, of course; perhaps many; maybe all. But Gilman's choice of texts, while large, is still particular, and does not include very much of the popular kind of culture that newspaper editors and police officers in nineteenth-century London were much more likely to be reading or hearing or seeing. Gilman's analysis does not attempt to trace connections between his texts and the events in east London in any grounded way; instead, they are related in his work simply through the category of 'discourse'. Discourse as a result seems to become a free-floating web of meanings unconnected to any social practices. The practical problem posed by this sort of discourse analysis, then – where to stop making intertextual connections – can also be an analytical one – how to make the intertextual connections convincingly productive.

Discourse analysis II

The second form of discourse analysis which this chapter will explore often works with similar sorts of materials, but is much more concerned with their production by, and their reiteration of, particular institutions and their practices, and their production of particular human subjects. It is thus much more grounded in actual practices than is discourse analysis I. However, this emphasis too carries a methodological price, as we shall see.

Several of Foucault's books examine specific institutions and their disciplines: prisons, hospitals, asylums. For writers concerned with visual matters, perhaps the key text is *Discipline and Punish* (1977). Subtitled *The Birth of the Prison*, this is an account of changing penal organisation in post-medieval Europe, in which alterations in the organisation of visuality (and spatiality) are central. The book begins by quoting a contemporary account of a prolonged torture and execution carried out as a public spectacle in 1757. Foucault then quotes from a prison rulebook written eighty years later which is, as he says, a timetable. Foucault's questions are: how (rather than why) did this change in penal style, from spectacular punishment to institutional routine, take place? And with what effects? As well as a new institution and a new understanding of punishment, Foucault describes in *Discipline and Punish* the emergence of a new set of professions who defined who needed punishment and who could exercise that punishment, and of a new subjectivity produced for those so punished: what he called the 'docile body'. This was the body subjected to these new penal disciplines, the body which had to conform to its 'constraints and privations, obligations and prohibitions'.

A key point of Foucault's argument is that in this new regime of punishment, these docile bodies in a sense disciplined themselves, and Foucault argues that this was achieved through a certain visuality (for general discussions of the role of visuality in the work of Foucault, see Jay (1993) and Rajchman (1988)). As is well known, Foucault (1977: 195–228) demonstrates the importance of visuality for the production of a certain kind of subject by discussing a plan for an institution designed by Jeremy Bentham in 1791. Bentham called this building a panopticon, and suggested it could be used as the plan for all sorts of disciplining institutions: prisons, but also hospitals, workhouses, schools, madhouses. The panopticon was a tall tower, surrounded by an annular building. The latter consisted of cells, one for each inmate, with windows so arranged that the occupant was always visible from the tower. The tower was the location of the supervisor but because of the arrangement of its windows, blinds, doors and corridors, the inmates in their cells could never be certain that they were under observation from the tower at any particular moment. Never certain of invisibility, each inmate therefore had to behave 'properly' all the time: thus they disciplined themselves and were produced as docile bodies. 'Hence the major effect of the Panopticon: to induce in the inmate a state of conscious and permanent visibility that assures the automatic functioning of power' (Foucault 1977: 210). This sort of visuality, in which one subject is seen without ever seeing, and the other sees without ever being seen, Foucault called surveillance, and he argued that since it was an efficient means of producing social order, it became a dominant form of visuality throughout modern capitalist societies.

Foucault suggests that institutions like the panoptic prison work in two ways: through their apparatus and through their technologies. Foucault was actually rather inconsistent in his use of these terms, and I will make a clearer distinction between them than that found in his work. An institutional apparatus is the forms of power/knowledge which constitute the institutions: for example, architecture, regulations, scientific treatises, philosophical statements, laws, morals, and so on, and the discourse articulated through all these (Hall 1997: 47). Hence Foucault described Bentham's panopticon as an apparatus: at once an architectural design and a moral and philosophical treatise. The institutional technologies (sometimes difficult to differentiate from the apparatus) are the practical techniques used to practise that power/knowledge. Technologies are 'diffuse, rarely formulated in continuous, systematic discourse . . . often made up of bits and pieces . . . a disparate set of tools and methods' (Foucault 1977: 26). An example might be the design of the windows and blinds in the panopticon.

This emphasis on institutional apparatus and technologies gives a different inflection to this second kind of discourse analysis. It shifts attention away from the details of individual images and towards the processes of their production and use. An example of this kind of work would be the accounts of photography by John Tagg (1988) and Alan Sekula (1989). Both are interested in photography because, more than any other visual medium, it is regarded as showing the truth of things, how things really looked when the shutter snapped. In order to critique this truth claim, they understand photography as nothing more than an effect of the institutions in which it is put to work. As Tagg (1988: 63) writes:

> Photography as such has no identity. Its status as technology varies with the power relations that invest it. Its nature as a practice depends on the

institutions and agents which define it and set it to work . . . Its history has no unity. It is a flickering across a field of institutional spaces. It is this field we must study, not photography as such.

Tagg and Sekula both explore the use of photography as evidence by various institutions in the second half of the nineteenth century – the police, orphanages, photography studios making *cartes de visites*, public health officials – in order to argue that it was these uses that made photographs appear to be truthful records. And to do this they explore a wide range of other sources to show how institutional practices worked.

This particular Foucauldian approach has also been used very effectively in studies of two institutions that deal centrally with visual objects, the art gallery and the museum (Bennett 1995; Hooper-Greenhill 1992). These accounts explore how visual images and objects are produced in particular ways by institutional apparatuses and technologies (as 'art', for example) and how various subjectivities are also produced, such as the 'curator' and 'the visitor'. And Lidchi (1997) has given a careful account of the various technologies of museum and gallery display areas: the detailed and usually highly conventionalised ways in which objects are displayed, interpreted, distributed in museum and gallery spaces, and the dominance of a certain kind of distanced looking in those spaces. Both kinds of work rely on a range of different texts, from architecture plans to treatises on the need for the working class to visit museums, from anthropological theories to captioning and labelling practices in museums. They also often rely on trying to reconstruct the spaces of these institutions, using photographs or visiting the buildings.

However, this type of discourse analysis frequently pays little attention to the specific ways of seeing invited by an image itself. Images, in this kind of work, are the effects of other things, and therefore it is those other things – institutions – which gain critical attention. Nor has this kind of Foucauldian work paid much attention to the way that 'power is exercised from innumerable points, in the interplay of nonegalitarian and mobile relations' (Foucault 1979: 94). Bennett (1995), in his fascinating study of the birth of the museum, for example, explicitly says he is simply not interested in what museum visitors did or thought about the museums they were visiting, and thus begs the question of how far these museums really were productive of the subjectivity of those visitors. And Tagg and Sekula have been criticised for paying little attention to any visualities other than those of dominant institutions. Lindsay Smith (1998), for example, takes them to task for not looking at a wide enough range of nineteenth-century photographic practices, and in particular for neglecting the kinds of domestic photography practised by a number of women in the mid-nineteenth century. Looking at these kinds of photographs, Smith argues that they do not replicate the surveillant gaze of the police mug-shot or the family studio portrait: they thwart that classifying gaze by strategies such as blurred focus, collage and over-exposure.

Foucault's own arguments, as I have noted, explicitly acknowledge the multiplicity and incommensurability of discourses, but exploring specific examples of this has not so far been undertaken by these Foucauldian analysts. Perhaps, as I suggested at the beginning of this section, this is the lingering legacy of semiology's uninterest in, to quote Slater again, 'the relations and practices within which discourses are formed and operated'.

CONCLUSIONS

This chapter is clearly not an exhaustive account of all the methodologies that might usefully be applied to visual materials. Nor has it been comprehensive in its coverage of the three methods it has discussed (for a fuller discussion, see Rose 2001). However, I hope I have been able to sketch the implications of adopting either of these methods. I also hope to have made two points that are prior to specific choices about research methods. The first of these is that there is scope for much more work that engages as carefully with visual images as it does with written materials, and vice versa. This is not simply a comment about unconquered academic territory. It is also a comment driven by a particular sense of how visual images work. Although I do think that each and every visual object has its own set of potentialities, its own particular set of qualities (and that compositional interpretation is a good way to get at those), I do not think that those qualities simply exist, ready to be encountered in a primary scene between critic and image. Rather, those qualities and potentials are differentially mobilised, depending on where and how an image is shown. And one important context (although not the only one) for the display of visual materials is the written materials that accompany them in more or less close proximity. Our understanding of the effects of visual materials will be much richer, I think, if we pay more attention to the written texts that are so often implicated in their effects.

The second point I hope to have made is that the choice to use one research method rather than another is never simply a technical one. It is also driven by a number of theoretical considerations. Hence my decision to discuss semiology and discourse analyses at some length. Although often blurred in practice, it seems to me that there are important differences between these kind of methodologies, particularly in terms of where they locate meanings and effects. While semiology looks to deep structures within an image, discourse analysis looks to the effects of particular texts and institutions in practice. These two positions allow different kinds of research questions, and encourage different methods. The fact that they have not been sufficiently distinguished – the fact that certain elements of semiology apparently continue to inflect what discourse analysis does – might explain why the complex, messy, site- and audience-specificity of visual materials has not yet been sufficiently acknowledged.

Finally, I have commented that none of the methods I have described, when put to work by contemporary critics of visual culture, pays much attention to the spectators who animate visual images by looking at them. Visual images do not just emanate meaning in some kind of vacuum, despite claims to the contrary. Meaning is made with them, from them, against them, by particular people in particular places. Their audiences are fundamental to their effects. Developing that claim also requires developing some rather different methodological tools, and in particular, ones less influenced by a certain kind of semiological practice whose legacy is perhaps still too pervasive.

REFERENCES

Acton, M. (1997), *Learning to Look at Paintings*, London: Routledge.

Bal, M. (1996), *Double Exposures: The Subject of Cultural Analysis*, London: Routledge.

Bal, M. and N. Bryson (1991), 'Semiotics and art history', *Art Bulletin* 73, 174–208.

Ball M. S. and G. W. H. Smith (1992), *Analyzing Visual Data*, London: Sage.

Bann, S. (1998), 'Art history and museums', in M. A. Cheetham, M. A. Holly and K. Moxey (eds), *The Subjects of Art History: Historical Objects in Contemporary Perspective*, Cambridge: Cambridge University Press, pp. 230–49.

Barrett, M. (1991), *The Politics of Truth: From Marx to Foucault*, Cambridge: Polity Press.

Barthes, R. (1973), *Mythologies*, trans. A. Lavers, London: Paladin.

Barthes, R. (1977), *Image–Music–Text*, ed. and trans. S. Heath, London: Fontana.

Bennett, T. (1995), *The Birth of the Museum: History, Theory, Politics*, London: Routledge.

Bolton, R. (1989), 'In the American West: Richard Avedon Incorporated', in R. Bolton (ed.), *The Contest of Meaning: Critical Histories of Photography*, London: MIT Press, pp. 261–82.

Cosgrove, D. (ed.), (1998), *Mappings*, London: Reaktion Books.

Cosgrove, D. and S. Daniels (eds) (1998), *The Iconography of Landscape*, Cambridge: Cambridge University Press.

Doyle, R. (2002), *Rory and Ita*, London: Jonathan Cape.

Elkins, J. (1996), *The Object Stares Back: On the Nature of Seeing*, New York: Simon and Schuster.

Foster, H. (ed.) (1988), *Vision and Visuality*, Seattle: Bay Press.

Foucault, M. (1972), *The Archaeology of Knowledge*, trans. A. M. Sheridan Smith, London: Tavistock Publications.

Foucault, M. (1977), *Discipline and Punish: The Birth of the Prison*, trans. A. Sheridan, London: Allen Lane.

Foucault, M. (1979), *The History of Sexuality, Volume I: An Introduction*, trans. R. Hurley, London: Allen Lane.

Fyfe, G. and J. Law (1988), 'Introduction: on the invisibility of the visible', in G. Fyfe and J. Law (eds), *Picturing Power: Visual Depiction and Social Relations*, London: Routledge, pp. 1–14.

Gage, J. (1993), *Colour and Culture: Practice and Meaning from Antiquity to Abstraction*, London: Thames and Hudson.

Gill, R. (1996), 'Discourse analysis: practical implementation', in J. T. E. Richardson (ed.),
    Handbook of Qualitative Methods for Psychology and the Social Sciences, Leicester: British
    Psychological Society, pp. 141–56.
Gilman, S. (1990), ' "I'm down on whores": race and gender in Victorian London', in D.
    Goldberg (ed.), *The Anatomy of Racism*, Minneapolis: Minnesota University Press, pp.
    146–70.
Green, N. (1990), *The Spectacle of Nature: Landscape and Bourgeois Nature in Nineteenth-
    Century France*, Manchester: Manchester University Press.
Grunenberg, C. (1999), 'The modern art museum', in E. Barker (ed.), *Contemporary Cultures of
    Display*, London: Yale University Press in association with The Open University, pp. 26–49.
Hall, S. (1980), 'Encoding/decoding', in Centre for Contemporary Cultural Studies Culture,
    Media, Language: Working Papers in Cultural Studies, London: Hutchinson, pp. 128–38.
Hall, S. (1997), 'The work of representation', in S. Hall (ed.), *Representation: Cultural
    Representations and Signifying Practices*, London: Sage, pp. 13–74.
Harley, J. B. (1992), 'Reconstructing the map', in T. J. Barnes and J. S. Duncan (eds), *Writing
    Worlds: Discourse, Text and Metaphor in the Representation of Landscape*, London: Routledge,
    pp. 231–47.
Hodge, R. and G. Kress (1988), *Social Semiotics*, Cambridge: Polity Press.
Hooper-Greenhill, E. (1992), *Museums and the Shaping of Knowledge*, London: Routledge.
Iversen, M. (1986), 'Saussure v. Pierce: models for a semiotics of visual art', in A. L. Rees and
    F. Borzello (eds), *The New Art History*, London: Camden Press, pp. 82–94.
Jay, M. (1993), *Downcast Eyes: The Denigration of Vision in Twentieth-Century French Thought*,
    Berkeley: California University Press.
Kress, G. and T. van Leeuwen (1996), *Reading Images: The Grammar of Visual Design*,
    London: Routledge.
Latour, B. (1999), *Pandora's Hope: Essays on the Reality of Science Studies*, Cambridge, MA:
    Harvard University Press.
Leiss, W., S. Kline and S. Jhally (1986), *Social Communication in Advertising: Persons, Products
    and Images of Well-Being*, London: Methuen.
Lidchi, H. (1997), 'The poetics and politics of exhibition other cultures', in S. Hall (ed.),
    Representation: Cultural Representations and Signifying Practices, London: Sage, pp. 151–222.
Matless, D. (1996), 'Visual culture and geographical citizenship: England in the 1940s',
    Journal of Historical Geography 22: 424–39.
Mirzoeff, N. (1999), *An Introduction to Visual Culture*, London: Routledge.
Monaco, J. (2000), *How to Read a Film: Movies, Media, Multimedia*, 3rd edn, London: Oxford
    University Press.
Nead, L. (1988), *Myths of Sexuality: Representations of Women in Victorian Britain*, Oxford:
    Blackwell.
Potter, J. and M. Wetherell (1987), *Discourse and Social Psychology*, London: Sage.
Potter, J. and M. Wetherell (1994), 'Analyzing discourse', in A. Bryman and R. G. Burgess
    (eds), *Analyzing Qualitative Data*, London: Routledge, pp. 47–66.
Rajchman, J. (1988), 'Foucault's art of seeing', *October* 44, 89–117.
Rose, G. (2001), *Visual Methodologies: An Introduction to the Interpretation of Visual Materials*,
    London: Sage.
Saussure, F. de [1916] (1983), Course in General Linguistics, trans. R. Harris, London: Gerald
    Duckworth.
Sebald, W. G. (1996), *The Emigrants*, London: The Harvill Press.
Sekula, A. (1989), 'The body and the archive', in R. Bolton (ed.), *The Contest of Meaning:
    Critical Histories of Photography*, London: MIT Press, pp. 342–88.

Slater, D. (1983), 'Marketing mass photography', in H. Davis and P. Walton (eds), *Language, Image, Media*, Oxford: Basil Blackwell, pp. 245–63.

Smith, L. (1998), *The Politics of Focus: Women, Children and Nineteenth-Century Photography*, Manchester: Manchester University Press.

Stafford, B. M. (1984), *Voyage into Substance: Art, Science, Nature and the Illustrated Travel Account, 1760–1840*, Cambridge, MA: MIT Press.

Tagg, J. (1988), *The Burden of Representation: Essays on Photographies and Histories*, London: Macmillan.

Taylor, J. C. (1957), *Learning to Look: A Handbook for the Visual Arts*, Chicago: Chicago University Press.

Thornham, S. (1997), *Passionate Detachments: An Introduction to Feminist Film Theory*, London: Arnold.

Tonkiss, F. (1998), 'Analysing discourse', in C. Seale (ed.), *Researching Society and Culture*, London: Sage, pp. 245–60.

Williamson, J. E. (1978), *Decoding Advertisements: Ideology and Meaning in Advertising*, London: Marion Boyars.

CHAPTER 6

Discourse Analysis

Gabriele Griffin, University of Hull

INTRODUCTION

Discourse analysis is concerned with the investigation of language,[1] both written and oral,[2] as it is actually used (as opposed to an abstract system or structure of language). It is different from textual analysis (see Chapter 9 in this volume) in that it assumes from the outset that language is *invested*, meaning that language is not a neutral tool for transmitting a message but rather, that all 'communicative events' (Van Dijk 2001: 98) – whether these be, for instance, readings of novels, plays, poetry, a notice on a billboard, a conversation, or an interview – constitute 'a particular way of talking about and understanding the world (or an aspect of the world)' (Phillips and Jørgensen 2002: 1) both on the part of the producer (the writer, the speaker) and on the part of the consumer (the reader, the audience). As such, discourse analysis references both a theory of language use – language use as not neutral but invested – and a method for analysing language in use.

Discourse analysis has two components. One is the investigation of patterns in language use, for instance the kind of personal pronouns – such as 'I' or 'we' – used by an individual speaker/narrator and the impact of this use on the authority status of the speaker/narrator. The other relates to patterns of language use as activity or process, for instance how much verbal space a speaker occupies in a conversation. The aim of discourse analysis is to produce an analysis or 'explanatory critique' (Fairclough 2001: 235–6) of how and to what purpose language use is invested through the deployment of specific textual features (lexical, grammatical, semantic), in order to facilitate understanding of its effects and the possibility of resistance to that investment. It thus explores 'the links between language use and [socio-cultural] practice' (Phillips and Jørgensen 2002: 69).

WHAT IS DISCOURSE?

The term discourse itself has multiple meanings (see Mills 1997, especially pp. 1–26). Thus, it may refer only to the spoken word, or to all utterances written and verbal, or to a particular way of talking that delineates a specific domain with its own particular vocabularies and sets of meaning such as legal discourse, medical discourse, scientific discourse. Discourse may also refer to a specific set of statements within a given context, a 'regulated practice which accounts for a number of statements' (Foucault 1972: 80) such as religious discourse or sermons, for example, or fairy tales, which have definable characteristics and features established and maintained through the regulations that govern what you can and cannot utter as part of these genres or sub-genres, and how you can articulate it. Thus, the conventions of a fairy tale allow for it to begin with 'Once upon a time . . .' but not with 'Beloved in Christ . . .', an opening more appropriate to a sermon. Discourses then simultaneously make certain utterances possible while suppressing others.

Discourses also produce different kinds of truth claims or effects. For instance, we understand fairy tales both as 'made-up' stories or fictions, and as myths, and the opening 'Once upon a time . . .' signals the commencement of a certain kind of story that we do not expect to be literally true but which – as fairy tale – delivers, *inter alia*, a particular sort of moral message. If a priest or a vicar were to start a sermon with 'Once upon a time . . .' this would create interdiscursivity (the mixing of different discourses with different types of truth claims). This in turn would destabilise her narrative and raise questions about its truth value since sermons are intended to convey partly a literal truth (for example, Christ did die on the cross and rose again after several days of burial) and partly a moral message. To start a sermon with 'Once upon a time . . .' would undercut the literal truth element of the sermon and render questionable the truth effect a sermon is meant to produce. In *The Time of the Angels*, Iris Murdoch captures the imperatives of the discourse of sermons hilariously and tragically in the exploits of the figure of Carel Fisher, rector of St Eustace Watergate, who has lost his faith in institutional religion (1978: 30):

> He introduced curious variations of his own into the ceremonial of his services and even into the liturgy. He began a sermon by saying, 'And what if I tell you that there is no God?' and then left his congregation to fidget uneasily during a long silence. He once conducted a service from behind the altar. He was given to laughing in church.

The novel here portrays the normative structure of discourses, showing that 'discursive frameworks demarcate the boundaries within which we can negotiate [meaning]' (Mills 1997: 18). By raising questions about the existence of God,

Carel steps outside these boundaries. The excerpt from the novel indicates a further aspect of discourse, namely that it assigns subject positions both to the speaker/narrator and to the listener/reader. Carel's boundary violations regarding the subject position he should adopt – metaphorically by affirming the existence of God, and spatially by speaking from in front of the altar – lead to unease among the congregation who do not know how to respond to these transgressions. Discourse then has 'meaning, force and effect within a social context' (Mills 1997: 13), in this instance in relation to the congregation, hence the emphasis in discourse analysis on the impacts or effects of discourse in the social.

Carel's boundary violations signal the extent to which discourse 'normalises' or 'naturalises' certain discursive conventions through their iterative performance, to the extent that only at the point of violation may we become aware of the existence of those norms. Part of the effect of discursive structures is precisely such naturalisation which serves to reinforce the boundaries between different kinds of discourse, and introduces the notion that change involves violation in what has been described as 'the order of discourses', that is 'a limited range of discourses which struggle in the same terrain' (Phillips and Jørgensen 2002: 27). One example commonly used of such struggles is the contest between traditional and alternative medical discourses. Such struggles concern the dominance of a specific discourse in a given field and indicate that the hegemony or pre-eminence of a given discourse is not set in stone but achieved through struggle and therefore subject to change. One struggle and change of this kind can be observed in feminist appropriations of certain literary forms such as fairy tales: texts like Angela Carter's *The Bloody Chamber* have served both to highlight the gendered conventions that govern traditional fairy tales and to explode the truth claims these make about relations of power – for instance, between the wolf and Little Red Riding Hood. The change in perception that such appropriations have brought about, both in relation to the genre in question and in relation to its truth claims, signal a key aspect of discourse: the fact that it can be the object of change through being used in different ways from what is 'normally' the case. Effective contestations of specific discourses result in socio-cultural changes, and discourse analysts are partly concerned with how these changes can be brought about.

Access to discourse is not equal (Mills 1997: 13). In the episode from Murdoch's novel, for example, Carel speaks while the congregation sits in silence. Similarly, in Jane Austen's *Mansfield Park*, the fate of the 'fallen' woman Maria is conveyed not through her narration but via the merger of the omniscient narrator's voice with the reported ruminations of Sir Thomas, Mansfield Park's ineffectual patriarch:

It ended in Mrs Norris's resolving to quit Mansfield, and devote herself to her unfortunate Maria, and in an establishment being formed for them in another country – remote and private, where, shut up together with little society . . . it may be reasonably supposed that their tempers became their mutual punishment.

Such silencing of women regarded as having disgraced themselves is common in nineteenth-century novels, providing insights into the portrayal of social structures during the period. Its rendition in Austen's novel signals the differential access to power and speech that diverse groups in society have.

As the examples above show, texts such as novels both *are* and *portray* discourses, and may be analysed in terms of both these dimensions. Sara Mills cites John Frow who states: 'The discursive is a socially constructed reality which constructs both the real and the symbolic and the distinction between them. It assigns structure to the real at the same time as it is a product and a moment of real structures' (Mills 1997: 50). It is for this reason that Phillips and Jørgensen (2002: 69) argue that the analysis of a discursive instant should include:

- an analysis of the discourses and genres articulated in the production and consumption of the text
- an analysis of the linguistic structure
- considerations about whether the discursive practice reproduces or, instead, restructures the existing order of discourse and about what consequences this has for the broader socio-cultural practice.

The analysis of textual features such as narrative voice (who speaks), grammar, wording and so on provides insights into 'the ways in which texts treat events and social relations and thereby construct particular versions of reality, social identities and social relations' (Phillips and Jørgensen 2002: 83).

VARIETIES OF DISCOURSE ANALYSIS

As a brief outline of the various versions of discourse analysis that are currently commonly used shows (see, for example, Phillips and Jørgensen 2002; Wetherall et al. 2001; Mills 1997), discourse analysis, situated on an intersection between linguistic and social theory (see Kress 2001), has come to the fore as a research method since the 1970s in a number of humanities and social sciences disciplines including linguistics, literature, sociology, psychology and politics. In all these different subjects, variants of discourse analysis have been produced that reflect their disciplinary context and related theoretical assumptions. Wetherall et al. (2001b: 6) distinguish six distinct discourse analytical research traditions:

1. Conversation analysis and ethnomethodology
2. Interactional sociolinguistics and the ethnography of communication
3. Discursive psychology
4. Critical discourse analysis and critical linguistics
5. Bakhtinian research
6. Foucauldian research

These traditions share certain traits, in particular their focus on language use as the object of research; the assumption that language is not a neutral means for conveying a message but rather shapes our perceptions of the world; that such shaping takes place within hierarchical structures of power which are both formulated and upheld by language, and can also be changed through the changing use of language; and that actual use offers possibilities for change or resistance to dominant discourse through being situated at particular moments in time and in particular contexts.

At the same time, these traditions differ in terms of:

- the degree to which they view the world as partially or wholly constructed through discourse
- the types of discourse they focus on (for example, written, spoken, 'naturally occurring', discursive or non-discursive, institutional)
- the assumptions they make about the enunciating subject (that is, the extent to which they ascribe agency to the subject in having or not having control over her language use and what change she may be able to generate through that use, as opposed to subjects being viewed as objects of and constructed by discourses)
- their focus on the structures of discourse or its effects
- the contexts in which they analyse discourse
- the knowledges they seek to produce.

These issues can be pursued by the reader via Wetherall et al. (2001b). The point of mentioning all this here is to indicate that discourse analysis is not a unitary research method but one that takes different forms in different contexts, dependent upon the research one wishes to conduct, and within what academic discipline. Discourse analysis as a research method also continues to evolve.[3] In the following I shall predominantly draw on the critical discourse analysis associated, *inter alia*, with the linguist Norman Fairclough (for example, 1989, 1992, 1995, 2000; Chouliaraki and Fairclough 1999) in order to discuss what kind of research one might conduct using discourse analysis, what kind of knowledge discourse analysis produces, and what some of the issues related to the use of discourse analysis as a research method are.

CRITICAL DISCOURSE ANALYSIS

Fairclough's version of critical discourse analysis (CDA) distinguishes discursive from non-discursive dimensions of communication, and is concerned with the ways in which discourses act to produce and change the world. It attempts to engage critically (hence 'critical' discourse analysis) with the discourses produced by dominant institutions such as the government in order to show how the texts they produce (re)create particular versions of the world (for example, Fairclough 2000, Van Dijk 2001). Fairclough's critical discourse analysis is thus also a theory of the subject and of agency in that it is concerned with the relationship between language, the subject and social processes, viewing the subject as capable of influencing perceptions of the world, and thus of changing things, through her use of language. Following Fairclough and Wodak (1997), Phillips and Jørgensen (2002: 60–4) identify six common features among the diverse versions of critical discourse analysis that exist:

1. the understanding that *language and discursive practices* (how texts are produced and consumed) *contribute to the constitution of the world*
2. the notion that discourse is both *constituted* by and *constitutes* the socio-cultural world
3. the focus on *actual language use* within a given context as the object of research
4. the notion that *discourse is invested*, and contributes to the (re)production of power relations in society and to the interpretive schema operating within a given society
5. the notion that *discourse is historically situated*, hence contingent and subject to change
6. the demand that discourse analysis should be concerned with a *critical* examination of language in order to promote change.

Language thus simultaneously refers to 'the world' and constructs it through embuing it with particular meanings. When Jane Austen in the opening sentence of *Pride and Prejudice* claims that 'It is a truth universally acknowledged, that a single man in possession of a good fortune, must be in want of a wife', she is not so much proclaiming a neutral and objective fact as mustering all her rhetorical force to offer a particular construction of a specific kind of 'single man'. That rhetorical force sets out both to avow a certain view and simultaneously and implicitly to disavow other ways of seeing. It thus seeks to set up Austen's particular view of a 'single man' as *the* only way of viewing him, without, however, making that explicit by referencing either an author or a narrator figure through qualifying the statement by a phrase such as 'in my opinion'. Austen's rhetorical resources include, for example, the use of the present tense and indicative verb form ('it is') which suggest fact and underscore validity, followed by a truth claim reinforced through an adverbial/adjectival assertion of generalisability ('a truth *universally acknowledged*') – in order to lend persuasiveness to her view and assert the normativity of a position that would not necessarily be shared, for example, by gay men who might be single and in possession of a good fortune but not in want of a wife. Thus, whilst constructing a world of normative heterosexuality, Austen's introduction simultaneously attempts to close down the possibility of other ways of reading the situation of a man in the position described. Here we are already in the midst of discourse analysis which, as this brief example demonstrates, involves the close textual analysis of the linguistic and semantic features of a text, in order to establish the meanings the text seeks to impose on the world and, by implication, on the reader. Such an analysis may focus on a small segment of text, or, as is more common, range over a larger amount of text, from a brief paragraph, to all the plays by and attributed to Shakespeare, or the entire output of a particular journal, magazine, or newspaper such as the *Edinburgh Review* (the term used to described large sets of texts or data such as the latter is corpus, or corpora in the plural). However, rather than merely describing a text's linguistic features, the purpose of discourse analysis is to reveal how such features set up and replicate particular world views. Thus, the fact that Jane Austen describes 'a single man in possession of a good fortune' as 'in want of a *wife*', as opposed to, for instance, 'friends', indicates the commitment to marriage the text seeks to promote in its focus on heteronormativity. The kind of knowledge discourse analysis may then produce is an understanding of the implicit rules and norms that govern language use in a specific context in order to make explicit the ideological assumptions that govern that use and, by making the latter explicit, to point to possibilities of resistance, or other ways of reading. As Roberts Scholes (1982: 16) suggested, we need to view the literary text as 'the product of a person or persons, at a given point in human history, in a given form of discourse, taking its meanings from the interpretive gestures of individual readers using the grammatical, semantic, and cultural codes available to them.'

One effect of this is that discussions of discourse and of discourse analysis tend to focus on texts in areas that produce ideological contention. Mills (1997), for instance, discusses sexist and racist discourses as a way of laying bare the operations of language use in the articulation of particular value systems. Similarly, Fairclough, in *New Labour, New Language?* (2000: vii) seeks to reveal how 'manipulating language to control public perception' is a vital aspect of New Labour politics. We are all familiar with the ways in which the language of business and institutions seeks to (re)present 'problems' as 'opportunities', to provide a positive and supposedly energising 'spin' on a difficult situation. Many special issues of *Discourse and Society* have been devoted to the ways in which contentious political situations have been variously and contradictorily represented in the different discourses that politicians and others employ to influence public opinion.[4]

WHAT KINDS OF TEXTS?

This brings us to the question of what kinds of texts might be analysed using discourse analysis within the frame of English studies. Here the first thing to note is that whilst English studies has sometimes been narrowly viewed as the study of 'literature' (that is, the study of high literary forms and of a set of specific authors' works),[5] the question of what is literature, and indeed, what is its purpose, raised particularly vigorously in and since the canon debates of the late 1970s and early 1980s, has itself become a matter of contestation. The effect of this has been that the field of English studies at the beginning of the twenty-first century has expanded to encompass all manner of texts and all manner of writers who were not part of the 'canon of literature' that formed the backbone of English teaching until the mid-1970s. For example, in the 1980s and particularly the 1990s, there was a turn in English literature towards science; this was promoted by the drive of public (educational) policies towards enhancing the 'public understanding of science' as part of the demise of the welfare state and the promotion, inaugurated under the Conservative government of Margaret Thatcher and continued under the Labour government of Tony Blair, of 'consumer choice' and 'individual responsibility'. This turn has meant that different kinds of texts from science, including from fields such as medicine, biology, zoology and anthropology, have been (re)visited by English literature scholars in order to explore the inter-relationship between the kinds of narratives we produce about our world in different domains and the impact that these narratives have. One need only think of works such as Gillian Beer's *Darwin's Plots* (1983), or Jonathan Sawday's *The Body Emblazon'd: Dissection and the Human Body in Renaissance Culture* (1995), to recognise the impact of this 'turn to science' on English studies as a field. Discourse analysis as a research method for English studies may not, then, be confined to the study of 'literature' as a high cultural form but can be applied to many different kinds of texts, including, not least, verbal ones such as interviews with, for instance, writers. In Chapter 7 of this volume, for example, Rachel Alsop briefly discusses the ways in which cultural critic Mary Louise Pratt has described ethnographic narratives as either utopic or dystopic, depending on their narrative arc and on how the ethnographer positions herself in her narrative. Studies of ethnographies as texts with specific narrative structures may well then, and indeed do in the context of travel writing, for instance, form part of what might be termed English studies. The point is that the field of English studies has widened considerably during the past thirty years. The kind of texts a researcher working with discourse analysis as a research method might focus on thus depends on the knowledge she wants to produce: she may focus on high cultural texts but is not restricted to these.

WHAT LEVEL OF ANALYSIS?

As previously stated, discourse analysis may be carried out on very brief texts (for instance, one of the shorter short stories of Bertolt Brecht or Jorge Luis Borges), or on extensive bodies of text or corpora. This means that no discourse analysis will ever be complete since it is beyond the scope of a single research project to analyse all the textual features contained in any but the briefest text. When conducting discourse analysis, a researcher therefore of necessity has to be selective, concentrating on certain textual features at the expense of others. This also means that all analyses are partial, influenced by the researcher's agenda, and thus – just like the texts under scrutiny – historically situated. Taylor therefore makes the points that 'the analyst must decide how much detail the data encompass', and that the data thus 'are not given but need to be selected according to the analyst's focus' (2001: 313).

To mitigate the effects of the selectivity of the researcher when analysing different discourses, many writers on discourse analysis as a research method recommend that the researcher make a description of the research process part of her analysis, and that she be as explicit as possible in her description of how she conducted her research, and the choices she made (for example, Taylor 2001; Phillips and Jørgensen 2002). This requires reflexivity on the part of the researcher, the ability to think critically about her actions and reactions in relation to the texts studied. Explicitness, transparency and reflexivity are the key words here, even as the issue remains of researchers themselves being formed by the discourses they examine and the question of how they can step outside these to reflect on their own practices. Such reflection on one's research practice, still largely uncommon in English studies, is routinely practised in other disciplines such as women's studies and is one of the valuable practices that could usefully be adopted in English.

WHAT TOOLS?

When conducting discourse analysis, researchers need to utilise the variant of discourse analysis best suited to their material and the knowledge pursued. Thus, in analysing, for example, a dramatic text or conversations in novels, a researcher may use the tools of conversation analysis in order to understand how turn-taking (who speaks and in what sequence) in 'making conversation' is structured in the plays or novels in question.[6] As discourse analysis, such a description needs to go beyond the charting of who speaks and when, to an analysis of the meaning of that turn-taking, for example what it reveals in terms of the relative power a given speaker has to occupy verbal space. Such an analysis could then be further enhanced by discussing the function each speaker adopts when they take their turn to speak, for instance in initiating or blocking a topic, supporting or dissenting from the previous speaker's viewpoint.[7] Such analyses can reveal much about the social structures (re)produced in a text. They can also – if conducted over a large group of texts and in comparative fashion – provide insights into the conventions of particular genres and particular periods, that is, they can illuminate the differences between dialogue in drama of the absurd and in naturalistic drama, or the differences in (re)producing conversations in modernist and realist novels, or the differences between dialogue in pulp fiction and in 'highbrow' writing.

In producing such analyses the researcher has recourse to, and will bring to bear upon the texts she is analysing, knowledge outside of those texts, derived from her understanding of the culture she is working in and the knowledge she has already acquired of what, for instance, constitutes pulp fiction as opposed to 'highbrow' writing, or of periodisation (the situating of a text within a given period, the latter itself, of course, a construct). She will have to consult other texts on these subjects, and her research will thus consist of more than 'discourse analysis', involving possibly archival research, the application of certain theoretical models regarding 'literature', and so on. Discourse analysis is then always used in conjunction with other modes of enquiry or research methods, even if these are only recall of previous knowledge.

There are many different textual features to which a researcher doing discourse analysis may choose to pay attention. These depend importantly on the perspective the researcher brings to bear on her material. A feminist perspective may direct her to pay particular attention to the way in which gender operates in a given text: how women and men are represented within it through, for instance, linguistic features such as the nouns that are used to refer to them, or semantic features such as the kinds of words ('lady', 'bitch', 'bloke', 'lad') that are used to describe women and men and the specific meanings or biases that attach to these words in the researcher's culture. A postcolonial perspective may direct her to focus on constructions of race. Such constructions, though possibly posing as 'merely descriptive', are never simply just that but also express power relations in a given culture by attaching different values to different positions within the discourses in question. Classificatory systems like the ones used in the Census or on equal opportunities forms are thus never 'neutral' but invested with values that serve to differentiate and discriminate between the different groups that are constructed through these classificatory systems. Donna Haraway (1989, 1991) has famously shown how the construction of the animal world in zoological and biological texts serves to (re)produce in the description of animals the dominant structures of the describing human societies whilst suppressing all those data that fail to fit into those classifications and might challenge them. An analyst can thus show how discourses enable us to speak about the world in particular ways, simultaneously enabling certain modes of talk whilst suppressing others.

This insight into the operations of discourse links the latter to issues of power and hegemony (the imposition of a single dominant meaning). Different theoreticians of discourse have produced different versions of how power and discourse inter-relate, but they all agree that power, and of course powerlessness, are expressed and maintained, but also challenged, through discourse. Indeed, discourse is viewed as functioning as a site of struggle over meaning, with particular instances of discursive use seeking temporarily to fix meaning in a specific way (Phillips and Jørgensen 2002: 29). Austen's definition of 'a single young man in possession of a good fortune' in *Pride and Prejudice* is a good example of this. The most influential theoretician of the relation between discourse, power and knowledge is Michel Foucault.[8] Foucault (1970, 1972) viewed discourse as both highly regulated and as productive of knowledge, at once constraining in producing the objects and effects of which it speaks, but at the same time creating knowledge by rendering certain discursive positions as acceptable or legitimate and others as not. Thus, for instance, in a PhD thesis it is legitimate or acceptable to refer to other academics' work in one's field (though hierarchies of knowledge production prevail and recourse to certain authors' works, for instance, carries more kudos than recourse to others') but not to knowledge communicated by 'my aunt Maisie writing on the wall of my bedroom at night'.

The question is, who determines what is legitimate and what is not? Foucault describes power as 'dispersed throughout social relations' (in Mills 1997: 20) and thus as not accruing to particular individuals or positions, and not operating merely in a top-down structure. A PhD student may, for instance, feel relatively powerless in relation to her supervisor and the object of that supervisor's instructions, but quite powerful in relation to students she teaches on a part-time basis where her discourse sets the agenda. The discourse of spiritualism may not have much status in science but will be highly influential in certain churches. Power, then, is relative; it is not inherent in discourse or any particular discourse *per se* but is the result of the use of specific discourses in particular contexts by certain individuals and groups. Within these situations, particular discourses produce specific knowledges and truths. The operations of 'power/knowledge' – to borrow a key phrase from Foucault – are the effects of power struggles between competing discourses in the same terrain. Such struggles are evident every time politicians from opposing parties are interviewed on the same issue, and in academic texts where authors compete through critical engagement with other writers in the same field to establish the 'supremacy' of their discourse – a convention often in evidence in literature reviews of theses, for example. Discourse analysis is, then, in part about laying bare the operations of power, of how knowledge and truth are (re)produced by and in certain discourses, and about the effects these have.

To do this requires the analysis of a given discourse, focusing on (Phillips and Jørgensen 2002: 145):

- the aspects of the world to which the discourses ascribe meaning
- the particular ways in which . . . discourses ascribe meaning
- the points on which there is open struggle between different representations
- any understandings naturalized in . . . discourses as common-sense.

Such an analysis is conducted by looking for patterns in text, looking at variations from patterns and at systematic absences. Patterns may be discerned at lexical, grammatical and semantic level, both within a particular text and across a range of texts. A practical way of identifying the features of a given discourse the researcher wants to focus on is to mark up the text to be analysed. Traditionally, this was done by literally marking a text, using, for example, different colours to underline or highlight different aspects of a text. This marking might be done according to a coding scheme predetermined at the outset of the analysis or one that evolves as the analysis progresses. Thus, you might look for every instance where a text such as *Pride and Prejudice* references 'marriage', either directly or indirectly, to begin to build up an analysis of Jane Austen's representation of marriage in her work. This could then be compared to other writers' use of 'marriage', either from the same period or from later periods to determine, for instance, how typical her representation of marriage is for her period, or how such representations have varied over time. One important issue here is that the word 'marriage' may never itself be mentioned so that you may be looking for associated vocabularies such as 'wife'. Additionally, you may need to identify the context in which 'marriage' is alluded to, therefore being interested not only in the particular instance but also in the context in which it is used. This, of course, complicates the research process since it requires more sophisticated coding to highlight both the reference to marriage itself (directly or indirectly) and the specificity of the context in which it occurs. The process is also complicated by using large bodies of text, for instance multiple works by an author, or a range of texts within one genre.

COMPUTER-AIDED DISCOURSE ANALYSIS

It is here that computer-aided analyses have come to the fore in the past twenty years or so since these allow the establishment and retrieval of large data sets so that, once the admittedly lengthy process of coding the text electronically has been completed, the analysis of that coding can be done much more efficiently. A word of caution, however: a computer-aided analysis of a given discourse is only as good as the coding you did. This is an issue when you code a text to pursue one kind of analysis, only to find that later on you want to analyse the same text by focusing on somewhat different textual features. And there is a further word of caution: a computer will not do the analysis for you; rather, it functions as a tool to store, organise, retrieve and display data, but how it does so depends both on the computer package you have chosen and on the ways in which you have coded your text or data. Your coding thus already imposes an interpretation on the text as well as the boundaries of that interpretation. Eben Weitzman (2003) provides a useful meta-discursive overview of the different kinds of software packages that are available to undertake 'computer assisted qualitative data analysis' (CAQDAS), of which discourse analysis represents one variety.

Discourse analysis can be done 'qualitatively' and 'quantitatively', that is non-numerically or numerically. As qualitative analysis it focuses, in English studies, on the interpretation of 'non-uniform' text (Smedt et al. 1999: 79), that is text which is not highly structured compared to, for example, answers to closed questions in a questionnaire that require you simply to tick 'yes' or 'no'. Novels, plays, most poems, interviews, conversations, dialogue in film and so on all constitute 'non-uniform' text. As quantitative research, discourse analysis is concerned with counting the frequencies of words, phrases, particular grammatical structures or lexical features in order, for instance, to show what the key concepts underpinning a text are, or, within authorship attribution research, in order to identify the typical language use of a particular author so as to reveal whether or not a work is likely to have been written by that author. Indeed, much use of computers in English studies since the 1970s has been devoted to the production of scholarly critical editions (see Smedt et al. 1999: 63–88), the tracing of genealogies of manuscripts, and concordances (lists of words in their context) showing where particular words are used in texts such as the Bible or in Shakespeare's plays (see also Chapter 12 in this volume).

Traditionally, scholarly critical editions and concordances have been done manually, that is through the marking-up of text by hand, through comparisons of hard copies of different editions of texts, and so on. Not only can this be labour-intensive and time-consuming, it may also require access to specialist libraries or collections such as the Manuscript Room in the British Library.

The latter can be difficult as well as expensive for those not living in close proximity to such collections, and where different versions of a text are located in
libraries in different cities (say at the University of Texas, and in libraries in
Cambridge and London), it may require investments beyond the means of the
researcher, especially a postgraduate. This is where digital archiving, the conversion of hard copies of text into computer data that can be downloaded from
the worldwide web, has been enormously helpful in facilitating certain kinds of
textual research.[9]

Digital archiving is done with the help of software packages, either
specifically developed for a project, or generic (Smedt et al. 1999: 39–53).
Lewins (2001: 304) distinguishes two types of software packages for use in
qualitative data analysis: 'text retrievers' or 'text-based managers' which can
automatically generate information on word frequencies and retrieve text in
context, and 'code and retrieve' or 'code-based theory builders' which allow
thematic analyses and interpretation of texts, for instance through the coding
of all instances where marriage is referred to in Jane Austen's *Pride and
Prejudice*.[10] One text retriever easily available to users of Microsoft Word 97 and
later Word versions is the 'Autosummarize' feature found under 'Tools' which
enables one to identify the most important concepts used in a text according to
word frequency. This tool will also provide a text summary and place it at the
beginning of the text, rather like the abstract that may be required when one
submits an article to a journal. Among the code and retrieve packages, which I
shall discuss below, are the software packages QSR NUD*IST, ATLAS.ti,
KWALITAN, the Ethnograph, and WinMAX. Software packages can be
expensive but (computer centres in) universities frequently hold licences for
such software which then allows university-based researchers access to that
software. Weitzman (2003) provides a useful set of questions a researcher
should ask herself when deciding on a software package for her research – a
determining factor may, however, simply be what is available in your university.[11]

In order to understand the process of conducting discourse analysis, and to
facilitate conceptualising such research when conducting computer-based discourse analysis, it is helpful to start by learning to categorise or code the material one wants to examine manually. The process of coding is critical for the
discourse analytical process since codes both reproduce the interpretive frame
with which you approach your material, and produce building blocks for your
analysis (hence the phrase 'theory builders'). Coding can be done in two main
ways (Fielding 2001). Both will impact on the analysis you produce. Thus, you
can code in an open manner, meaning you code everything that you consider of
interest in a text, and then refine those codes through repeated re-reading and
re-coding, resulting in, for instance, the merger of certain codes that seem
similar, or the creation higher-order categories under which sets of codes are

subsumed. Alternatively, you may decide in advance what kinds of codes you want to apply because you want to analyse your texts from a particular perspective. As a feminist you might concentrate on textual features that mark gender effects in the text, for example. Or, from a socialist perspective you may want to show how a particular discourse uses economic metaphors to suggest the need for a market-driven approach to politics or education. In such a case, your codes may be theory-based (that is, based on the particular perspective you have) and you may create them before you start applying them to the text, rather than looking to see what you find in the text, as is the case with open coding. You may then let codes emerge from the text as you (repeatedly) work through it, or develop codes prior to applying them. This process takes time, and researchers need to build this time into their project timetable. What type of coding method you adopt depends on the kind of analysis you want to perform.

In order to facilitate the application of codes, it is useful to develop a codebook in which you note each code label (for example, 'marriage'), a definition of the code describing why you developed it, any qualifications (for instance, if you do not want the code to apply to common-law marriages), and an example. This codebook will help you to be consistent in the application of the codes, especially if you are coding over a long period of time or co-coding with others. You should also produce brief coding instructions (as reminders for yourself and others applying the codes) to indicate what you want to be encoded (for example, individual words, whole sentences, aspects of narrative structure). You are then in a position to begin the coding process.

Different software packages have different ways of enabling you to code. NUD*IST, for instance, encourages you to code in a hierarchical manner which will facilitate structured thinking but which may not be suitable if you want to conduct open coding. With open coding ATLAS.ti may be more helpful because it does not privilege the hierarchical organisation of ideas or codes. The process of using the software package involves importing the text to be analysed, then going through it systematically highlighting the words or sections of text you want to code, and then applying the code. Once you have coded your material, 'code and retrieve' packages such as NUD*IST and ATLAS.ti allow you to retrieve, by code, the chunks of text you are interested in. They also allow you to view the material in context so that you can understand where the particular bit of text was used. The retrieved material can be saved as a separate file and printed as a 'report', or it can, in these software packages, be used to create new 'supercodes' or meta-categories, allowing further analysis. Seeing all the pieces of text that relate to a particular code fragments that text in what some would describe as a postmodern fashion but, at the same time, it enables you to focus on those textual fragments and to find patterns that might not be obvious as you flip from page to page in the hard copy of a text trying to establish patterns.

NUD*IST and ATLAS.ti also allow several other functions that facilitate analysis of the text. One of these is the writing of analytic memos that will help you to remember, for instance, why a particular piece of text struck you as important. All researchers have the experience of underlining text in a hard copy because something struck them about that word or passage, only to find that when they go back to it later, they can no longer remember why they underlined it in the first place. The memo facility enables one to note such reasons so that one can later retrieve them and follow up one's thinking. Another useful function of these packages is that they allow you to produce graphics of the relationships between codes, for instance in the form of a spider gram with the code 'marriage' at the centre and other related codes such as 'wife', 'dowry', 'suitor' grouped around the code. This allows you to structure and to visualise relations between the concepts and themes that occur in your material.

In sum, NUD*IST and ATLAS.ti allow one to search texts, mark them up, link and re-organise data and represent one's own observations related to the texts being analysed. Learning to use such a software package takes some time. Additionally, the preparatory process for analyses with (and indeed without) CAQDAS can be time-consuming, especially when one deals with large corpora. However, as Weitzman puts it (2003: 16–17): 'the speed of the computer quickly pays for that investment' through the speed of the process when searching text (thus enabling many and multiple searches), the ability to quickly redefine codes and reassign chunks of text which means that one can revise one's analysis at will, and the ability to follow up a variety of ideas with much less cost to oneself in terms of time and effort. As Weitzman suggests (2003: 17): 'The speed of the computer alone can change what researchers even contemplate undertaking.' All of this may result in a much more detailed knowledge of the texts one is working on than was previously possible.

CONCLUSION

Discourse analysis is a useful research method for investigating ideological dispositions evident in texts. The systematic nature of its focus on patterns of, and in, language use, especially in relation to large sections of text/s, enables computer-aided analyses. The acquisition of the relevant skills requires time and effort from the researcher and raises the question of the utility of such acquisition in a research method that is evolving theoretically and practically, and given that one may work with this research method for only a limited period of time. Weitzman rightly suggests that the question of one's longer-term research intents needs to be considered when making such an investment. Smedt et al. make the point that learning how to use software packages provides researchers with proficiency in software tools, analytical skills in how to deal with non-uniform data, the ability to create information structures from complex data sets, text capture and manipulation techniques, understanding of metadata and version control, all of which 'are important parts of *document management*' and are relevant to an increasing range of research, commercial and other spheres of activity (1999: 79). Discourse analysis thus enhances both a researcher's research capacity and creates process- and content-specific knowledges that are useful across many different kinds of activity. As Norman Fairclough's work shows, it can also determine your research future and field.

REFERENCES

Austen, Jane [1814] (1966), *Mansfield Park*, Harmondsworth: Penguin.

Austen, Jane [1813] (1972), *Pride and Prejudice*, Harmondsworth: Penguin.

Beer, Gillian [1983] (1985), *Darwin's Plots: Evolutionary Narrative in Darwin, George Eliot and Nineteenth-Century Fiction*, London: Arc Paperbacks.

Burton, Deirdre (1980), *Dialogue and Discourse: A Sociolinguistic Approach to Modern Drama Dialogue and Naturally Occurring Conversation*, London: Routledge and Kegan Paul.

Chouliaraki, Lilie and Norman Fairclough (1999), *Discourse in Late Modernity: Rethinking Critical Discourse Analysis*, Edinburgh: Edinburgh University Press.

Crystal, David (1987), *The Cambridge Encyclopedia of Language*, Cambridge: Cambridge University Press.

Fairclough, Norman (1989), *Language and Power*, London: Longman.

Fairclough, Norman (1992), *Discourse and Social Change*, Cambridge: Polity Press.

Fairclough, Norman (1995), *Critical Discourse Analysis: The Critical Study of Language*, London: Longman.

Fairclough, Norman (2000), *New Labour, New Language?*, London: Routledge.

Fairclough, Norman (2001) 'The discourse of new Labour: Critical discourse analysis', in M. Wetherall et al. (eds), *Discourse as Data: A Guide for Analysis*, London: Sage, pp. 229–66.

Fairclough, Norman and Ruth Wodak (1997), 'Critical discourse analysis', in Teun Van Dijk (ed.), *Discourse as Social Interaction – Discourse Studies: A Multidisciplinary Introduction*, vol. 2, London: Sage.

Fielding, Jane (2001), 'Coding and managing data', in Nigel Gilbert (ed.), *Researching Social Life*, 2nd edn, London: Sage, pp. 227–51.

Foucault, Michel (1970), *The Order of Things: An Archaeology of the Human Sciences*, London: Tavistock.

Foucault, Michel (1972), *The Archaeology of Knowledge*, trans. A. M. Sheridan Smith, London: Tavistock.

Haraway, Donna (1989), *Primate Visions*, New York: Routledge, Chapman and Hall.

Haraway, Donna (1991), *Simians, Cyborgs, and Women: The Reinvention of Nature*, London: Free Association Books.

Heritage, John [1997] (2004), 'Discourse analysis as a way of analysing naturally occurring talk', in David Silverman (ed.), *Qualitative Research: Theory, Method and Practice*, London: Sage, pp. 200–21.

Kress, Gunther (2001), 'From Saussure to critical sociolinguistics: The turn towards a social view of language', in M. Wetherall et al. (eds), *Discourse Theory and Practice*, London: Sage, pp. 29–38.

Lewins, Ann (2001), 'Computer assisted qualitative data analysis', in Nigel Gilbert (ed.), *Researching Social Life*, 2nd edn, London: Sage, pp. 302–23.

Mills, Sara (1997), *Discourse*, London: Routledge.

Murdoch, Iris [1966] (1978), *The Time of the Angels*, Frogmore, St Albans: Triad/Panther Books.

Phillips, Louise and Marianne Jørgensen (eds) (2002), *Discourse Analysis as Theory and Method*, London: Sage.

Potter, Jonathan [1997] (2004), 'Conversation analysis and institutional talk: analysing data', in David Silverman (ed.), *Qualitative Research: Theory, Method and Practice*, London: Sage, pp. 222–45.

Sacks, Harvey (2001), 'Lecture 1: Rules of conversational sequencing', in M. Wetherall et al. (eds), *Discourse Theory and Practice*, London: Sage, pp. 111–18.

Sawday, Jonathan (1995), *The Body Emblazon'd: Dissection and the Human Body in Renaissance Culture*, London: Routledge.

Scholes, Robert (1982), *Semiotics and Interpretation*, New Haven: Yale University Press.

Silverman, David (ed.), [1997] (2004), *Qualitative Research: Theory, Method and Practice*, London: Sage.

Smedt, Koenraad, Hazel Gardiner, Espen Ore et al. (1999), *Computing in Humanities Education: A European Perspective*, Bergen: University of Bergen.

Taylor, Stephanie (2001), 'Evaluating and applying discourse analytic research', in M. Wetherall et al. (eds), *Discourse as Data: A Guide for Analysis*, London: Sage, pp. 311–30.

Van Dijk, Teun (2001), 'Principles of critical discourse analysis', in M. Wetherall et al. (eds), *Discourse Theory and Practice*, London: Sage, pp. 300–17.

Weitzman, Eben A. (2003), 'Software and qualitative research', in Norman K. Denzin and Yvonne S. Lincoln (eds), *Collecting and Interpreting Qualitative Data*, London: Sage, pp. 310–39.

Wetherall, Margaret, Stephanie Taylor and Simeon J. Yates (eds), (2001), *Discourse as Data: A Guide for Analysis*, London: Sage.

Wetherall, Margaret, Stephanie Taylor and Simeon J. Yates (eds), (2001), *Discourse Theory and Practice*, London: Sage.

Wilhelmi, Nancy O. (1994), 'The language of power and powerlessness: Verbal combat in the plays of Tennessee Williams', in Cynthia Goldin Bernstein (ed.), *The Text and Beyond: Essays in Literary Linguistics*, Tuscaloosa: University of Alabama Press, pp. 217–26.

Wodak, Ruth and Michael Meyer (eds), (2001), *Methods of Critical Discourse Analysis*, London: Sage.

Wooffitt, Robin (2001), 'Researching psychic practitioners: Conversation analysis', in M. Wetherall et al. (eds), *Discourse as Data: A Guide for Analysis*, London: Sage, pp. 49–92.

NOTES

1. There is some debate and diversity among discourse analysis theorists regarding the question of whether 'discourse' refers only to written and oral texts or also to other sign systems such as visual signs and body language. My focus in this chapter is predominantly on written and oral texts although it should be noted that many texts – from illuminated manuscripts to novels such as W. G. Sebald's, to auto/biographies – contain non-textual materials (for example, images, colouring) that contribute to, and are part of, the meaning of the text.

2. Some theorists (for example, David Crystal 1987) define discourse analysis as focusing exclusively on spoken language; the more common approach is to view it as pertaining to both written and spoken language usage.

3. For ongoing discussions about discourse analysis, see the journal *Discourse and Society* in which some of these debates are aired. See also Phillips and Jørgensen (2002), Wodak and Meyer (2001) and Wetherall et al. (2001a) for historicising accounts of the development of discourse analysis.

4. Two special issues in 2004 (15/2–3; 15/4), for instance, were devoted to 'Interpreting tragedy: the language of 11 September 2001', and 'Genetic and genomic discourses at the dawn of the twenty-first century' respectively.

5. Mills discusses the construction of 'literature' as an object of enquiry as part of her introduction to the ways in which discourses have been mobilised to create and sustain classificatory systems, quoting Foucault's definition of discourses as 'practices that systematically form the objects of which they speak' (Foucault 1972: 49, in Mills 1997: 17).

6. See Deirdre Burton (1980) and Nancy O. Wilhelmi (1994).

7. Conversation analysts have developed a whole range of vocabularies to describe conversational (inter)actions. See, for example, Wooffitt (2001), Potter (2004), Heritage (2004), Sacks (2001).

8. For an extended discussion of his work on this, see Mills (1997).

9. The Arts and Humanities Data Service (AHDS) supports digitisation projects and provides information about these (http://ahds.ac.uk). For guides about digital resources, see www.jisc.ac.uk/resourceguides/

10. See also Weitzman (2003: 319–22); http://www.content-analysis.de/quantitative.html; and http://caqdas.soc.surrey.ac.uk

11. Weitzman also provides information about free software downloadable from the worldwide web such as AnSWR and EZ-Text (2003: 331).

CHAPTER 7

The Uses of Ethnographic Methods in English Studies

Rachel Alsop, University of Hull

What is ethnography? Is it relevant to English studies? And, if so, how? This chapter is concerned with these questions. In academia, ethnography as a research methodology is typically associated with the social sciences, most usually, although not exclusively, with the discipline of anthropology. It is chiefly a qualitative research strategy that relies primarily on participant observation and concerns itself in its most general sense with the study and interpretation of cultural behaviour. The conventional image of the ethnographer is of the academic who goes out into the field (traditionally a distant land of whose people and way of life little was known) and lives closely alongside the people for an extended period of time, observing social interactions, customs and rituals (Hammersley and Atkinson 1983; van Maanen 1995). While in the field the ethnographer records his or her observations by making fieldnotes and then, on leaving and returning home, produces a written ethnographic study of that particular community.

The aims of this chapter are to explore the process of undertaking ethnographic research, to untangle the methodological pitfalls and possibilities of an ethnographic research strategy and to assess its use in and usefulness for English studies. The image of the ethnographer depicted above is a simplistic one, which conceals not only the complexities of actually doing ethnographic research (as well as the scope of ethnographic subject matter), but also questions of how to read and interpret ethnographic texts. Importantly, ethnography refers to both a process of research and to the research account, the ethnographic report, that is compiled from the research. In short, it is both a 'method of study and a result of such study' (van Maanen 1995: 4). Whilst both these strands of ethnography – the research process and the research text – are of potential relevance to the field of English studies, this chapter focuses primarily on ethnography as a research process. The chapter begins by examining key debates within ethnography and then moves to an analysis of the specific and varied ways in which ethnographic research is applicable to English studies. Within the latter discussion, particular attention will be paid to travel writing and audience response criticism as examples of subject areas in English studies where ethnographic research techniques are effectively deployed.

WHAT IS ETHNOGRAPHY? ISSUES AND DEVELOPMENTS

The ethnographer is both storyteller and scientist. (Fetterman 1998: 2)

Writing Culture: The Poetics and Politics of Ethnography (1986), edited by James Clifford and George E. Marcus, represents a watershed in the understanding and practice of ethnography. This volume, originating predominantly from a set of seminars at the School of American Research in Sante Fe, New Mexico in April 1984, confronts the relative absence of critical reflection on the process and products of ethnographic research, challenging the hitherto dominant conceptualisation of ethnographies as able to convey an objective, unmediated reality. The collection articulates the emergent understanding of ethnographies as themselves social constructions and not, as had been conceived previously, unambiguous representations of the 'truth'. As van Maanen articulates elsewhere, gone were the days '[w]hen ethnography was read as a straight-ahead cultural description based on first hand experience an author had with a strange (to both author and reader) group of people' (1995: 1). Instead, ethnographies were now recognised as themselves 'inventions' of culture, 'something made or fashioned' (Clifford 1986: 6), that are 'inherently *partial* – committed and incomplete' (Clifford 1986: 7). Importantly, *Writing Culture* emphasises the textual nature of ethnography, declaring that whilst it is erroneous to regard ethnography as 'only literature', ethnography is nevertheless 'always writing' (Clifford 1986: 26).

In line with developments elsewhere within research methodology debates, the significance of the impact of the researcher on the collection and writing-up of data, acknowledging crucially the power relations between researcher and researched, became central to the refashioning of understandings of ethnographic practice and texts. The ethnographer, it was now recognised, intervenes in two key, inter-related domains. The first intervention is in the collection and analysis of the data (for instance, in the designation of the field to be studied, decisions on whom to observe, how actions and words are interpreted, and what is seen as significant, as well as in the ways in which the ethnographer's presence impacts on the actions and words of the observed). The second key intervention by the ethnographer is in the construction of the written narrative that reflects on and communicates the research conclusions.

Thus, in all parts of the research process, the ethnographer is part of the research and not merely a neutral, impartial observer.

Traditionally within anthropology ethnographers have published two key texts from their fieldwork experience: the ethnography of the particular culture under scrutiny, and an account of the ethnographer's personal experience of the fieldwork process (a research biography). Indeed, it is common and recommended practice for the ethnographer to keep a research diary to note his or her personal reflections on the time in the 'field'. If contained within one text, the personal account is usually confined to the early sections of the ethnography with the bulk of the text devoted to an 'objective' evaluation of the cultural practices in question. The separation of the ethnographic descriptions of the culture under study from personal narrative (and the confinement of the personal narrative to the 'margins') was symptomatic of the uneasiness within anthropology and ethnographic research more generally about how to reconcile the perceived contradiction between subjective and objective accounts of fieldwork (Pratt 1986). How to embrace the experiences of the researcher within the field but still to fulfil the scientific demands of social science enquiry has been an enduring problem for ethnographers. In *Writing Culture* Mary Louise Pratt contemplates this uneasy juxtaposition of personal experience and 'objective' evaluations, emphasising, however, the importance of subjective reflections within ethnographies to frame the cultural descriptions. 'Personal narrative,' she argues,

> mediates this contradiction between the engagement called for in
> fieldwork and the self-effacement called for in formal ethnographic
> description, or at least mitigates some of its anguish, by inserting into
> the ethnographic text the authority of the personal experience out of
> which the ethnography is made. (1986: 33)

Janice Radway's (1997) study of the US Book-of-the-Month club and of middlebrow literary culture is a useful example within the field of literary studies where a predominantly ethnographic analysis productively entwines the author's subjective responses into the research account. Her narrative, which draws on a lengthy, interactive period of research, is intensely autobiographical, reflecting on her own place within the research project not only in relation to the research process but also to the subject matter. As Radway observes:

> this project became as much my story as it was theirs, I place myself
> within the tale as a character inhabiting the same world occupied by the
> people and institutions I was trying to understand. What I try to
> provide . . . is a sense of the process through which I came to recognize

that the impingement of my own history on my present activity had everything to do with what I saw and could begin to say about it. (1997: 14–15)

A greater attention to reflexivity in both the research process and research writings, recognising how the ethnographer's experience within the field unquestionably colours the data obtained, potentially breaks down the confrontation between 'subjective' and 'objective' commentary. Instead of playing a role at the margins, awareness within ethnographic research that the impact of the researcher cannot and should not be extracted from the research process places the personal account of fieldwork centre stage. Feminist researchers have played a key role here in highlighting the power relations at play in the research process (Roberts 1981). Feminist research has at its core not only a concern to make visible, to analyse and to challenge gender (and other associated) inequalities but also an awareness of 'the political and ethical issues involved in the research process' (Maynard 1994: 14; see also Letherby 2003). It is a question not just of *what* is studied but *how* it is studied, and, importantly, of how the actual process of research impacts on both the research findings and those involved in the research (for a discussion of feminist ethnography, see Skeggs 1994). Postcolonial critiques have similarly engaged with issues of power relations within research, highlighting and challenging the ways in which some ethnography (and indeed anthropology as a discipline) has been entwined with the exploitative relations of colonial enterprise (Mills 1991; Pratt 1992; Clifford 1997).

Ethnography fundamentally is a mode of research conducted in a natural, as opposed to an artificial, setting such as a laboratory (Hammersley and Atkinson 1983: 2). The ethnographer finds out about other cultures, or features of a culture (for English studies, this may relate to the cultural dimensions of literature or language, as illustrated in more detail below), by undertaking prolonged periods in the 'field', participating and observing in all or certain relevant aspects of social life. Whilst participant observation is central to ethnography, this method of research can be supplemented by interviews, document analysis, consideration of novels, magazines, photography, even the analysis of statistical information if found to be relevant, although ethnographic research does tend to favour qualitative research over quantitative. Significantly, ethnography is 'multimethod research' (Reinharz 1992: 46). The ethnographer is interested in 'collecting whatever data are available to throw light on the issues with which he or she is concerned' (Hammersley and Atkinson 1983: 2). As has been argued elsewhere, ethnography is better understood as a research methodology rather than a research method (Skeggs 1994). It is a 'theory of the research process' which can employ a variety of different research methods (Skeggs 1994: 76). As an example, Radway's study of the

Book-of-the-Month club (1997), discussed previously, utilises an array of different research methods, including participant observation, interviews with Book-of-the-Month club staff, and document analysis (examining, among other things, readers' reports and internal memoranda) as well as autobiographical insight in her evaluation of the organisation.

Although there is much debate as to what makes a project researching cultural behaviour distinctively 'ethnographic' (Wolcott 1995), there is some consensus that what is central to and specific about an ethnographic research methodology is the depth and length of engagement with the subject matter, of the ethnographer's immersion in the 'field'. During the fieldwork period, the process of collecting data is largely unstructured in that the ethnographer does not embark on fieldwork with pre-set ideas of what to research and how to codify, but is instead led by what he or she encounters during the period of fieldwork (Hammersley 1990: 2). Importantly, the collection of data and the analysis of the data start at the same time, with the ethnographer reflecting from the outset on the data amassed (Fetterman 1998). It is not a question of gather the data first and scrutinise them later but a constant process of contemplation and analysis.

Across the broad reach of ethnographic research there are different emphases and approaches. Van Maanen (1995) attempts to classify ethnographic research into five possible types: ethnographic realism; confessional ethnography; dramatic ethnography; critical ethnography; and self- or auto-ethnography. Ethnographic realism refers to the type of ethnographic research critiqued above, which has been condemned for lacking reflexivity and an acknowledgement of power relations within the research process. Here the presence and impact of the researcher is absent in the ethnographic text. The aim is to produce an objective picture of the cultural activity under scrutiny, 'a clear, unmediated record of a knoweable world' (van Maanen 1995: 7), through the researcher being there, observing, taking notes and reporting what has been seen. This is typical of early ethnographic accounts. By contrast, in confessional ethnography the role of the researcher in the research process is central, thereby moving 'attention from the signified (the studied culture) to the one who, quite literally signifies (the ethnographer)' (1995: 8). Here the focus is on the process by which the ethnographer undertakes the research. The information produced about the culture under study is therefore located at a particular point in time and as a result of a particular research/ethnographic intervention. Radway's study of the Book-of-the-Month club, discussed above, is one such example (1997). Thirdly, dramatic ethnography, van Maanen postulates, has clear cross-overs in style with novels and other fictional accounts and might focus in particular on one episode or occurrence within a specific community. Here, he argues, 'ethnographies present unfolding stories and rely more on techniques drawn from literary fiction and personal essays than from plain-speaking, documentary techniques – the style of nonstyle – drawn from scientific reports' (1995: 9). Critical ethnography, on the other hand, situates the culture within a wider framework whether that is socio-economic, historic, symbolic or otherwise. Finally, self-ethnographies or auto-ethnographies centre on the culture of the ethnographer him- or herself, thereby eradicating the differentiation between the 'signified' and the 'signifier' (van Maanen 1995: 10; see also Clifford 1986: 9 for a discussion of indigenous ethnography). Boyarin's ethnographic study of his own involvement at a Jewish yeshiva (a school where biblical and Talmud texts are studied) is one such example of the auto-ethnographic style of research (Boyarin 1992a; 1992b).

Clearly, the image of the ethnographer painted in the opening paragraph of this chapter is outdated and misleading. The scope of ethnographic research is much wider, including studies of the cultures of faraway shores but also studies closer to home, or even at home. What constitutes the 'field' is being remoulded. The earlier notion of the field as a singular and fixed location, somewhere else and somewhere distant, has been eroded with the growth of indigenous and multi-locale ethnographies (Clifford 1997). Whilst Western researchers still dominate the academic landscape, the emergence of ethnographic studies by indigenous non-Western researchers has begun to unsettle the West's domination of ethnographic knowledge production. Furthermore, ethnographic research has begun to include 'microethnographies' (Wolcott 1995) which deal with specific social phenomena, such as 'medical ethnography, school ethnography, occupational ethnography, organizational ethnography, family ethnography' (van Maanen 1995: 10) to name just a few examples. And, as is discussed below, within English studies there is significant scope for the development of microethnographies, focused on particular aspects related to literature, literacy and language.

Thus, whilst ethnography is central to the task of cultural anthropology (Hammersley 1990), ethnography remains an interdisciplinary phenomenon and is – and can be – successfully used as a research tool in a variety of different disciplines, including English studies. It is the objective of the following sections to explore further the ways in which researchers working within English studies do, and can, deploy ethnographic research techniques.

ETHNOGRAPHY FOR ENGLISH STUDIES

As indicated above, ethnographies are of significance to English studies both as a research process and a research text. This section will begin by exploring four key ways in which ethnographies are of relevance to scholars in this field, before moving on to examine in more depth two specific areas of English studies where ethnographic research can be appropriate: travel writing and audience response criticism.

Firstly, ethnographies are of interest as an object of enquiry in themselves, as literary works. As indicated above, an increased understanding of the textual dimensions of ethnographic research, of its position as both a narrative construction and a scientific pursuit (Fetterman 1998; Clifford 1986; Pratt 1992), affirmed the scope of ethnography to straddle both the arts and social sciences. But, as Clifford observed, there is still a resistance by some anthropologists (and relevant funding bodies) to the depiction of ethnography as a literary as well as a scientific endeavour:

> To a growing number, however, the 'literariness' of anthropology – and especially ethnography – appears as much more than a matter of good writing or distinctive literary style. Literary processes – metaphor, figuration, narrative – affect the ways cultural phenomena are registered, from the first jotted 'observations' to the completed book, to the ways these configurations 'make sense' in determined acts of reading. (1986: 4)

Thus, for those working in English studies, ethnographies have a value and relevance as texts. Baine Campbell, for example, argues that as ethnographies (of the past at least) have been presented as conveying the truth of a situation, they constitute 'a perfect test case for analytical work that tries to posit or explain the fundamental fictionality of all representation' (2002: 263). Pratt is also concerned with the narrative constructions of ethnographies and identifies particular tropes within ethnographic writing (1986; 1992). Ethnographies often start with the depiction of the arrival of the ethnographer in the field. This, she argues, tends to follow two distinctive formats: the utopian and the anti-utopian. In the former the ethnographer is greeted enthusiastically by the members of the community he or she wishes to observe and welcomed into the fold. In the latter the arrival is met with scepticism, suspicion or even hostility. The task of the ethnographer is to confront and negotiate such difficulties in order to conduct the proposed fieldwork. As Baine Campbell asserts:

> The very fact that rhetorical tropes and allegorical structures can be uncovered or simply pointed out in ethnographic texts has revealed . . . that ethnographic writing was a kind of representation as wedded to an inherited medium and the associative rip tides of the unconscious as is poetry or political propaganda. (2002: 273)

For any literary student or researcher analysing the textual constructions and narrative strategies of ethnography, an understanding and appreciation of the practice of ethnographic research methods is, of course, vital. However, such literary analysis of ethnographic research matter is overwhelmingly concerned with ethnography as a research text rather than as a research process. Here, ethnography is not utilised itself as a research methodology but instead constitutes the object of research, with other research methods employed (for example, textual deconstruction) to facilitate the process of enquiry.

In a second related way, ethnographic research is pertinent to English studies as a means of evaluating the extent to and the ways in which literary works draw on ethnography in the construction of narrative. Whilst the discussion above has focused on the literary analysis of texts explicitly presented as ethnographies, here the attention is moved to uncovering and exploring the possible ethnographic basis of other forms of literature not customarily defined as ethnographic, but where the narrative draws on ethnographically produced material. Examples for such investigation include George Orwell's *Road To Wigan Pier*, Nell Dunn's *Poor Cow*, or even Shakespeare's *The Tempest*. What is at stake is the extent to which the authors use ethnographic research strategies to research and write their accounts (or, indeed, the ethnographic work of other writers) as well as the manner in which ethnographic techniques are deployed.

Whilst this second mode of enquiry examines the use of ethnography in seemingly 'non-ethnographic' styles of writing (and again it does not utilise ethnography as research method but instead explores the use of ethnography by another writer), a third function of ethnography in English studies is as a research tool for writers. The emphasis has subtly shifted here from analysing the ways in which other writers have used ethnographic techniques in their writing to *actively* using ethnographic research strategies in one's own literary compositions. 'People-watching', it is widely agreed, is central to many forms of creative writing and this falls most definitely within the realms of 'participant observation', itself a staple of ethnographic research. Ann Hoffmann's *Research for Writers*, which is primarily a guide to help writers research their projects, argues that 'a writer's raw material is derived principally from a study of other human beings, their complex relationships, their strengths and weaknesses and idiosyncrasies, as well as their history' (1996: 4). Yet whilst the guide covers research resources such as the printed media, biography and autobiography and official records, there is no separate section on or detailed discussion of 'participant observation'. Dymphna Callery, offering advice for would-be writers, similarly acknowledges the usefulness of participant observation in preparing the background for a written piece: 'If your story or drama is set on a fishing boat research on the spot will prove far more useful than reading a book' (2000: 159). In short, she suggests microethnographic research. Indeed, whilst 'people-watching' or 'participant observation' are credited as integral to the research process for many writers, guides on research methods for writers typically fail to explore ethnography as a possible research strategy, thereby omitting any careful analysis of its usefulness for this purpose.

Fourthly, ethnography can be utilised in English studies as a method of studying literary (or, indeed, linguistic) behaviour, for example as a means of exploring the social context in which literature is both produced and consumed or the cultural framework of oral communication. Here, 'ethnographies of reading' or 'ethnographies of language' are salient to students and researchers in English studies and anthropology as well as other related fields. As Boyarin notes, the distinctions between literary and anthropological scholars undertaking ethnographies of reading are 'not so much methodological as chronotopic – between those who are learning to include textuality as one of the fields of interaction they study in the present, and those who are learning to see fields of interaction shaping and surrounding the remains of the past' (1992a: 2).

In relation to the analysis of literary behaviour, ethnographic strategies enable an in-depth and interactive analysis of the social conditions and aspects of literary pursuits. As Long asserts, the popular image of writing and reading as solitary activities belies the social and collective facets of such literary endeavours. In relation to writing, she notes that writers are engaged, for instance, in 'reading other writers, discussing ideas with other people, and writing to and for others in a language whose very grammar, genres, and figures of speech encode collectivity' (1992: 181). Similarly, what is available to read and what we decide to read is *socially framed* (1992: 192), influenced by publishers, academics, literary reviewers, book clubs, reading groups and so on. As she states,

> collective and institutional processes shape reading practices by authoratively defining what is worth reading and how to read it. In turn this authorative framing has effects on what kinds of books are published, reviewed, and kept in circulation in libraries, classrooms and the marketplace, while legitimating, as well, certain kinds of literary values and correlative modes of reading. (Long 1992: 192)

Moreover, reading is often enjoyed as a collective and social pursuit, as is witnessed by the long history and current growth of reading groups in the UK, US and elsewhere (Hartley 2002; Long 1992).

In exploring the social context of literary production and consumption, possible avenues of research might include microethnographic studies of writers' colonies, reading groups, literature festivals, book signings, book clubs, English classes or poetry readings as well as macroethnographic studies of literacy (or, indeed, oral forms of communication) within specific cultures or societies. Boyarin, for example, an advocate of ethnographic studies of literature, undertook an ethnographic study of his involvement in a yeshiva in Lower East Side, New York (1992a; 1992b). Radway's (1997) study of the US Book-of-the-Month Club also explicitly acknowledges the ethnographic element of the research process, as does her earlier study of romance reading, which is discussed in more detail below.

Not all potentially ethnographic research in this field necessarily acknowledges the ethnographic dimensions of the research process. For example, Jenny Hartley's study of reading groups in the UK (2002) could be classified as an ethnographic piece of research, although it is not explicitly presented nor framed as such. Whilst much of the data on reading groups is acquired through questionnaire research, Hartley also draws on her own lengthy involvement in reading groups, both as a facilitator and a member (2002: 38), as well as her participant observation of other reading groups first contacted through questionnaires (2002: 89). Whilst Hartley does not package the research as ethnographic and tends to highlight the questionnaire research over the other research methods used when discussing research methodology, the detail of the discussion would not have been possible without Hartley's intense and prolonged involvement in reading groups.

To consider further the role of ethnography in English studies, the following analysis focuses on two areas of the discipline in which the use of ethnographic research is particularly relevant and which have, to this point in the chapter, remained relatively unexamined: travel writing and audience response criticism. The aim is to illustrate in more depth through these two case studies the various ways in which ethnographic research techniques can be productively deployed.

As is illustrated further below, in travel writing there is a long history of ethnographic research dating back to the sixteenth century when travel accounts, often produced by sailors, merchants and missionaries, became widespread. Travel writing is a genre that overlaps, encompasses and integrates both factual and fictional literary modes and, in so doing, draws on a range of research techniques and textual strategies, including ethnography, both as a research methodology and as a form of writing. Travel writing is of interest to scholars working within English studies in a number of ways. Firstly, ethnographic travel accounts are open to textual deconstruction and literary analysis. As discussed below, Pratt (1992) identifies various similarities and continuities between the often denigrated genre of travel writing and the seemingly more 'serious' field of academic anthropology. Likewise, the more literary styles of travel writing, or indeed literature that embodies travel as a key motif, can be evaluated in terms of their ethnographic bases: where, for instance, does autobiography or fictional prose give way to ethnographic observations? Finally, ethnography is of significance for analysts of travel writing and for the writers of travel literature. Ethnographic research methodology is the research tool with which travel writers can study, get to know and interpret the cultural behaviour encountered.

Audience response criticism is part of literary analysis concerned with the social consumption of literature. It focuses on the reception and negotiation of texts by audiences and, importantly for this discussion, it has an established history of using ethnographic research methodologies to explore literature within a cultural context. Here, the concern is not only with how texts are approached and interpreted by readers (individually or collectively) but how the social activity of reading (or, indeed, watching, if the text is performed) links into, is sculpted by, and in turn moulds other aspects of social and personal life.

TRAVEL WRITING

Only recently has travel writing, 'the varied body of writing that takes travel as an essential condition of its production' (Rubiés 2002: 244), been accorded serious consideration within academia. This 'vast, little explored area' (Hulme and Youngs 2002b: 1) encompasses a range of different styles and approaches, including, amongst others, the travelogue, the autobiographical novel, the journalistic narration and the scientific report. Travel writing is interdisciplinary, covering, for instance, anthropology, geography, history, literature, media studies. Ethnography clearly has a place in some travel writing. As Rubiés asserts, 'the description of peoples, their nature, customs, religion, forms of government, and language is so embedded in travel writing . . . that one assumes ethnography to be essential to the genre' (2002: 242). Although it would overstate the case to see all travel writing as ethnographic – Bill Bryson's travel novels, for example, are based primarily on autobiographical humour rather than ethnographic method (Hulme 2002) – an understanding of ethnographic research methods may be required in order to appraise, to analyse and indeed to produce travel writing.

Travel writing has a lengthy history. For as long as people have travelled they have narrated accounts of their journeys in oral, pictorial or written forms. One need only think of the Bible and its numerous tales of travel (Hulme and Youngs 2002b: 2), Homer's *Odyssey*, or more recently *Don Quixote*, to appreciate that well established history. In the modern epoch, travel writing began to flourish in the sixteenth century with the greater global movements of people producing and requiring written documentation of journeys, for instance, maps and accounts of lands visited, peoples and terrains encountered. Missionaries, explorers, sailors, pirates, ambassadors, scholars and merchants (among others) were all involved in the accumulation of travel writing in this period, which developed understanding of the physical and social world through first-hand observation and fed back into the huge expansion at this time of philosophical and scientific knowledge more generally (Hulme and Youngs 2002a; Sherman 2002).

Many of the early accounts draw on ethnographic research methods in their production. Indeed, we can see the early roots of ethnography in the travel writing of the sixteenth century. In this period a standard format for reporting information acquired through travel was established. 'Relations', as they were known, aimed to produce systematic accounts of the economic, geographical, social and political aspects of the place visited through supposedly neutral observation. Such was the organisation of the production of this knowledge that instructions were published for travellers detailing the ways in which information should be recorded, with suggested headings for the categories to be covered (Rubiés 2002: 252). As Rubiés asserts, 'in the earlier centuries of European expansion, travel writing generated ethnography as a matter of course' (2002: 243).

Between the nineteenth and twentieth century the more scientific travel writing generated by scientists, explorers, ethnographers and other travellers gave way to a upsurge in more literary styles of travel writing (Carr 2002; Hulme 2002; Rubiés 2002). From the twentieth century literary travel writing, whilst not completely replacing ethnographic travel writing, became the more popular and dominant form within the genre.

> If in the nineteenth century, travel writing might often be produced by
> missionaries, explorers, scientists, or Orientalists . . . in texts in which
> the purveying of privileged knowledge was a central concern,
> increasingly in the twentieth century it has become a more subjective
> form, more memoir than manual, and often an alternative form of
> writing for novelists (Carr 2002: 74).

Indeed, after the Second World War travel writing became much more possible as a basis for a career as a writer (such as Paul Theroux) rather than something that writers did in addition to their usual and better acknowledged work. Additionally, the interconnections between travel writing and more journalistic styles of writing became more pronounced (Carr 2002).

The emergence of scientific anthropology in the twentieth century served to cement ethnographic research methods within academia and to marginalise and denigrate the genre of travel writing. There are clear continuities between the ethnographies of the travel writing in the early modern period and those conducted under the auspices of academic anthropology in the twentieth century. Pratt, for instance, recognises the tensions evident in both areas between the personal narrative and the more impersonal, distanced cultural descriptions, along with a similarity of written conventions and tropes utilised in both forms (1986; 1992). She illustrates, for example, how the arrival scenes in modern ethnographies resemble those of earlier forms of travel writing.

As anthropological ethnographers have started to recognise the intrinsic partiality of all research (including ethnographies), the literary qualities of ethnographic writing, the significance of the routes in and out of the field on what is studied therein, now grappling with issues of reflexivity and textual construc-tion, the carefully observed distinction between anthropological texts and some travel accounts has started to erode, potentially blurring the disciplinary borders (Pratt 1986; Pratt 1992; Clifford 1997). Whilst anthropology's own internal debate about the distinctiveness of its disciplinary position and its particular brand of ethnography continues (Clifford 1997), what is of greater significant here for researchers within the field of English studies are the crossovers and interactions between the research practices of the arts and the social sciences, the permeability of disciplinary borders and the importance of looking beyond one's own disciplinary backyard when contemplating research methods.

AUDIENCE RESPONSE CRITICISM

The study of how audiences respond encompasses potentially a wide variety of textual forms and participatory settings. The focus could be a written text (novel, play, magazine, newspaper), a performance (on stage, on the screen, in the street, in a sporting arena), a documentary, a newsreel, a photograph, a bill-board, an oil painting – the list goes on. Likewise, the 'audience' could be a con-ventional audience in a theatre, the reader/s of a novel (alone, in a reading group, in a classroom), a viewer of television (either solitary or in a group, for example a family watching TV), and so forth. Its objective is to explore how texts and/or performances are negotiated, interpreted and given meaning by the reader or viewer.

With reference to the written text, audience research, usually discussed under the banner of reader response criticism, challenges the notion that meaning is located within the text, that the author is the originator of meaning and that the text is self-sufficient (Freund 1987; Radway 1991; Leitch 1995). Instead, the reader is seen as the source of meaning, neither passive nor invis-ible. In consequence, texts are conceptualised as having no pre-existing, fixed or singular meaning. Readings are multiple, differentiated potentially by the gender, age class, geographical and temporal location and so on of the reader (see, for example, Flynn and Schweickart 1986 for a discussion of gender and reading). The body of work forming reader response criticism is broad and diverse. Of particular interest in this chapter are the ways in which ethno-graphic research has been utilised to investigate the social activity of reading and the understandings of the texts produced. Ethnographic research enables the exploration of the consumption of literature within defined social and his-torical settings and by specified groups of readers.

Radway's *Reading the Romance*, first published in 1984, is an example of how an ethnographic research methodology can be deployed to explore the reception of literature amongst its readers. Radway, a literature specialist interested in popular culture, was part of a growing movement within American studies in the US in the 1970s and 1980s interested in the cultural and social dimensions of literature production and consumption. As textual analysis constituted the established and dominant form of literary research, the move towards a more culturally located understanding of American literature represented a radical and hotly debated departure from accepted practice. It also necessitated the use of research methods within the study of literature more commonly associated with social science scholarship. At the University of Pennsylvania where Radway took up employment in the 1970s, American studies scholars were pioneering the use of ethnographic research methods within the discipline.

Radway's particular interest here was in 'ethnographies of reading' (1991: 4). Her research into the reading of romances by women sought therefore to produce an ethnographically-based account of romance reading, 'designed initially to see whether it was possible to investigate reading empirically so as to make "accurate" statements about the historical and cultural meaning of literary production and consumption' (1991: 4). At the outset, Radway was concerned with the ways in which women interpret romances. However, her research revealed that equally significant was the value accorded by the women to the actual activity of reading. A distinction was made therefore by Radway between the meaning of the text and the event of reading (1991: 7). For the women the act of reading was, she concluded, 'a declaration of independence' (1991: 11) and a way of resisting the demands placed upon them as wives and mothers. Women, she observed, were utilising 'traditionally female forms [the reading of romance novels] to resist their situation *as women*' (1991: 12). Interestingly, Radway, whilst acknowledging that potentially there are as many different interpretations as readers, argues that patterns can be detected, suggesting that 'similarly located readers learn a similar set of reading strategies and interpretative codes' (1991: 8). Although her original project was not comparative, she did conclude that a comparative dimension in audience research would be useful, looking not only at the impact of a variety of social variables (for example, age, class, geographical location and so on) but also exploring the experiences of those women who do read romances with women who do not.

When originally conducting the research, Radway saw scientific research methods such as ethnographies as a way of uncovering an objective reality, a way of 'telling it as it is'. In her introduction to the second edition of the book (1991), Radway reflects on the research methods utilised and the ways in which the text was received and interpreted. Subsequently influenced by the ethnographic studies of the Birmingham Centre for Cultural Studies amongst others, Radway discusses in this later edition the limitations of her own research and of ethnographic methods more generally.

I also no longer want to argue theoretically that ethnographies of reading should *replace* textual interpretation because of their greater adequacy to the task of revealing an objective cultural reality. Rather, I would claim that they can be fruitfully employed as an essential component of a multi-focused approach that attempts to do justice to the ways historical subjects understand and partially control their own behaviour in a social and cultural context that has powerful determining effects on individual social action. (Radway 1991: 5–6)

Nonetheless, Radway's study illustrates the role ethnographic research methods can play in literature-based disciplines such as English and American studies. Whilst Radway rightly acknowledges that ethnographic research should not be viewed as the only, the most valid or the principal research method for these areas, her work nevertheless demonstrates that ethnographic research methods are suitable and productive for some avenues of research within literature-based subjects.

Another useful example of how ethnographic research methods can be utilised in the study of texts and their meanings is *Reading National Geographic* (1993) written by Catherine A. Lutz and Jane L. Collins. Lutz and Collins, both anthropologists by background, were interested in the part that *National Geographic* magazine plays in moulding Americans' awareness and comprehension of the world beyond the US. *National Geographic* is the third most heavily subscribed magazine in the US with a readership of around 37 million people worldwide (1993: 2) and is, the authors argue, 'one of the primary means by which people in the United States receive information and images of the world outside their own borders' (1993: 1). It is a high-status magazine with significant social credibility that has as its focus the cultural and biological diversity of the globe, with a sizeable portion of its stories covering the developing world.

Lutz and Collins investigated the production and consumption of the *National Geographic* in the US. Their project, they argue, was 'not at all about the non-Western world but about its appropriation by the West, and *National Geographic*'s role in that appropriation' (1993: 2). They used a range of research methods to explore the ways in which *National Geographic* is produced, and what is covered within the magazine, as well as how readers of the magazine respond to its contents. Regarding the latter, Lutz and Collins focused on audience responses to the photographic images within the magazine since these are 'one of the most culturally valued and potent media vehicles shaping American understandings of, and responses to, the world outside the United States' (1993: xii).

In investigating the production of the magazine, the researchers conducted a number of interviews with staff of the *National Geographic*, including editors and photographers. They also observed various stages of the process of production, planning meetings, the lay-out of a particular story, the mock-up of the magazine and so on. They write in detail, for example, of one of the weekly planning meetings they attended, chaired by the editor, commenting on the decision-making and managerial processes (discussions, for instance, on what was to be included, omitted and commissioned) and on the social interactions and hierarchies within the organisation (it was, they noted, 'a participatory dictatorship' dominated by white males). Elsewhere, they also remark on observations from their casual encounters in the offices of the *National Geographic*, for example, after the editor had vetoed the inclusion of one particularly graphic image in the magazine Lutz and Collins note that the photograph could still be seen on the walls of a number of different offices in the *National Geographic* building.

Lutz and Collins' research, whilst not consciously defining itself in the text as 'ethnographic', has been classified elsewhere as an example of how ethnographic research methods can be deployed in the analysis of text and images (van Maanen 1995). Lutz and Collins are both anthropologists and, in line with ethnographic research methodology, use a range of research strategies to amass their data, including both qualitative and quantitative methods. They not only blend a mixture of interviews, document and image analysis and participant observation but they also locate themselves as one-time consumers of the magazine:

> Our parents and grade-school teachers led us to *National Geographic*, and there we found immense pleasure in the views of fantastically decorated forest people, vivid tropical fish and flowers, and the expansive sense of a world, large, diverse, and somehow knowable . . . Both of us were implicated deeply and early in the seductive representations of the third world produced by *National Geographic*. In fact, like many anthropologists who have described to us the effect of the magazine on them, we can, in part, root our life's work in our early reading of it. (Lutz and Collins 1993: xi–xii)

In this sense, Lutz and Collins can be defined as indigenous ethnographers. Their fieldwork does not take them into an 'other' culture but instead they focus on an aspect of their own culture. Whilst they are on new ground in the offices of the magazine where they investigate the production process, they are familiar with, and have experience of, consuming *National Geographic*. Their research field, they acknowledge, was 'not overseas . . . but was in the homes and offices where *National Geographic* is read and produced' (1993: xii).

Although participant observation formed part of the research conducted, both in relation to the production and consumption of the magazine, it is useful to consider briefly the extent to which participant observation was constituent of the whole research strategy. Anyone considering a similar project could seek a greater degree of participant observation by securing work within the proposed institution (for example, with a publisher), either paid or unpaid, perhaps shadowing an employee, a photographer or an editor for example. Clifford, in considering the disciplinary distinctions of anthropology, comments on Susan Harding's ethnographic study of Christian Fundamentalism in the US. Her research, he notes, investigates a multitude of discourses constructing Christian Fundamentalism, examining printed and visual media (newspapers, television programmes), and undertaking participant observation in church and its surrounding community. However, as Clifford points out, what makes Harding's work distinctively anthropological is her 'insistence that a crucial portion of her ethnographic work must involve *living with* an evangelical Christian family' (1997: 62). For Clifford, anthropology is not about exotic travel but about 'intensive/interactive styles of research' (1997: 89). Whilst Harding's sojourn with an evangelical Christian family was not the central plank of the research but just one of the research methods deployed, it did, in Clifford's opinion, produce the depth and intensity of ethnographic research characteristic of anthropological study.

For most people seeking to conduct ethnographic research within English studies, the question of whether the research methods are sufficiently 'interactive and intensive' to conform to the disciplinary demands of anthropology may be an irrelevance. What this example illustrates, however, are the varying extents to which participant observation can be conducted, and the different styles of ethnographic research. Whilst anthropology may demand a particularly intensive form of ethnographic research and a deeper level of participant observation, this does not mean that this level of intensity and interaction is out of bounds for those researchers working outside anthropology, such as in English studies.

CONCLUSIONS

Ethnography is a research strategy which seeks to explore and interpret cultural behaviour through prolonged and deep engagement and interaction with the subject, employing prospectively a variety of research methods, including participant observation. Whilst the explicit use and acknowledgement of an ethnographic research methodology in English studies is still relatively uncommon and pocketed in certain areas, ethnographic methods do represent a potentially fruitful mode of investigation for many avenues of enquiry within the field. Indeed, the genres of travel writing and audience response criticism, as outlined above, constitute two valuable examples of the productive employment of ethnographic strategies.

Ethnography is of additional interest to researchers within English studies because of its dual function as a storytelling and a scientific enterprise. Ethnography refers not only to the research process but also to the product of the research, the written text, and is itself a literary artefact worthy of critical attention by literary scholars. Significantly, the study of ethnography, both as a research process and a research text, exposes its interdisciplinary foundations and underlines the value of a broad-based, multidisciplinary approach to research and scholarship.

REFERENCES

Baine Campbell, Mary (2002), 'Travel writing and its theory', in P. Hulme and T. Youngs (eds), *The Cambridge Companion to Travel Writing*, Cambridge: Cambridge University Press, pp. 261–78.

Boyarin, Jonathan (1992a), 'Introduction', in J. Boyarin (ed.), *The Ethnography of Reading*, Berkeley: University of California Press.

Boyarin, Jonathan (1992b), 'Voices around the text: The ethnography of reading at Mesivta Tifereth Jerusalem', in J. Boyarin (ed.), *The Ethnography of Reading*, Berkeley: University of California Press.

Boyarin, Jonathan (ed.) (1992c), *The Ethnography of Reading*, Berkeley: University of California Press.

Callery, Dymphna (2000), 'Writing for stage', in J. Newman, E. Cusick and A. La Tourette (eds), *The Writer's Workbook*, London: Arnold.

Carr, Helen (2002), 'Modernism and travel (1880–1940)', in P. Hulme and T. Youngs (eds), *The Cambridge Companion to Travel Writing*, Cambridge: Cambridge University Press, pp. 70–86.

Cervantes, Miguel de (1986), *Don Quixote*, London: Allen and Unwin.

Clifford, James (1986), 'Introduction: partial truths', in J. Clifford and G. E. Marcus (eds), *Writing Culture: The Poetics and Politics of Ethnography*, Berkeley: University of California Press.

Clifford, James (1997), *Routes: Travel and Translation in the Late Twentieth Century*, Cambridge, MA: Harvard University Press.

Clifford, James and George E. Marcus (eds) (1986), *Writing Culture: The Poetics and Politics of Ethnography*, Berkeley: University of California Press.

Dunn, Nell (1988), *Poor Cow*, London: Virago.

Fetterman, David M. (1998), *Ethnography: Step by Step*, London: Sage.

Flynn, Elizabeth A. and Patrocinio P. Schweickart (eds), (1986), *Gender and Reading: Essays on Readers, Texts and Contexts*, Baltimore: Johns Hopkins University Press.

Freund, Elizabeth (1987), *The Return of the Reader*, London: Methuen.

Hammersley, Martyn (1990), *Reading Ethnographic Research: A Critical Guide*, Harlow: Longman.

Hammersley, Martyn and Paul Atkinson (1983), *Ethnography: Principles in Practice*, London: Routledge.

Hartley, Jenny (2002), *The Reading Groups Book*, Oxford: Oxford University Press.

Hoffmann, Ann (1996), *Research for Writers*, London: A. and C. Black.

Hulme, Peter (2002), 'Travelling to write (1940–2000)', in P. Hulme and T. Youngs (eds), *The*

Cambridge Companion to Travel Writing, Cambridge: Cambridge University Press, pp. 87–104.

Hulme, Peter and Tim Youngs (eds) (2002a), *The Cambridge Companion to Travel Writing*, Cambridge: Cambridge University Press.

Hulme, Peter and Tim Youngs (2002b), 'Introduction', in P. Hulme and T. Youngs (eds), *The Cambridge Companion to Travel Writing*, Cambridge: Cambridge University Press, pp. 1–16.

Iser, Wolfgang (1995), 'Interaction between text and reader', in A. Bennett, *Readers and Reading*, Harlow: Longman.

Leitch, Vincent B. (1995), 'Reader-response criticism', in A. Bennett, *Readers and Reading*, Harlow: Longman.

Letherby, Gayle (2003), *Feminist Research in Theory and Practice*, Buckingham: Open University Press.

Long, Elizabeth (1992), 'Textual interpretation as collective action', in J. Boyarin (ed.), *The Ethnography of Reading*, Berkeley: University of California Press.

Lutz, Catherine A. and Jane L. Collins (1993), *Reading National Geographic*, Chicago: University of Chicago Press.

Maynard, Mary (1994), 'Methods, practice and epistemology: The debate about feminism and research', in M. Maynard and J. Purvis (eds), *Researching Women's Lives from a Feminist Perspective*, London: Taylor and Francis, pp. 10–26.

Mills, Sara (1991), *Discourses of Difference: An Analysis of Women's Travel Writing and Colonialism*, London: Routledge.

Orwell, George (1959), *The Road to Wigan Pier*, London: Martin Secker and Warburg.

Pratt, Mary Louise (1986), 'Fieldwork in common places', in J. Clifford and G. E. Marcus (eds), *Writing Culture: The Poetics and Politics of Ethnography*, Berkeley: University of California Press, pp. 27–50.

Pratt, Mary Louise (1992), *Imperial Eyes. Travel Writing and Transculturation*, London: Routledge.

Radway, Janice A. (1991), *Reading the Romance: Women, Patriarchy and Popular Literature*, Chapel Hill: University of North Carolina Press.

Radway, Janice A. (1997), *A Feeling for Books. The Book-of-the-Month Club, Literary Taste, and Middle-Class Desire*, Chapel Hill: University of North Carolina Press.

Reinharz, Shulamit (1992), *Feminist Methods in Social Research*, Oxford: Oxford University Press.

Roberts, Helen (ed.) (1981), *Doing Feminist Research*, London: Routledge and Kegan Paul.

Rubiés, Joan Pau (2002), 'Travel writing and ethnography', in P. Hulme and T. Youngs (eds), *The Cambridge Companion to Travel Writing*, Cambridge: Cambridge University Press, pp. 242–60.

Sherman, William H. (2002), 'Stirrings and searchings (1500–1720)', in P. Hulme and T. Youngs (eds), *The Cambridge Companion to Travel Writing*, Cambridge: Cambridge University Press, pp. 17–36.

Skeggs, Beverley (1994), 'Situating the production of feminist ethnography', in M. Maynard and J. Purvis (eds), *Researching Women's Lives from a Feminist Perspective*, London: Taylor and Francis, pp. 72–92.

Van Maanen, J. (1995), 'An end to innocence: The ethnography of ethnography', in J. van Maanen (ed.), *Representation in Ethnography*, London: Sage.

Wolcott, Harry F. (1995), 'Making a study "more ethnographic"', in J. van Maanen (ed.), *Representation in Ethnography*, London: Sage.

CHAPTER 8

Numbers and Words: Quantitative Methods for Scholars of Texts

Pat Hudson, Cardiff University

This chapter considers the virtual absence of statistical techniques and quantitative methods from literature studies and the arts more generally. It starts by defining the nature and boundaries of literary analysis and of literature as a discipline, and asks how literature specialists generally encounter numbers. It then explores why there is a tension between quantitative and qualitative approaches to research and argues that literary studies are impoverished by the continued avoidance of quantification. Finally, some basic computational and statistical procedures and techniques, likely to be useful to literature research, are introduced. It is suggested that these elements should be included in research training across the arts disciplines.

THE NATURE AND BOUNDARIES OF LITERARY CRITICISM

Literature research and literary criticism, as currently practised, confine themselves almost exclusively to textual analyses, scarcely ever mentioning or using numbers. Yet those disciplines that are near neighbours of literary studies, particularly linguistics and sociology, are amongst the most vigorous and innovative users of quantitative methods and of computer-aided research techniques based upon counting and probability calculus. This seems paradoxical. Although some of the technical excesses of quantitative analyses in adjacent disciplines justifiably discourage emulation, the almost total absence of any sort of quantification in studies of literary texts is a mystery. Literature research covers a spectrum of approaches that overlap at the margins with linguistics on the one hand and with sociological and cultural studies, including history, on the other, but the degree of common research approaches at the overlapping margins is generally minuscule. The scope for using social scientific, statistical

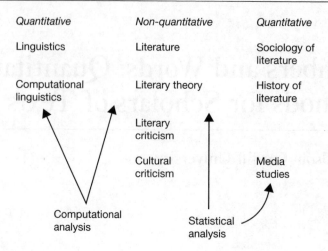

Figure 8.1 Literary studies: disciplinary and research methods boundaries

and computer applications in literature research, as in so many branches of the arts and humanities, is great but its actual use appears to be negligible. The divisions in methodology and approach are illustrated in Figure 8.1.

LITERARY RESEARCHERS, TEXTS AND NUMBERS

As a historian not fully familiar with attitudes to quantification in the arts, yet charged with exploring the absence of such method, I decided to seek advice at the outset in writing this chapter from my colleague Catherine Belsey, Professor of Critical and Cultural Theory at Cardiff University. Despite the particular deconstructionist leanings of the Cardiff Department, the reply I received is probably not atypical of academics in literature departments more generally:

> I'm sorry to say that I'm no use to you whatever. To my undying shame, I don't even know what quantification is. And my computer is no more than a word processor, but faster. I'm so sorry. I don't even know who to refer you to.[1]

To begin to understand why there is such antipathy to quantification and to identify the drawbacks of rigid and exclusive adherence to non-quantitative approaches in literature studies, it is useful to ask what encounters literature specialists commonly have with numbers and the nature of their response.

In literary works themselves numbers are most often encountered in relaying such matters as dates, incomes, prices, wealth or inheritance. Their use appears rarely to be questioned by academics analysing the texts. Numbers and their context within broader grammatical or situating frames receive much less scrutiny than words, and the meaning or veracity of a quantified amount is rarely questioned. For example, the second chapter of Jane Austen's *Sense and Sensibility* is peppered with financial details about inheritance, division and disposition of wealth but the figures themselves have attracted little comment, in relation to historical or real values, for example, or even as to why, in alliterative terms, so much numerical detail is given – onomatopoeically – almost like a cash register.

One should, however, question the idea that the selection and use of numbers can be taken for granted as some neutral, value-free aspect of a text, identifiable with information or fact, in contrast to the literature or fiction that surrounds it. In Terry Eagleton's view of what counts as literature, this practice is strongly contested. He unsettles the assumption of the neutrality of numbers, in this case a date, by using the description of a cathedral as being built in 1612. He suggests that we imagine that the reader is someone from a culture where diachronic values are suppressed, where dates and chronologies are rarely invoked but where, in the case of buildings, the direction in which they face is of infinitely greater importance. The literary quality and the cultural relativism of what, at first sight, appears to be a standard or neutral description is fully exposed.[2]

Despite the normative, relative and stylistic attributes of most numbers that appear in texts, a search of English-language journals relating to literature and literary criticism over the past decade (those available electronically – hence easily searchable) demonstrates that numbers, where they are used at all by academics, are employed to convey dates, values and amounts, but are little questioned in relation to emphasis, style or context. By far their most frequent use is in dates of publication of works cited! Exceptions appear where research strays into the neighbouring disciplines of sociology or history. But even here it remains possible to write histories of the novel with no reference to numbers produced, prices, consumption data or sales figures. Only where the study of literature involves the study of broad trends in the content and plot or study of readerships or readership responses do numerical citations increase and tabulations appear.

For example, Joseph McAleer's history of Mills and Boon, *Passion's Fortune*, uses quantitative as well as visual and qualitative evidence.[3] Figures 8.2 and 8.3 give examples of McAleer's use of bar charts to convey information about sales of differently priced editions and the profitability of the company. Edward Copeland's excellent *Women Writing About Money: Women's Fiction in England, 1790–1820* employs bar charts to illustrate the frequency of depictions of different aspects of marriage in *The Lady's Magazine* during the Napoleonic War period (Figure 8.4). However, these are the only numerical analyses in a

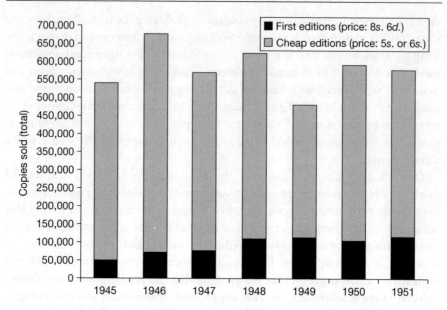

Figure 8.2 Annual fiction sales of Mills and Boon Ltd, 1945–51 (Source: Joseph McAleer (1999), *Passion's Fortune: The Story of Mills and Boon*, Oxford: Oxford University Press, p. 86. By permission of Oxford University Press.)

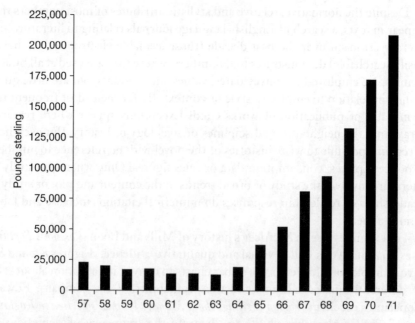

Figure 8.3 Annual net profit of Mills and Boon Ltd, 1957–71 (Source: Joseph McAleer (1999), *Passion's Fortune: The Story of Mills and Boon*, Oxford: Oxford University Press, p. 115. By permission of Oxford University Press.)

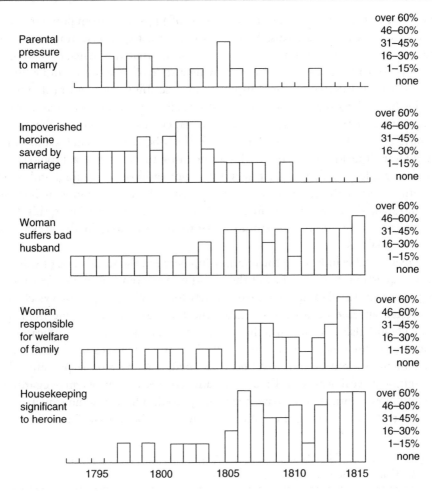

Figure 8.4 Plot analysis bar charts from *The Lady's Magazine*, 1793–1815 (Source: Edward Copeland (1995), *Women Writing about Money: Women's Fiction in England, 1790–1820*, Cambridge: Cambridge University Press, p. 63.)

book suffused with, and focused upon, pecuniary and financial references, and it is, instructively, about plot lines rather than monies, their meaning or their disposition.[4]

In *The Alienated Reader* (1991), which straddles the divide between literary and sociological analysis, Bridget Fowler gives circulation figures for nineteenth-century journals, differentiating between those 'saturated with the ethos of dependent femininity and familism' [sic] and those with a feminist and radical orientation.[5] By demonstrating that the circulation of the former was up to eighteen times greater than the latter and that radical journals were short-lived, she emphasises the ideological weight of passive femininity.

Fowler employs content analysis in a sample of 144 stories from popular magazines of the 1920s and 1930s. Although the criteria for the selection of stories are not discussed, the 'sample' is used to argue that the magazines sought popularity with their readers by employing a style of melodrama and realism (1991: 52–3). Figures are also employed in describing sales and profitability ratios for various sorts of fiction, global sales figures for *Harlequin* and other imprints, and the shelf life of American paperback romances in the 1980s (1991: 26–7). An important aspect of Fowler's book is her analysis of contemporary questionnaire data which she uses to construct a typology of women readers, their literary tastes, their motivations for reading, and their politics. Although her questionnaire design, tabulations and conclusions would struggle to pass muster in a 'hard' social science environment, this does represent a rare attempt to employ quantitative methods in the service of literary analysis.

Fowler's table indicating the relationship between the social class of women in her questionnaire sample and their reading preference is shown in Figure 8.5. The very small sample size, particularly for certain groups (such as class 1 representing élite occupations) makes the findings somewhat questionable. One should also question whether occupations are a reasonable indicator of social class for this purpose and exactly how the categories of 'Legitimate', 'Middlebrow' and so on have been defined. Figure 8.6 perpetuates the definitional weaknesses of Figure 8.5 and creates new problems regarding exactly how political views have been categorised. There is some explanation in the text, but categorisation and the drawing of boundaries between cate-

Figure 8.5 Class and reading preference (Source: Bridget Fowler (1991), *The Alienated Reader*, London: Harvester Wheatsheaf, p. 129.)

Class	Women's occupation	Total occupations	Legitimate	Middlebrow	'Cookson'	Romantic	Radical
1	1	2 (2%)	1	1	0	0	0
2	23	25 (22%)	15	3	4	2	1
3 Non manual	40	41 (36%)	6	10	16	8	1
3 Manual	10	16 (14%)	3	1	6	6	0
4	5	7 (6%)	0	0	5	2	0
5	23	24 (21%)	1	1	11	8	3
Total	102	115	26	16	42	26	5

Notes: Women have been classified by their positions in the labour-market; where these are not known or they are students or houseworkers, they have been classified by their husband's work, or (where single) their father's work. The Registrar-General's categories of (paid) work are used.

Figure 8.6 Reading preferences and views on politics and feminism (Source: Bridget Fowler (1991), *The Alienated Reader*, London: Harvester Wheatsheaf, p. 155.)

Reading group	Political radical	Elements of radicalism	Not radical	Feminist	Elements of feminism	Traditional views on women
Legitimate (26)	16 (64%)	4 (16%)	5 (20%)	19 (73%)	2 (8%)	5 (19%)
Middlebrow (16)	4 (25%)	2 (13%)	10 (63%)	6 (38%)	3 (19%)	7 (44%)
'Cookson' (42)	9 (23%)	13 (33%)	18 (45%)	14 (34%)	10 (24%)	17 (41%)
Romantic (26)	3 (11%)	3 (11%)	20 (78%)	3 (13%)	10 (38%)	13 (50%)
Radical (5)	4 (80%)	1 (20%)	0	4 (100%)	0	0
Total	36 (32%)	23 (21%)	53 (47%)	46 (41%)	25 (22%)	42 (37%)

* Numbers and percentages are slightly divergent from reading group totals due to unclassifiable responses.

gories is a perennial problem with questionnaire results and with other sorts of raw statistical data. Fowler admits that some responses were unclassifiable. Figure 8.7 attempts to summarise attitudes to literature on the part of different types of reader. The difficulties of framing leading questions and of categorising responses are clearly revealed here. The table allows much information to be conveyed but there are weaknesses of questionnaire design and interpretation.

The examples of quantitative analysis in English literature research quoted in this section were hard to find and are weak demonstrators of the potential of numerical analysis for scholars of texts. The next part of this chapter explores reasons for, and the implications of, privileging words over numbers as a prelude to explaining how quantitative methods might be employed in textual analysis and literature studies.

THE COMPLEMENTARITY OF WORDS AND NUMBERS

The writing of Oliver Wendell Holmes serves as an introduction to the issues at stake in privileging words (in the form of detailed descriptions of individual cases) over numbers (amassed in aggregated categories of data) on the assumption that the former are uniquely able to capture the experience of individuals. Holmes was a medical practitioner as well as a novelist, treating patients with puerperal fever, amongst other complaints, and using his medical experiences to inform his novels. Jane F. Thrailkill's study of Holmes has shown that his recognition of the pattern of the disease amongst seventy-seven patients, which he tabulated in a two-page chart, indicated a clustering of incidence of the symptoms. This led him to reject the idea that it was caused by individual

Figure 8.7 Attitudes to Literature (Source: Bridget Fowler (1991), *The Alienated Reader*, London: Harvester Wheatsheaf, p. 143.)

| | Reading group | | | | | |
	Legitimate	Middlebrow	'Cookson'	Romantic	Radical	Total
Like to read novels about 'how things really are'?						
Yes	24 (93%)	8 (50%)	28 (67%)	8 (31%)	5 (100%)	73 (63%)
Sometimes, also likes fantasy	2 (8%)	1 (6%)	1 (2%)	0	0	4 (3%)
No	0	5 (31%)	9 (21%)	15 (58%)	0	29 (25%)
No answer	0	2 (13%)	4 (10%)	3 (12%)	0	9 (8%)
						115
Reasons for reading						
Interest in critical ideas of writer[1]	15 (56%)	5 (31%)	12 (29%)	0	3 (60%)	35 (30%)
Distraction or pleasure[2]	0	1 (6%)	4 (10%)	10 (38%)	0	15 (13%)
Distraction or pleasure[3]	9 (35%)	7 (44%)	15 (36%)	7 (27%)	1 (20%)	39 (34%)
Interest in a record of lived experience[1]	16 (62%)	7 (44%)	28 (67%)	9 (35%)	4 (80%)	64 (56%)
Interest in an imaginary world of harmony[1]	9 (35%)	5 (31%)	7 (17%)	9 (35%)	1 (20%)	31 (17%)
						184
Enjoyment of a formula in romantic novels and family sagas						
Pleasure in a formula	0	4 (25%)	16 (38%)	20 (77%)	0	40 (35%)
Dislike of a formula	23 (88%)	9 (56%)	17 (40%)	3 (12%)	5 (100%)	57 (50%)
Structure important, *not* romantic formula/other	2 (8%)	1 (6%)	3 (7%)	0	0	6 (5%)
No answer	1 (4%)	2 (13%)	6 (14%)	3 (12%)	0	12 (10%)
						115

Notes:
1. *Either sole reason stated or given with other reasons.*
2. *Sole reason.*
3. *Combined with other reasons.*

bodily or moral failing (the dominant view at the time) and instead to argue that doctors were infecting their patients. This went against the belief that disease could only be treated by understanding the detailed pathology of individual cases: that the 'incommensurable' particularity could only be investigated by novelistic means in the form of detailed individual case notes.[6] Holmes' combination of the latter approach with a respect for the science of numbers in turn had an impact upon the characterisations in, and the message of, his novels, particularly *Elsie Venner: A Romance of Destiny* (1861). In *A Mortal Antipathy* (1885) a character argues that novelistic or particularistic description not balanced by aggregation and abstraction might cause 'great damage, wrong, loss, grief, shame and irreparable injury'.[7]

By examining the novelistic thinking of doctors who rejected the theory of contagion, Thrailkill emphasises that narrative form can be individually rich but at the same time socially blind. By treating each woman's illness individually, physicians unwittingly spread a disease that, before the discovery of bacteriology, could be made visible by a simple analysis of the pattern of incidence in numerous cases: by considering the social as well as the individual pathology. In this attention to social pathology, Holmes anticipates the path-breaking innovations in social statistics pioneered by Emile Durkheim in his studies of suicide. Holmes does not plump for one approach to the exclusion of the other. Rather, he settles for the idea that words, as much as numbers, are inadequate substitutions for the thing itself, but that the two are all we have, and can be usefully combined.

Similarly, with an entirely different Holmes, Sir Arthur Conan Doyle clearly expresses the contrast between the two approaches (social scientific/deductive and individual/narrative/inductive) in his Sherlock Holmes novels. Whilst making Dr Watson, the man of science, the plodding fall guy to Sherlock's superior opiate-induced intuition, the interpretation of clues and scientific method, induction and deduction, are combined in the solution of his most intriguing crimes. In Conan Doyle's *The Cardboard Box* (1892) severed ears in a parcel sent to Miss Cushing are immediately identified by Holmes as anatomically identical to the ears of the recipient. Whilst Watson deduces nothing, Holmes leaps to the assertion that the victim is a close relative of Miss Cushing.[8]

QUALITATIVE/QUANTITATIVE TENSION AND BIFURCATION

Even on the boundaries of literary research where social, cultural and historical context and analysis are invoked and the need for quantification becomes more urgent, numbers are hard to find in studies of literature. Rarer still are examples of the complementary use of numerical and textual analysis. This is because of the strong tension, if not complete bifurcation, that exists between quantitative and qualitative research in this field and in the humanities more generally. Too often the choice of research approach – between qualitative and quantitative – is seen as an either/or question. What is seen as at stake is not just a choice of research method but of research methodology, of epistemological position, and this is where the perceived incompatibility lies. Literary critics disparage overly systematic modes of research and understanding.[9] They see quantification as the method of positivistic enquiry geared to the possibility of objectively approaching reality: the polar opposite of the nuanced and relativistic understandings possible from their preferred hermeneutic and narrative methodologies expressed solely in prose. Many quantifiers, on the other hand, disparage the unsystematic and particularistic methods characteristic of the humanities. Thus, each side tends to misunderstand, to caricature and to talk past the other.

In *Poetic Justice: The Literary Imagination and Public Life* Martha Nussbaum argues that the novel is uniquely able to represent the empirical experience of particular individuals and that its *ethical* importance is magnified in a world where most disciplines, and the language of civil society, is so oriented towards aggregated numerical data, statistical evidence and averages (1995: 26–7).[10] She echoes the perspective of Mary Poovey who argues that 'the individual human being . . . is obliterated by the numerical average or aggregate that replaces him'.[11] Her much-cited and broader work *A History of the Modern Fact* (1998) sustains a fashionable critique of what she sees as the assumed neutrality and the primacy of numerical representation in modern society.[12] But Nussbaum's and Poovey's argument fails to recognise that much effort is spent in statistical studies guarding against bias and attacking the neutrality hypothesis. More importantly, what eludes such interpretations is the fact that detailed description or narrative shares many of the same problems of categorisation, bias, rhetorical presentation and distortion that afflict quantitative approaches. The postmodern world of media hype is created by language. Textual researchers are thus concerned more than ever to emphasise the absence of an anterior reality, independent of spoken and written language: that the researcher is engaged to study representations and cultural productions rather than reality. Ironically, this is just what literary traditionalists have found so difficult to accept in quantitative methods. Also, like statistics, hermeneutic methods have blind spots. They are good for conveying and suggesting some things, bad for others. Literary analysts may be more reflexive, self-critical and alert to the representational rather than the real significance of their findings than are mathematicians, but few of the latter lack this awareness and there is no methodological reason for the assumption that numbers carry positivistic dangers and that words do not.

THE SIMILARITIES BETWEEN WORDS AND NUMBERS

Quantitative and humanistic approaches are by no means as methodologically distinct as their present champions make out. If this is accepted, the barriers to the use of quantification in the arts are lowered. Those opposing quantification often argue that it attempts to impose an inappropriate scientific methodology upon the analysis of complex human behaviour and to force evidence into classificatory straitjackets that allow too little for diversity and unpredictability. It is also claimed that the statistical techniques themselves are so imbued with the values and prejudices of those who were responsible for creating them that they are of little use in wider contexts. But it would be a mistake to think that the theories and techniques of statistics are any more tainted in this way than other sorts of theories, ideas and concepts used in the human sciences. It is perhaps surprising that the intense discussion of the subjective and normative nature of qualitative approaches and of the problems inherent in language, vocabularies and linguistic structures has not resulted in a greater thawing of the qualitative/quantitative divide. Postmodern and poststructuralist debates about the values, beliefs, assumptions, categories, dialogics and monologics embedded in the language of source documents and literary texts have a counterpart in long established critiques of quantification and its power to restrict understanding by narrowing the scope of discourse to things neatly and subjectively categorised and enumerated in monologic or didactic expression.

Postmodern orientations in the social sciences and in the arts have nevertheless made quantification the focus of much criticism. In particular, statistical methods have been identified almost exclusively with positivistic enquiry and with attempts to mould society along particular lines.[13] For many postmodern critics, numbers represent the cutting edge of the modernity that they detest. Numbers are seen as exercising power over individuals, particularly through the creation of statistically verifiable behavioural and physical norms against which an oppressive category of abnormality is created.[14] Yet quantification is not alone in doing this. It is inherently no less and no more than a language and it shares characteristics with other languages. All languages contribute to the creation of the society they purport merely to describe or to mediate. All languages share with quantification the production of oppressive categories which promote or extol certain individuals or groups and condemn others. It is the case that quantification appears as, and is promoted as, more objective and more rigorous in its hold on reality than qualitative accounts. It is also potentially more hegemonic and inflexible across time and space than other languages: it follows an internationally accepted set of rules and assumptions that change only slowly. Such distinctions between the language of words and the language of numbers call for vigilance but should not blind us to the problems that quantification shares with narrative or qualitative approaches. The force of linguistic structures, manners of delivery, rhetoric, style and storytelling need careful evaluation and reflexivity as do numbers and their use. One could argue that words carry subtleties of connotation and context, and fertile ambiguities, which allow more effective communication. But what words gain in flexibility they lose *vis-à-vis* numbers in precision. Both carry problems and a mix of the two can only be desirable for many sorts of investigation. Unfortunately, we are too often presented with a mutually exclusive choice between words and numbers as if each represented an entirely different approach to knowledge.

NUMBERS AS A LANGUAGE

The methodological similarity of the two approaches can be better appreciated by further considering numbers as a language. W. G. Sebald, whose corpus of work inspires by crossing the boundaries between the personal and the social, between fact and fiction and between literature and social analysis, provides a good example of the use of numbers in literary expression. In *On The Natural History of Destruction* (2003) he argues that the saturation bombing of civilian targets in German cities in 1943 caused destruction on a scale that was impossible for contemporaries to articulate.[15] The bombing was thus largely obliterated from the retrospective understanding of those affected.

> The reality of total destruction, incomprehensible in its extremity, pales
> when described in such stereotypical phrases as . . . 'all hell was let
> loose', 'we were staring into the inferno', 'the dreadful fate of the cities
> of Germany', and so on and so forth. Their function is to cover up and
> neutralise experiences beyond our ability to comprehend . . . (2003: 25)

The capacity of everyday language to go on functioning as usual was lost and the authenticity of experiences directly recalled was filtered through stock phrases and second hand responses.

Even the 'literature of the ruins', a distinct genre of the late 1940s and 1950s that one might expect to be expressive of the reality of urban destruction, appears to Sebald as 'an instrument already tuned to individual and collective amnesia' (2003: 9). He also criticises the literature of the immediate postwar period which, with the exception of Heinrich Böll's novel *The Angel was Silent* (not published until 1992), ignored realism, 'succumbing . . . to the temptation to make the real horrors of the time disappear through the artifice of abstraction and metaphysical fraudulence.'[16] 'Language . . . proves inadequate as a cure for the precarious condition of a man losing faith in the world' (2003: 166).

Sebald thus explains his need to supplement the impoverished accounts of individual eye witnesses, survivors and the literature of a generation with a synoptic view based on a wide range of official documents and popular sources, quantitative and qualitative. These together form his literature:

> It is true that the strategic bombing survey published by the allies, together with the records of the Federal German Statistics Office and other official sources, show that the Royal Air Force alone dropped 1 million tons of bombs on enemy territory; it is true that of the 131 towns and cities were attacked, some only once and some repeatedly, many were almost entirely flattened, that about 600,000 German civilians fell victim to the air raids and 3.5 million homes were destroyed, while at the end of the war 7.5 million people were left homeless, and there were 31.1 cubic metres of rubble for everyone in Cologne and 42.8 cubic metres for every inhabitant in Dresden. (2003: 3–4)

Sebald describes an air raid on Hamburg when:

> 10,000 tons of high explosive and incendiary bombs were dropped . . . weighing 4,000 pounds . . . (including) fire bombs weighing up to 15 kilograms . . . fires . . . covered some 20 square kilometres . . . rising 2,000 metres into the sky . . . At its height the storm lifted gables and roofs from buildings, flung rafters and entire advertising hoardings through the air, tore trees from the ground and drove human beings before it like living torches. Behind collapsing facades the flames shot up as high as houses, rolled like a tidal wave through the streets at a speed of over 150 kilometres an hour . . . The glass in the tramcar windows melted; stocks of sugar boiled in the bakery cellars . . . The smoke had risen to a height of 8,000 metres. (2003: 27–8)
> . . . victims (were) reduced to ashes by the heat, which had risen to 1,000 degrees or more . . . the remains of families consisting of several people could be carried away in a single laundry basket. (2003: 28–9)

Eagleton defines literature as a form of expression where the 'texture, rhythm and resonance of words are in excess of their abstract meaning'.[17] My argument here is that numbers can be used in a similar way, and the lengthy quotations from Sebald's work demonstrate this supremely well.

QUANTITATIVE METHODS: SOME BASIC DEFINITIONS

Having established a case for considering the usefulness of numbers as a language and the usefulness of counting to researchers in the humanities, I shall now consider what sorts of quantitative techniques might be of most use in the analysis of literature, of texts and of literature-related phenomena. The first point to make is that quantitative methods in the text-based humanities can be divided into two main categories: computational and statistical. *Computational methods* in the humanities concern the computer-aided storage, retrieval, interrogation and analysis of texts (see also Chapter 12 in this volume). This can take many forms but is largely based upon quantification. These methods are generally found at the interface between literature studies and linguistics but there is no reason why they should be confined to this periphery. *Statistical methods* concern the display and analysis of quantitative data. In the humanities/literature studies this might be data on literary output, classifications of literature or readerships, or readership opinions from questionnaire or interview material. Statistical methods might also concern the analysis of plots or other content in narratives and can overlap with computational analysis. Computers are often used alongside statistics to facilitate analysis or the presentation of statistical data.

COMPUTATIONAL METHODS

Computational methods have expanded enormously with the growing sophistication and easy accessibility of information technology in recent decades. Such methods can be used to assist in analysing various features of texts: aspects both of style and content.[18]

At its most simple, once a text has been transcribed into machine-readable form, various software programmes can be used easily to retrieve particular words, word strings, or phrase and sentence structures which facilitate the study of literary expression. Text retrieval and concordance programmes were amongst the earliest to be employed in text analysis, the most basic operations being to count the number of occurrences of specific words, to assist in indexing, and to retrieve (through concordance) particular words within the context of their accompanying phrase or sentence. Software can enable one to pick out words of similar construction and allow for spelling variations. Text analysis software can also generate collocations which show pairs of words which co-occur frequently, for example pound and flesh and flesh and blood in *The Merchant of Venice*.[19] Some concordance programmes can generate a list of all the collocates of a given word. Such exercises not only speed up traditional analyses of the form or style of literary expression but they can also reveal patterns that are not easy to spot with the naked eye, particularly in a very large or variable work (just as was the case with Wendell Holmes and the social pathology of puerperal fever revealed in the statistical pattern of incidence). Collocation analysis from the outset resulted in a variety of vocabulary studies and 'dialectology'.[20]

Computers are most useful for finding features within a literary work and counting occurrences of those features. They can also locate specific words or patterns within a text or collection of texts and thus point the researcher to further areas of enquiry. Not surprisingly, one major and longstanding use of such computations has been to assist in establishing the authorship of works and especially in helping to settle disputes about authorship.[21] The assumption that one can begin to identify authorship through the frequency with which certain word patterns or sentence structures occur is of course debatable, not least because an author might use different vocabularies and structures for different sorts of writing and/or might change their characteristic patterns over time as their craft matures. However, authorship identification programs can highlight the degree to which different works have common patterns and they can thus give the researcher grounds for rejecting or being more confident about a particular conclusion. Early and overconfident examples of author identification in the 1970s gave this method a bad name. Many literary scholars regarded the results as counter-intuitive and worth little but as programmes become more sophisticated, employing intelligent systems softwares that learn patterns and features from the text for themselves as one feeds it in, the method is likely to generate more valuable and acceptable results.

It is, however, important to note that languages vary in their computability when it comes to the analysis of stylistic content or stylometry. The more rigid the rules of grammar, punctuation and expression, the more difficult it is, generally speaking, to identify variations between particular authors and personal idiosyncrasies. In Japanese, for example, it is the writer's choice where one word ends and another begins, there are fewer rules about how words should be ordered within sentences, and the choice of appropriate conjunctions in sentences is much freer than in English. Perhaps for this reason, more effort has been devoted to computer-aided authorship analysis in Japanese than in English literature, as with the debates over the authorship of the last ten chapters of *The Tale of the Shining Prince Genji*, debatably the world's first novel, written in the eleventh century.[22]

LITERARY ANALYSIS EMPLOYING COMPUTATIONAL METHODS

When one moves from basic concordance, collocation and stylometric research to the engagement of computers in literary analysis and criticism, the chorus of opposition from traditionalists increases, sometimes with good cause. Some of the early computer applications in literary studies exhibited poor practice and obtained poor results. Thus, much contemporary objection from traditionalists is based upon a misunderstanding of current best-practice computer use. Best practice involves the use of computers to generate evidence to support or refute hypotheses based on other methods or to be more systematic or complete in the coverage of texts studied. Computers do not have a mind of their own and are only as good, or as bad, as the researcher who employs them (as could be said about libraries, archives or filing cabinets).

Most uses of computational methods for literary analysis depend upon concordance and word-count applications of various degrees of sophistication. The influence of one author upon another has been studied by attempting to identify the echoes of one author in the text of another. At their most effective, these involve a great deal of manual mark-up and tagging of the text before the investigation can commence and a considerable amount of passing back and forth between what the computer throws up and the researcher's own evaluation of the echoes. The best such research appears where computational techniques are used as a facilitator or adjunct to traditional methods and where automation is accompanied by great care in interpreting results. Ian Lancashire has, for example, investigated repeated phrases in a number of different texts from Chaucer to Margaret Atwood whilst Lessard and Hamm have used a computer program to identify repeated structures in Stendhal.[23] In a similar way, the study of genres can be furthered by computer-aided analysis of vocabulary, and there have also been developments in the use of computers to study sound patterns in verse and in the structure of dramas.[24]

Content analysis can be used to analyse the substance as well as the form of a text. Richard Merrit analysed eighteenth-century newspapers in this way to examine at what point Americans developed a separate nationalistically-oriented identity. He analysed regularities of speech, vocabulary and images.[25] Some of the more sophisticated content analysis currently being developed involves the use of cognitive science and mental mapping where the relationships between ideas, beliefs, attitudes and information available to an author are studied to understand how semantic decision-making takes place in the creation of a text.[26] The dangers of this sort of analysis are, of course, manifold. It rests entirely on the assumption that the written word (in journalism, novels or whatever) does reflect social and political attitudes. This value judgement underpins the research but is not a weakness of the computational method itself. More important for our purposes is the point that quantification in this sort of study is not neutral because the researcher has selected the variables to be counted and considered (particular words, word strings or collocations in the text) and has already decided that these are the most significant as expressions of identity. Again, however, this is not a criticism or weakness of quantification *per se*, and it has a direct counterpart in problems commonly encountered in qualitative work as with the choice of text or section of text for detailed analysis for particular purposes.[27]

STATISTICAL METHODS

Statistical methods employed in the arts and elsewhere can be divided into two distinct categories: descriptive and inferential. *Descriptive statistics* are techniques employed to improve the communication and display of numerical information in an analytical context. *Inferential statistics* are techniques of greater technical sophistication employed to interrogate possible meanings and implications of available data. Inferential statistics go beyond data rearrangement and display to consider cause and effect, based largely upon probability theory.

Descriptive statistics

Descriptive statistics are extremely useful for researchers in the humanities. The most common need of such researchers is to comment upon data extracted from documentary or oral sources but such data is rarely discovered or collected in a form immediately useful for the researcher's purpose. Much can be gained by re-arranging and summarising such numerical data and displaying it in the form of visually effective tables, figures or graphs in order to convey the information more effectively and thus to comment upon its meaning.[28]

We have already seen some examples of this in the bar charts and tables above. Figure 8.8 gives another example. It shows a set of pie charts depicting the age composition of the British population for various years. Such data might be useful for considering the changing popularity of different forms of children's literature over time, for example. The pie chart is a simple display technique useful for a wide range of purposes.

In re-arranging data in order best to summarise and to access their meaning, averages are often calculated as a way of representing common experience. With histograms or graphs of continuous interval data as in Figure 8.9, the mean value bisects the area under the curve.

What is often not recognised by researchers in the arts is that averages by themselves can be misleading. They are most useful when accompanied by some indication of the range of the observations. Charles Dickens berated the politicians with 'addled heads who would take the average of cold in the Crimea during twelve months as a reason for clothing a soldier in nankeens on a night when he would have frozen to death in fur.'[29] In his example the highest and lowest temperatures are as, if not more, important than the average, because of the wide range involved and the dire consequences of the extremes. There are several useful ways of expressing the range of a set of figures. There are also several different ways of expressing or calculating an average, each appropriate to particular questions or sorts of data. The most common, as with Dickens' example, is the so-called arithmetic mean where all values are

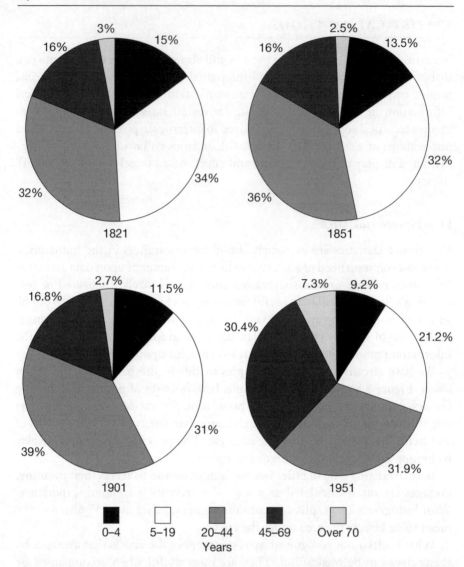

Figure 8.8 Pie charts of age composition of the British population for various years (Source: Pat Hudson (2000), *History by Numbers*, London: Edward Arnold, p. 76.)

added and divided by the number of observations, but this can be misleading in many cases. The mode – the most commonly occurring observation – can often be more useful, in collocations for example. In Figure 8.9 the mode is sixty-eight (the highest bar of the histogram), the mean a little higher. The median value is also often used in analysis. The median is the value of the middle observation when the range of values is ranked in size order. Figure 8.10 is a pictogram, an effective way of displaying the characteristics of a range

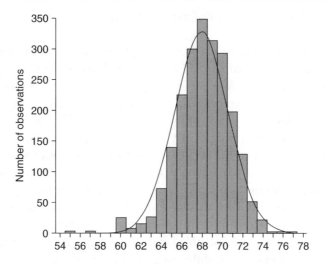

Figure 8.9 Frequency distribution (histogram and graph) showing numbers of poems with naturalistic themes published 1970–90 (hypothetical data)

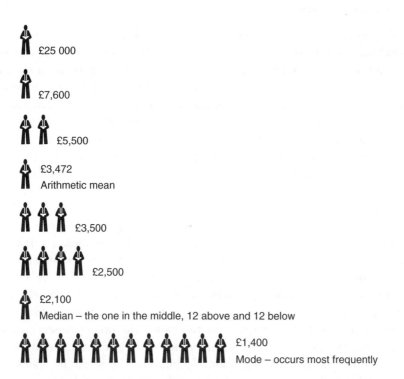

Figure 8.10 Pictogram of yearly expenditure on hardback fiction by a sample of bibliophiles (hypothetical data)

of data. In this case the three different ways of referring to an average are also indicated.

Another common device used in descriptive statistics is the formation of indices which is employed to yield a clearer indication of the composition of data or their change over time. An index (pl. indices) is a way of recording variation in a time series (movement of a variable over time) and is effected by converting all values to a percentage of the value of the variable in a certain so-called base year/day/month. It is especially useful in highlighting movements in one or more time series when the original units are complex or different from one another. For example, if you had sales figures for a particular author over time in numbers and royalties in pounds for another author over the same period, the two time series could be directly compared if converted to indices rather than left in the original, different units. Indices are further useful as they enable new composite time series to be assembled from the original data. For example, if the sales figures for a number of different authors, within a genre, were available yearly for a twenty-year period, these could be used to form a composite index of variation in popularity of the genre taking the figures as a whole.[30]

Inferential statistics

Exploration of anything like the full potential and range of techniques of statistical inference are beyond the scope of this short chapter. The reader should consult one or more of the range of introductory statistical texts for the social sciences and arts to find out more.[31] The most important elements concern assessment of the existence and strength of relationships between variables over time or across space or subject matter and the assessment of their likely causal connection, if any. For instance, we may have sales figures for a number of popular thrillers of the 1990s together with a measure of their literary quality (on a scale of one to ten, for example – the result of a canvas of experts in the genre). We may wish to know if sales are related to literary quality assessed in this way. The simplest way of exploring this hypothesis would be to plot the two variables (sales and literary quality) on a scatter graph. Figure 8.11 shows various types of scatter graph. Where two variables are closely related, the points line up, sloping from left to right if the variables are positively related (that is, they increase or decrease together) and downwards if the relationship is negative (that is, one increases as the other decreases). In our example, if sales increase with literary quality, we would expect to see an upward-sloping cluster of points on the scatter graph, and the closer the points cluster around a definite line the closer the relationship indicated. It is important to note that a scatter graph may indicate a relationship but only the researcher can suggest whether this is likely to be a causal relationship and in what direction causality might lie.

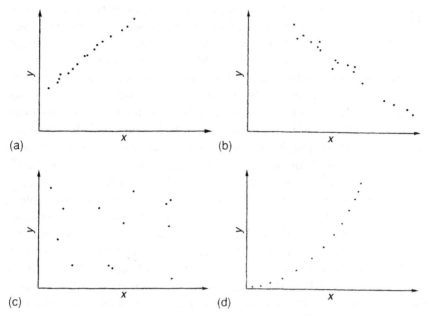

Figure 8.11 Scatter graphs with different indications (a) positive linear correlation indicated, (b) negative linear correlation indicated, (c) no correlation indicated, (d) no linear correlation indicated but a curvilinear or monotonic positive relationship is indicated. (Source: Pat Hudson (2000), *History by Numbers*, London: Edward Arnold, p. 146.)

The scatter graph is only the first and simplest way of examining variation in pairs of variables. Once a relationship appears to be indicated on the basis of a scatter graph, one can move on to test in a more sophisticated manner, and provide a measurement of, the closeness of relationships. This is especially useful if there are several potential causal factors that interest us. For example, we may be interested in the relationship between sales and price, sales and number of previous successful novels by the same author, sales and number of murders in the novel, or sales and page length. From initial scatter graphs that give an indication of the relative strength of possible causal connections, we can move on to employ correlation and regression analyses. These can give a firmer, measured indication of the relationship between variables based upon the principles of probability theory. In essence, the correlation coefficient (a measure of the strength of a relationship) depends upon asking what the chances of finding such a close relationship would be if there were no underlying relationship present – that is, if the observations were thrown up by accident. Regression analysis involves graphical construction of a line representing the closeness and pattern of movement between variables. When just two variables are being considered, the regression line is the line of best fit through the points on the associated scatter graph, and it can be extended beyond the available data as a predictive indicator. In our rather simplistic case, relating to sales of 1990s thrillers, we could use a regression line to predict, for example, by how much the price might have to be reduced, how many additional murders incorporated or how much literary quality increased (or decreased) to effect a particular increase in sales.

All this may sound potentially exciting and it is the case that research into many aspects of literature might be enhanced by using these techniques. However, in using statistical data and techniques in any field, it is easy to get carried away. The apparent sophistication of techniques, and the speed and accuracy with which graphs and calculations can now be executed using computers, is no substitute for careful thought at all stages of the research. Only if the original hypothesis regarding causal relationships is sensible and likely should statistical techniques be used to analyse them. For example, it is very bad statistical practice (though all too easy with computers) to run correlation exercises with all the variables one has, and then to invent explanations for those that are indicated statistically as being significantly related. Only the researcher can decide on the significance of statistical correlations. A second major pitfall is the temptation to engage statistical techniques without first asking: how reliable is the data? What biases does the data contain, how was it collected, is it a representative sample, and how well do the figures continue to measure exactly the same thing over time and space? Mistakes often occur in choosing statistical techniques that are inappropriate to the data at hand, perhaps because the data are insufficiently robust to withstand such fine levels of numerical analysis. Finally, it is worth repeating that statistical techniques are only useful if the researcher is able to judge wisely the result and its significance for the research in hand. What is statistically significant is not always significant in terms of the research itself. The researcher must judge.

CONCLUSION

Quantitative analysis is rare in the arts, and particularly in literature studies, largely because the choice of research approach is too often seen as a choice of methodology rather than method (a way of thinking about knowledge rather than a tool to gain knowledge). Yet there is no necessary reason to identify quantification with a hard-edged, scientific positivism from which narrative entirely escapes, nor with rigid categorisations and normative biases absent from qualitative analysis. Numbers and numerical analysis form a language like many others that can be used for good or ill: intelligently, sensitively and reflexively, or crudely and misleadingly. The computer revolution since the 1980s has created many new possibilities for quantification as a research tool in all fields. Because it has made quantitative analysis easy, it has too often, though not yet in literary studies, resulted in excessive quantification and poor research practice. This has given quantification rather a bad name, particularly in the arts. Quantifiers of the 1970s and 1980s were accused, often with good cause, of being 'statistical junkies' who had abandoned critical reasoning.[32] Today however, researchers are a deal more sophisticated about the ways in which statistical and computational techniques are used in all fields and are infinitely more sensitive about the pitfalls of both methods and data. Poststructuralist concerns have highlighted similar dangers in prose-based analysis: quantitative and qualitative methods are not so methodologically distinct or incompatible as their proponents often argue. As Peter Burke has stated:

> Statistics can be faked, but so can texts. Statistics are easy to misinterpret but so are texts. Machine readable data are not user friendly but the same goes for many manuscripts, written in illegible hands or on the verge of disintegration.[33]

In short, both quantitative and qualitative methods are only as good as the researcher who employs them. Quantitative methods are a research tool: a means to an end rather than an end in themselves, an adjunct to clear thinking rather than a substitute for it. If used wisely in this spirit, there is no reason why numbers cannot be a great deal more exploited and valued by researchers of literature than is currently the case.

NOTES

1. My thanks to Catherine Belsey for allowing me to quote her response. In later correspondence she explained her negative reaction to the excesses of computer-aided quantitative research in the 1970s, arguing justifiably that generous funding often produced results of the 'utmost banality'. She did, however, concede that the results of quantitative analysis did not have to be banal in principle.
2. Terry Eagleton (1996), *Literary Theory: An Introduction*, Oxford: Blackwell, p. 11.
3. Joseph McAleer (1999), *Passion's Fortune: The Story of Mills and Boon*, Oxford: Oxford University Press.
4. Edward Copeland (1995), *Women Writing About Money: Women's Fiction in England, 1790–1820*, Cambridge: Cambridge University Press.
5. Bridget Fowler (1991), *The Alienated Reader*, London: Harvester Wheatsheaf, p. 19.
6. Jane F. Thrailkill (1999), 'Killing them softly: childbed fever and the novel', *American Literature*, 71, 4, 679–707.
7. Oliver Wendell Holmes, *A Moral Antipathy*, *Works* 7: 110, quoted in J. Thrailkill (1999), 'Killing them softly'.
8. Cited by Carlo Ginzburg (1979), 'Morelli, Freud and Sherlock Holmes: clues and scientific method', *History Workshop Journal*, 7–36.
9. Explored in Elaine Scarry (ed.) (1988), *Literature and the Body: Essays on Populations and Persons*, Baltimore: Johns Hopkins Press, 'Introduction'.

10. Martha Nussbaum (1995), *Poetic Justice: The Literary Imagination and Public Life*, Boston: Beacon Press.

11. Mary Poovey (1994), 'Figures of arithmetic, figures of speech: the discourse of statistics in the 1830s', in James Chandler, Arnold J. Davidson and Harry Harootunian (eds), *Questions of Evidence: Proof, Practice and Persuasion Across the Disciplines*, Chicago: University of Chicago Press.

12. Mary Poovey (1998), *A History of the Modern Fact: Problems of Knowledge on the Sciences of Wealth and Society*, Chicago: University of Chicago Press.

13. This is not surprising given the history of statistics which is associated with the rise of powerful nation states aiming to gain greater control over the populace, and with the social thought and social policy of the late nineteenth century which had strong views about deviance and heredity. For an introduction to these aspects of the history of statistics, see Pat Hudson (2000) *History by Numbers*, London: Edward Arnold, pp. 26–50.

14. See, for example, Michel Foucault (1973), *The Order of Things*, New York Tavistock; Richard Rorty (1991), *Objectivity, Relativism and Truth*, Cambridge: Cambridge University Press; Nikolas Rose (1999), *Governing the Soul*, London: Free Association Books.

15. W. G. Sebald (2003), *On the Natural History of Destruction*, London: Penguin.

16. Ibid., p. 50, describing Hans Erich Nossack's *Nekyia*.

17. Eagleton, *Literary Theory*, p. 9.

18. The best introductions to these methods are found in Susan Hockey (2000), *Electronic Texts in the Humanities*, Oxford: Oxford University Press, and Susan Hockey (1980), *A Guide to Computer Applications in the Humanities*, London: Duckworth, which remains useful for the earlier history and basic understanding of this field.

19. This example is given in Hockey, *Electronic Texts*, p. 64.

20. Hockey, *A Guide to Computer Applications*, pp. 79–100.

21. For a survey of computer aided authorship attribution and stylometric analysis in this and other contexts, see D. Holmes (1994), 'Authorship attribution', *Computers and the Humanities*, 28: 87–106; D. Holmes (1998), 'The evolution of stylometry in the humanities', *Literary and Linguistic Computing*, 13: 111–17.

22. Arai Hiroshi (1997), 'The authorship problem of the last ten chapters of the Genji Monogatori', *The Hototsubashi Review* 117, 3 (in Japanese), which applies the rank correlation coefficient to look at the concordance of phrases in the first forty-four chapters compared with the last ten chapters. I am grateful to Mina Ishizu, research student, Cardiff University, for this reference and for discussion of Japanese language structure.

23. Ian Lancashire (1993), 'Chaucer's repetends from the General Prologue of the *Canterbury Tales*', in R. A. Taylor, J. F. Burke, P. J. Eberle, I. Lancashire and B. Merrilees (eds), *The Centre and Its Compass: Studies in Medieval Literature in Honor of Professor John Leyerle*, Kalamazoo, Western Michigan University, pp. 315–65; 'Computer-assisted critical analysis: a case study of Margaret Atwood's *Handmaiden's Tale*', in G. P. Landow and P. Delany (eds) (1993), *The Digital Word: Text-based Computing in the Humanities*, Cambridge, MA: MIT Press, pp. 291–318; 'Phrasal repetends and the Manciple's Prologue and Tale', in I. Lancashire (ed.) (1993), *Computer-based Chaucer Studies*, Toronto: Toronto Centre for Computing in the Humanities, pp. 99–122; 'Phrasal repetends in literary stylistics: Shakespeare's *Hamlet* III.I', in S. Hockey and N. Ide (eds) (1996), *Research in Humanities Computing 4: Selected papers from the 1992 ALLC-ACH Conference*, Oxford: Oxford University Press, pp. 34–68, Lessard, G. and J. Hamm, 'Verifying intuitions: research and repeated structures in Stendhal', in Hockey and Ide, *Research in Humanities Computing*. Examples quoted in Hockey, *Electronic Texts*.

24. See examples cited in Hockey, *Electronic Texts* pp. 27–35, 78–84, and Hockey, *A Guide to Computer Applications*, pp. 144–88.

25. Richard L. Merrit (1970), *Systematic Approaches to Comparative Politics*, Chicago: Rand Mcnally.

26. See for example, M. E. Palmquist, K. M. Carley and T. A. Dale (1997), 'Two applications of automated text analysis: analysing literary and non literary texts' in C. Roberts (ed.), *Text Analysis for the Social Sciences: Methods for Drawing Statistical Inferences from Texts and Transcripts*, Hillsdale, NJ: Lawrence Erlbaum Associates.

27. For a detailed overview of content analysis in literature studies, see http://writing.colostate.edu/references/research/content and Kimberly A. Neuendorf (2001), *The Content Analysis Guidebook*, Thousand Oaks, CA: Sage. Software options for textual analysis are examined in E. A. Weitzman and M. B. Miles (1995), *Computer Programs for Qualitative Data Analysis: A Software Sourcebook*, Thousand Oaks, CA: Sage. For further guidance on the use of computational techniques in the analysis of qualitative data, see A. Coffey and P. Atkinson (1996), *Making Sense of Qualitative Data: Complementary Research Strategies*, Thousand Oaks, CA: Sage; Ian Dey (1993), *Qualitative Data Analysis: A User-friendly Guide for Social Scientists*, London: Routledge; Soloman, R. and C. Winch (1994), *Calculating and Computing for Social Science and Arts Students*, Buckingham: Open University. Some idea of the range of computational techniques used in the study of literary texts (fiction, poetry, theatre, religious, philosophical and classical texts) from the inception of the computer to 1994 can be found in Conrad F. Sabourin (1994), *Literary Computing: Bibliography*, Montreal: Infolingua. For an overview of the related field of computational linguistics, see http://www.ifi.unizh.ch/CL.

28. For more detail and discussion of the techniques of descriptive statistics in historical applications and the arts, see Hudson, *History by Numbers*, pp. 51–135, and E. R. Tufte (1997), *Visual Explanations: Images and Quantities, Evidence and Narrative*, Cheshire, CT: Graphics Press.

29. Letter to Charles Knight, 30 January 1854 in Walter Dexter (ed.) (1938), *Letters of Charles Dickens*, 3 vols, London: Bloomsbury, vol. 2, p. 620, quoted by Ivanka Kovacevic and S. Barbara Kanner (1970) in 'Blue Book into novel: the forgotten industrial fiction of Charlotte Elizabeth Tonna', *Nineteenth-Century Fiction* 25, 2: 161.

30. For more on indices and their usefulness in historical and arts applications, see Hudson, *History by Numbers*, pp. 109–20.

31. Amongst the best introductions are A. Aron and E. N. Aron (1997), *Statistics for the Behavioural and Social Sciences*, New Jersey: Prentice Hall; C. Marsh (1988), *Exploring Data: An Introduction to Data Analysis for Social Scientists*, Cambridge: Polity; R. Soloman and C. Winch (1994), *Calculating and Computing for Social Science and Arts Students*, Buckingham: Open University; Charles H. Feinstein and Mark Thomas (2002), *Making History Count: A Primer in Quantitative Methods for Historians*, Cambridge: Cambridge University Press; Hudson, *History by Numbers*.

32. Lawrence Stone (1987), *The Past and the Present Revisited*, London: Routledge; Tony Judt (1979), 'A clown in regal purple: social history and the historians', *History Workshop Journal*, 7: 74.

33. Peter Burke (ed.) (1991), *New Perspectives on Historical Writing*, Cambridge: Cambridge University Press, p. 15.

CHAPTER 9

Textual Analysis as a Research Method

Catherine Belsey, Cardiff University

(I)

How important is textual analysis in research? What is it? How is it done? And what difference does it make? My contention will be that textual analysis is indispensable to research in cultural criticism, where cultural criticism includes English, cultural history and cultural studies, as well as any other discipline that focuses on texts, or seeks to understand the inscription of culture in its artefacts. And since textual analysis is in the end empirical, I shall set out to exemplify my methodological account with a single instance. The project is to imagine that Titian's painting of *Tarquin and Lucretia* constitutes material for research and to pose the kinds of questions a researcher might seek to answer, standing back from the exercise at intervals to assess the methodology involved in making a reading of the picture as 'text'.[1]

What, then – to pose the inaugural question as broadly and as baldly as possible – is going on in *Tarquin and Lucretia* (Figure 9.1)? The first and most immediate answer is a rape. Even to a viewer who does not know the story in advance, the position is clear from Tarquin's raised dagger; his knee between Lucretia's legs; his muscular dominance over her body, already placed visually at a lower level than his, and so subject to it; and from the white bedlinen draped over her thighs as the only available protection against violation. Her nakedness and the bed point to the sexual nature of the assault; they also show her to be defenceless.

This is a moment of considerable intensity. The painting arrests and fixes an instant immediately before the rape itself, offering to enlist the viewer in a kind of suspense. What we are invited to fear will follow is left to our imagination, and may well in consequence be experienced as more, not less, painful. Rape is a sustained action; its duration is part of the horror; and in that sense a still image cannot capture it. But this one comes close – partly by showing the

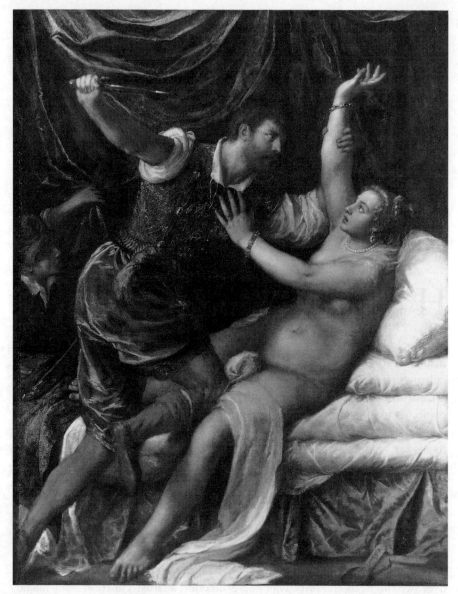

Figure 9.1 Titian, *Tarquin and Lucretia* (Reproduced by kind permission of the Fitzwilliam Museum, Cambridge.)

figures so evidently in motion, but above all by leaving the action to be completed in the spectator's mind.

Lucretia is evidently already in bed, and is taken by surprise. Human beings seem to be at their most vulnerable when they sleep, especially if they sleep without clothing. The female nude in general tends to hover between helplessness and sexuality. Where does the emphasis fall here? My second question, then, would be how the painting invites us to see Lucretia. Is she presented as a victim struggling to resist a brutal assault? Or is she offered as an object of desire for the spectator, as well as Tarquin?

Where, in other words, are our sympathies? The light comes from the left and falls on Lucretia's naked flesh. To that extent, the nude body of a woman, set against her bedlinen, is offered as a spectacle. On the other hand, the breasts, usually a focus for the erotic gaze, are here only indicated, rather than depicted. Meanwhile, two main composition lines draw attention to the violence rather than to her body itself: the diagonal line formed by the legs, and most sharply defined by Tarquin's, leads direct to her left shoulder, drawing the eye to the other diagonal formed by her left arm and his right. So the visual emphasis falls on what goes on between the figures. And because the woman seems to have no chance against Tarquin's greater strength and the threat indicated by the dagger, the occurrence seems to me to be on the whole more shocking than titillating.

But there is room for debate, and a researcher might well want to come back to this uncertainty, since it arguably constitutes part of what continues to hold the viewer's attention. Whatever the decision, the painting evidently plays a part in the history of gender politics. If, on the one hand, it confirms the view that images of the high-lit, naked female body objectify women, on the other hand it goes some way to substantiate a good deal that feminists have been arguing about rape since the 1970s. Rape, we have maintained, constitutes an assertion of force over vulnerability; it is as much about power as sex.[2]

(II)

Let us go back and look at the mechanics of that – I hope – fairly non-controversial preliminary analysis of this one text. What I have just done was bring together two assumptions I learned from feminist politics – about images of women[3] and the nature of rape – with a close look at the painting. That look was not exhaustive, for the moment, but it was close enough to pick out the detail of the white bedlinen that so ineffectually defends Lucretia's honour, and the composition lines, which seem to put the emphasis on the power relations.

How would we justify calling that the beginning of a research project? Stating that this painting is about rape hardly constitutes research, since it is no more than paraphrase. For the same reason, it is not research to reproduce Laura Mulvey's view that images of women in Western culture are tradition-ally presented for the male gaze, or Susan Brownmiller's contention that rape is more about power than sex. Bringing together the painting and 1970s femi-nism, however, might begin to look like the beginnings of a hypothesis – about

Titian's sexual imagery, or rape in art, or the history of attitudes to rape, or the cultural history of sixteenth-century Venice . . . .

To clear the ground slightly, then, I am assuming that there is a distinction between research and other forms of study. Research is expected to make a contribution to knowledge; it uncovers something new. Research is expected to be 'original' in the sense that it is independent: the contribution, whatever it is, originates, in that fairly modest sense, with the researcher. It does not have to be 'original' in the much more daunting sense that it springs fully armed from the head of the researcher without reference to any previous account. On the contrary, in fact: it is much more likely to involve assembling ideas that have not been brought together in quite that way before. And it does not have to shift the paradigm: the contribution can be quite small, a piece of the jigsaw. But research is expected to make a difference to the standard account of a topic, whatever that topic might be.

(III)

So far, my research on this painting has consisted of analysing the image fairly closely, in the light of something I bring to it from elsewhere. There is no such thing as 'pure' reading: interpretation always involves extra-textual knowledge. Some of this is general, part of the repertoire of knowledges that constitutes a culture; some of it is personal, a matter of one's own interests or biography; and some of it is derived from secondary sources. The first impulse of many researchers, confronted by an unfamiliar text, is to look up what others have said about it on the internet, in the library, in bibliographies provided for the purpose.

Secondary sources have their uses. They will soon make clear that the story of Lucretia is told by Livy and Ovid, and discussed by Saint Augustine. They will indicate the place of this painting in Titian's work, and provoke comparisons of his manner of painting with his contemporaries and his master, Giovanni Bellini. All this is valuable, if it leads to further textual analysis. Always read the sources and consider the analogues. Never take other people's word for it. This is the key to saying something new: what is distinctive about *this* text emerges as its difference from all the others.

Secondary material can be unduly seductive too, however. Textual analysis is hard – and, if it isn't, it ought to be. It is always much easier to do a literature search, or read an anthology of essays. It is easier, but less productive. What secondary sources usually provide is well informed, coherent and rhetorically persuasive arguments, which can leave the researcher convinced that whatever *can* be said *has* been said already. The way to use secondary sources is very sparingly indeed. I prefer to make a list of the questions posed by the text and arrive at my own tentative, provisional answers, and only then to read other people's interpretations.

But what prevents my account from being pure subjectivism, just my opinion? Suppose I put forward an outlandish idea? Suppose, say, instead of the convictions of 1970s feminism (which are, of course, impeccable!), I bring my own private preoccupations, and decide that the two figures represented are 'really' brother and sister, or that Tarquin is a woman in drag. What is to stop me calling that 'research' on the same basis? Or, how does textual analysis differ from free association?

It differs, I suggest, in terms of the way we conceptualise the role of a third party, a reader or, in this instance, the spectator. Take the uncertainty about the response the painting invites. I proposed that *Tarquin and Lucretia* invited the viewer to be more shocked than titillated, but also that this was open to discussion. How would we go about resolving the question – if, indeed, we can? My inclination would be to appeal to a supposed addressee: the lighting is there for a viewer; the composition lines are there to be interpreted. This is representation, not an event, and representation is made for someone, addressed to someone, even if the work never sees the light of day, or never reaches a spectator other than the artist.

How does this invocation of a third party advance the argument? Traditional forms of cultural criticism often have difficulty with this issue. The viewer is an individual, so the story goes, and brings individual expectations and values to the picture. Doesn't that just confirm that the text can mean anything we choose, whatever happens to strike us? That all readings are equal?

I do not think so. Roland Barthes notoriously champions the rights of the reader in his essay on 'The Death of the Author'.[4] The reader who is to be liberated by the proposed execution of the Author is no more, he maintains, than the 'destination' of the text. This polemic first appeared in 1967, only a year before workers and students took to the streets of Paris side by side. A product of its moment, the essay reads like a manifesto, and in it Barthes unmasks the Author as the alibi of the critical institution. Critics, he says, hug the text to themselves, claim a superior access (based on their research, of course) to the Author's intentions, and then explain the work in those terms, excluding all other possible interpretations. Criticism allots itself 'the important task of discovering the Author . . . beneath the work: when the Author has been found, the text is "explained" – victory to the critic'.[5]

The real tyranny, in other words, is exercised by the critical institution, which secures its authority by exerting a stranglehold on what is admissible as an interpretation. Scholarship – hunting down diaries, letters, autobiographies, recorded conversations, attributed remarks and general gossip – produces a conjectural author, and on the basis of this figure's equally conjectural character and views, it isolates an even more conjectural intention, which can then be invoked to fend off new readings of the texts themselves. 'To give a text an Author is to impose a limit on that text, to furnish it with a final signified, to close the writing,' Barthes insists.[6] In a follow-up essay, 'What is an Author?', Michel Foucault calls this same restrictive construct of the institution 'the principle of thrift in the proliferation of meaning'.[7]

Barthes's call-to-arms is perfectly perspicuous up to this point, though it is sometimes hard to tell that from some of the extraordinary commentaries and counter-attacks it seems to have generated. It concludes, still in the spirit of its time, by siding with the people: 'the birth of the reader must be at cost of the death of the Author'. In this final paragraph, however, it appears that the reader is not simply a person, not you or me, not, indeed, an individual at all. Here is what Barthes says:

> a text is made of multiple writings, drawn from many cultures and entering into mutual relations of dialogue, parody, contestation, but there is one place where this multiplicity is focused and that place is the reader, not, as was hitherto said, the author. The reader is the space on which all the quotations that make up a writing are inscribed without any of them being lost; a text's unity lies not in its origin but in its destination. Yet this destination cannot any longer be personal: the reader is without history, biography, psychology; he is simply that *someone* who holds together in a single field all the traces by which the written text is constituted.[8]

This utopian figure, without biography or psychology, does not exist in any material sense. To sustain the analogy with the French Revolution on which it depends, Barthes's manifesto has to locate the reader in the place of the people. The people in this context are not individuals, however, but an ideal type, the oppressed, who will rise up and seize control of their collective destiny. In the same way, Barthes's reader is the ideal addressee of the work, the representative of all those whose interpretations the institution has excluded. What is at stake, then, is not a person at all, but a position in relation to the text. To avoid the restrictive practices of the institution, to escape its 'thrift' and proliferate meanings, to uncover, in other words, something new, interpretation attends to all the quotations that make up the text, the traces by which it is constituted.

We are still absorbing the implications of that challenge, in my view. Barthes is certainly not proposing that we simply shift the authority from the head of the author to the head of the reader. The main problem for us now is that, while most people are very willing to surrender the authority of the author, along with intimidation by 'intention', they often want to replace it with the authority of the reader as individual. This was not Barthes's point at all. His reader is no more than the destination of the multiple writings and intertextual relations that make up the text itself. In other words, the essay does not support a vague subjectivism, in which the text means whatever it means to *me*, and there is nothing to discuss. On the contrary: 'to read' is a transitive verb. We read *something*, and that *something* exists in its difference. If *Tarquin and Lucretia* were no more than a blank space for the reader's fantasies, it would be indistinguishable from *The Venus of Urbino* or Tracey Emin's *Bed*. Barthes urges us to be more rigorous, not less.

(IV)

How is this to be done? By understanding the process of interpretation as the effect of a *relation* between a reader and a text. There may be dialogue within a text, but the text itself also engages in dialogue with the reader. Titian's *Tarquin and Lucretia depicts* a dialogue and a struggle: the exchanges *in* the text are violent. But it also enters into a relationship of dialogue *with a viewer*, and to that degree the painting itself plays a crucial part in constructing its addressee as destination, or defining how it can legitimately be read and the range of its possible interpretations.

This is not to say, however, that the text alone determines its own reading. The vocabulary of traditional criticism is imprecise when it says, 'the text "forces" us to see this feature or that; the text "makes" us rethink our attitudes'. No text can ever compel its reader to view it in a particular way. We should do better, in my view, to adopt a critical vocabulary that allows the text to 'invite' certain readings and 'offer' specific positions to its addressee.

Any serious textual analysis depends on a grasp of how meaning works. Meaning is not at the disposal of the individual, and not, whatever stout common sense may indicate, a matter of intention, an isolatable 'idea', fully formed prior to its inscription. We learn to mean from outside, from a language that always pre-exists us. Ideas do not come first and cast around for means of expression. On the contrary. A substantial element of education, for example, consists in acquiring a vocabulary, and it is this expanded vocabulary that permits us to think with greater clarity, to make finer distinctions.

If meaning is acquired from language, we can make words up, but they will become meaningful only if other people understand them. We can make up codes, but the same applies: they become languages only when they are intelligible, at least in principle, to another person.

Meaning, then, subsists in the relations between people, inscribed in sounds or images (including written shapes, and pictures, as here). It has its own materiality: meaning intervenes in the world, defining our understanding of values, requiring us to obey rules and, indeed, calling us to arms. But because it never appears in itself, as pure intelligibility, as idea, but is always inscribed in the signifier, in the sound or the image, meaning is never fixed, single or final. The signifier, Jacques Derrida insists, supplants any imagined idea, takes its place. What we have is always the signifier, never what it signifies. This is relegated beyond reach by the signifier itself, deferred.[9]

It follows that meaning is inevitably plural. On the other hand, as in dialogue, I exclude myself from the circuit of exchange altogether if, when you say, 'please shut the door', I hear 'pass me the pepper'. In practice, 'shut the door', which always seems to be the example that comes up in discussions of speech-act theory, is an exemplary case. The utterance is plural, to the degree that it would be perfectly legitimate in certain contexts to read it as meaning 'it is cold in here', or 'I am going to tell you a secret', or 'I am going to make sexual overtures to you'. And it is not always clear in advance which interpretation is appropriate. Meaning is plural. But not infinitely plural; only saints and psychotics see meanings as unique to them personally, and independent of the signifier.

The text, as a tissue of signifiers, makes certain demands on the textual analyst, and provides the material for analysis. That material is by no means an empty space, a vacancy into which we pour whatever we like; instead, the text itself participates in the process of signification. It reproduces or reiterates meanings, which always come from outside, and are not at the *artist's* disposal, any more than they are at ours. The work of art is in that sense always *citational*, constituted, as Barthes puts it, of quotations. *Tarquin and Lucretia* reiterates a familiar tale, quotes an existing narrative. And, in turn, the classical sources themselves re-inscribed a story already in circulation. But even when there is no narrative to cite, the text invokes intertexts: new female nudes signify in relation to existing female nudes, just as domestic interiors allude to other domestic interiors, and landscapes are intelligible in relation to the tradition of landscape painting. There is no moment of 'origin', but only breaks with what went before. In that sense, every iteration is always a reiteration. Research involves tracing these intertexts, and reading them attentively too, to establish the difference of the text in question.

At the same time, texts can only ever quote with a difference. 'Iteration alters, something new takes place.'[10] In *Limited Inc* Derrida makes the paradoxical point that, while a repetition is the *same* as the original utterance – or it would not be a repetition – it is also the case that a repetition is *never* the same as the original, or it would *be* the original itself. In other words, every time anyone uses a familiar mark or image, they shift its meaning very slightly in the process, precisely by quoting its previous occurrences, as well as changing its setting. In that sense, every text breaks with what went before. Maybe artists shift the meanings or break with the past more radically at times, but changing meanings is not the same as making them up.

The possible meanings of *Tarquin and Lucretia*, then, are to be found – or perhaps more accurately, supposed, hypothesised – in the relation between the painting and the viewer who is its destination. And each party – the picture and the spectator – contributes to the process of making it mean. The viewer faces the picture from a place outside it, and examines from that location the internal relations on the surface of the canvas.

As an instance of one elementary imposition of limits exerted by the painting itself, the optimum physical place of the spectator is fairly sharply specified by *Tarquin and Lucretia*. The picture is not visible, for example, from the back. What is more, it is not clearly visible from one side or the other, because the lines appear distorted from there. And from too close up, the *trompe l'oeil* effect disappears. The folds of the fabric, for instance, dissolve into lines on a flat canvas. An image in monocular, fixed-point perspective, as this is, addresses a viewer who stands in a specified place, directly in front of it, and with one eye closed. Only from there do we fully grasp the three dimensions simulated on a two-dimensional canvas. In this instance, Tarquin, Lucretia and the properly placed viewer form a triangle.[11]

The text exercises certain constraints, and yet we are not entirely at its mercy. A good textual analyst would be aware of the text's requirements on us, in this sense, but the same good analyst would also acknowledge that we might deliberately refuse the position the text offers, might choose to look at it from somewhere else. On close examination, Titian poses a puzzle: the very precise mimetic effects are apparently achieved by techniques that, viewed from close to, appear quite impressionistic, compared, for example, with Bellini. How, we might want to know, is it done? An analyst of Titian's brushstrokes would reject the optimum position of the viewer, would get close and lose the three-dimensionality in a good cause. Alternatively, the composition lines might draw my eye to the violence, but I remain entitled to look at the bedlinen. Engaged in dialogue, the textual analyst retains a certain independence.

How does this account of the reader's relative self-determination square with Barthes's account of a reader who is no more than the destination of the text? Barthes helps to locate meaning where it belongs, in the signifier, not in the head of either the author or the addressee. But at the same time, his essay retains a trace of structuralism. Fully alert to the differences that make up the *text*, Barthes here ignores the differences between *readings*. If the textual analyst understands all the quotations in the text, grasps all its intertextual allegiances, every trace by which it is constituted, how is it possible for interpretations to differ? How can we, after all, say anything new?

Thanks to poststructuralism, which breaks with structuralism by emphasising difference, we can see how interpretations come to differ from each other. Although meanings are not at our disposal, we not only iterate them with a difference, however infinitesimal; we also recognise them with a difference, however marginal, and for the same reason. Every time the signifier appears in a new location, it relates differently to its prior appearances, as well as its new surroundings; it *differs* from them in a distinct way, however infinitesimally. Every time it is recognised, it is capable of being seen in a new light, or related to different knowledges. The poststructuralist reader remains the destination of the text, but is at the same time differentially located in relation to it. If we maintain the sense of a dialogue between what we bring and what we find, the reading that results is likely to make – or to come to make – sense to other people, to be admissible, at least in the end, as interpretation, and not free association.

(V)

Any specific textual analysis is made at a particular historical moment and from within a specific culture. In that sense, the analysis is not exhaustive: it does not embrace all the possible readings, past and future. At the same time, it is able to be new. Suppose we return to the painting and analyse it from the specific point of view of the historical differences it inscribes. Is there anything there that seems to modern eyes to need accounting for? There is the costume, of course, and the bedding . . . but those differences are only to be expected. What else might we find?

One feature of this picture does seem odd. I have described Lucretia as naked. She is evidently already in bed, and she is now apparently attempting to get out of it, though Tarquin's body blocks her escape. But she is wearing at least one earring, a pearl necklace and two quite substantial bracelets, as well as a wedding ring. Surely this jewellery is very slightly out of place? Do people normally sleep in their portable property in this way? Not these days, I think. What, then, do we make of it? Even if Venetian woman habitually wore their jewellery in bed in 1570, the presence of these bracelets, the necklace and the earring seems to me potentially significant.

In the first instance, they might cause us to reopen the question of the overall project. This body is decorated, adorned, and to that degree correspondingly spectacular, an object of the gaze. Second, the jewels indicate Lucretia's wealth. Do other textual details confirm this? The bedlinen is very fine, almost translucent; is it silk perhaps? The valance is certainly silk. The edge of the pillow facing the viewer is delicately embroidered. Behind the figures, a looped bed-curtain also implies propriety and taste.

By now, our researcher, self-consciously outside the painting, and outside the historical moment when this story would have been familiar, will certainly have been prompted by secondary material to investigate its classical sources,[12] acknowledging in the process the degree to which 'a text is made of multiple writings'. In this instance, the picture retells a well known story; it cites – with an inevitable repetition, and an equally inevitable difference – a narrative that enjoyed wide currency at the time. The sources will have revealed that, while

Tarquin was the heir to the kingdom in the early days in Rome, before it became a republic, Lucretia was the wife of his friend and comrade-in-arms, Collatinus, who was evidently therefore of noble blood himself. Does the painting make a relation between rape and rank? Is the intensity of this image linked with the fact that the victim belongs to the rapist's own social class?

Lucretia's wedding ring is critically placed on the canvas, exactly at the centre measured horizontally, and one-third of the way down vertically. She is married, the spatial relations emphasise – and married to her rapist's friend, the story confirms. A new aspect of the research project I have sketched begins to surface in response to these observations, and it concerns the historical specificity of rape. Is it more culpable in Renaissance Italy if the victim is aristocratic and married? Regrettably, I think the answer is yes. The *Oxford English Dictionary* indicates that rape is etymologically theft ('rapacity' still indicates a propensity to lay hands on other people's goods). In medieval law, rape was a crime against the *property* of the husband or father. Consent came into the question in the first instance in order to distinguish between rape and adultery. It was not until humanism began to invest women with a will of their own that their wishes in the matter became the central issue. The virtue of aristocratic wives must have been a distinctly valuable object. Tarquin's theft of Lucretia's is correspondingly disgraceful.

Lucretia herself, whose propriety was part of what inflamed Tarquin in the first place, refused to live with the dishonour, but went on to reinstate her name in the high Roman fashion. Some of the interest the story seems to hold for the early modern period attaches, no doubt, to this subsequent affirmation of her own autonomy in her suicide.[13] How far does this painting align itself with a new humanist interest in the will of the victim?

(VI)

Without pursuing an answer here, I am suggesting that, while research entails unearthing information, it is the textual analysis that poses the questions which research sets out to answer. The reverse process tends to distort the text. And since the project of cultural criticism is to understand the texts – or rather, to read the culture in the texts – or since, in other words, the texts themselves constitute the inscription of culture, the appropriation of the text to illustrate a prior thesis seems to miss the point. Of course, in practice, it is never quite that simple: once the knowledge is lodged in your mind, it becomes part of what you bring to the text. But in principle, my idea is that the text has priority; ideally, the text sets the agenda.

So, let us get back to ours. Tarquin is fully, though informally, dressed, even if his disordered state is evident in the rolled-up sleeves and collapsing right stocking ('down-gyved', like Hamlet's[14]). These are rich clothes, and they are brilliantly coloured. Oil paint highlights the folds of the fabric with loving verisimilitude. The contrast between Lucretia's pale, naked, half-supine body and Tarquin's, defined by both costume and stance as dominant, driven, insistent, emphasises the tyranny of his lawless act.

This is royalty in disarray, in breach of the obligations of monarchy to enforce the law and protect the subject. As Livy tells the story, Lucretia's rape was an abuse of power so appalling that the Romans rose against it, abolished the monarchy, and installed the Republic. After her suicide, her dead body was paraded through the streets as the motive for a heroic revolt. The rape of the chaste Lucretia led to the overthrow of the Tarquin dynasty and its replacement by a form of government committed to less autocratic values.

The painting, then, does not confine its interest to sexual politics. State politics, too, contributes to its meaning, and the contest it depicts is not only between a woman and a man, but also between a class and its oppressor. On this reading, Lucretia's struggle against Tarquin stands in for the resistance of the patricians. No wonder the work draws attention to her wealth and taste, her well-appointed bed and the evident propriety of her elegantly dressed hair.

To stand back yet again from what I am putting forward as a research method here, the textual details may be overdetermined, may signify in more than one way. In other words, when we have considered a question raised by the text, we have not necessarily done with it. Lucretia's jewellery and the rich furnishings make the rape more shocking, according to the sexual politics of the period. But they also vindicate her right – or perhaps her obligation – to resist, as the representative of a class that deserves to be reckoned with.

Meanwhile, Tarquin's costume makes no attempt at historical accuracy. There is nothing Roman here. Comparison with contemporary paintings reveals that this is a Tarquin in modern dress, the costume of a wealthy Venetian in about 1570. Was this because Titian did not know any better? Or was he simply indifferent to history, like Shakespeare, who brings a striking clock into *Julius Caesar*? Alternatively, is there a quite different motive for anachronism here? What might the founding moment of the Roman Republic mean in the Venetian Republic in the second half of the sixteenth century?

Venice's heyday was now past. Instead, the Venetian empire was considerably diminished, and the city itself was threatened by the expansionist plans of the Ottoman Empire to the east. Could this picture be read as an appeal to the Venetian Republic to assert itself against the Turks? The Fitzwilliam Museum, where the painting hangs, places it between 1568 and 1571. *Tarquin and Lucretia* was sent to Titian's patron, Philip II of Spain, in 1571. In May that year, a treaty was signed between the Papacy, Venice and Spain to join forces against the Turks. And in October, at Lepanto, Don John of Austria led the allies to defeat the Ottoman Empire. This victory seemed to have beaten back

the Turks for good, and was greeted with great rejoicing.[15] What are the reso-
nances of a picture of the founding moment of republicanism, sent by the fore-
most painter of the Venetian Republic to the King of Spain at this historical
moment?

(VII)

Overcoming my own impulse to follow up this question, I again draw attention
to the methodological issues here. The textual analysis I am recommending is
anything but an empty formalism. It leads outwards into sexual politics, and
then into cultural and political history. But once again the text *itself* poses the
questions that scholarship may be able to answer, and not the other way round.
I rather suspect that, if we started from the cultural implications of the battle
of Lepanto, we might take quite a long time to get to Titian's *Tarquin and
Lucretia*.

Meanwhile, a related element of the painting would take us back into history
in a different way. Barely visible behind Tarquin, a shadowed figure, with what
appears to be a darker skin than the protagonists', holds apart the bed curtains
and watches the action. His expression is impossible to read: curiosity, outrage,
trepidation? Who is this enigmatic observer? The Latin sources reveal that
Tarquin backed his violence with a threat still more dangerous to Lucretia's
honour. He will, he says, kill her if she does not submit, and place a dead slave
in her bed to destroy her reputation. Adultery with a slave was evidently more
scandalous than rape by a king's son. Lucretia gives in.

To modern eyes the difference between monarchy and republicanism might
not seem as large as it did to the Romans themselves. The Roman Republic, too,
was founded on slavery. Slavery also played a part in the history of the Venetian
Republic. The slave trade was a crucial component of Venice's commercial
success in the early days, and slaves made an important contribution to the
economy of the household, as well as in the galleys that made Venice rich and
powerful. If domestic slavery diminished in the course of the sixteenth century,
the idea of slavery was by no means alien at this time. In 1539 Titian himself
painted a portrait of Fabricius Salvaresius with an African page, probably a
slave.

What does *Tarquin and Lucretia* invite us to make of its slave? Anything, or
not much? The figure is too indeterminate to be sure. But his inclusion in the
margins of the image has the effect of doubling the brutality of Tarquin's
tyranny: in front of Tarquin is a defenceless woman, whose resistance is heroic;
behind him is a slave, who has no real scope for resistance. The slave is not in full
possession of his own body, since it belongs to another. The painting thus enters
into the history of imperialism, in which some people become the property of

others and, as such, are expendable at the will of a tyrant. Is it anachronistic to detect a certain symmetry between the highlit Lucretia and the shadowy figure whose defencelessness redoubles hers?

Either way, the slave's death does not happen. Lucretia is subdued by the threat and no more is heard of the slave.

(VIII)

In each instance, I have suggested we address a question posed by the text. Where are its sympathies? What historical differences does it present? Are there any surprises? In other words, we start from a problem. This is a method of textual analysis I owe ultimately to psychoanalysis. It is only the caricatures of psychoanalysis that present it as claiming the key to all mythologies in the Oedipus complex, or answering all questions with the phallus before they are even posed.

In my view, the main value of psychoanalysis to cultural critics is not so much in its conclusions and explanations as in its way of reading. Freud listened attentively, and not only to the surface narrative. He worked on the assumption that a deeper or more subtle meaning was to be found in unlikely places: in incidental observations, denials, jokes, slips of the tongue. Freud concentrated on the detail that did not fit, that pulled against the coherence of the official, intentional story. And he treated these unexpected components of what was said as intellectual problems, which analysis would set out to solve. We do not have to agree with his solutions to admire the method. (Indeed, anyone with a rooted antipathy to psychoanalysis in its entirety might prefer to take as a role model the detective Freud most admired. Sherlock Holmes, like his descendant Miss Marple, and any number of television detectives, teases out the *in*coherence in the story, the puzzling detail that causes the obvious interpretation to unravel.)

Tarquin and Lucretia includes one element that does not fit the obvious narrative. Although not all that marginal, it does not stand out at first, not least because it seems to pull against the most likely reading. This detail is the angle of Lucretia's left arm. There is no muscular force there. If she were pushing Tarquin away, pushing as hard as she would have to against his evident insistence, we should expect that arm to be fully extended, rigid. It would be much more difficult to exert force with her arm bent. I cannot escape the feeling that Lucretia's left hand, the hand with the wedding ring on the third finger, placed at the horizontal centre of the canvas, is not resisting as firmly as it might.

Could this be a mistake? It is legitimate to ask. But this is a late work by a man who was by this time the most famous artist in Europe, and has never to this day lost his place in the pantheon of Renaissance painters. The arm in question is central, moulded in some detail, and highly lit. Nothing about its depiction appears accidental. And what about the rest of the body? Lucretia is in tears, but she is not self-evidently braced against Tarquin's assault. Is it possible, then, that Lucretia's resistance is in question?

The classical sources relate that she submits not just to superior force, but in the light of the danger the threat of the slave poses to her honour. By this means, she protects her husband and her name from disgrace. The visual space of the painting constructs a kind of ironic symmetry between the blond Lucretia and the dark slave, or between the highly lit Lucretia and the slave in deep shadow. Is it possible that the moment Titian has depicted is one not just of external struggle between the protagonists, but of inward struggle for Lucretia herself? Some of the intensity of the image for the viewer would then stem from the fact that the painting arrests the action at a turning-point, the instant when the chaste Lucretia reluctantly concedes the victory and ceases to struggle.[16]

Titian's triumph is that again and again he gives the impression of painting interiority made flesh. His hunched popes and desiring Venuses seem to put their emotions on display in his canvases. What an extraordinary painting this would be if Lucretia's body were depicted at the moment of transition between fighting off the rapist and yielding to him under duress.

(IX)

There is one more possibility. I venture this idea with some considerable (feminist) reservations. We *might* see Lucretia's bent elbow as indicating another kind of turning-point. The gesture of the hand on Tarquin's chest could almost be read as a caress. Once the thought has established itself, I find it difficult to dislodge. Could the transition in question be from resistance to pleasure? And does the theatricality of the painting lie in its capture of *that* moment in the struggle?

I would certainly do my best to overcome this unworthy speculation, if it were not for the fact that Lucretia's story was given currency in the early modern period by Saint Augustine, as well as Ovid and Livy. Augustine, who discusses the rape in *The City of God*, saw sexual desire in fallen human beings as the effect of an involuntary reflex, not subject to conscious control, or, as he would have put it, the will. The disobedience to us of our sexual organs, he believed, was a proper punishment for the disobedience of Adam and Eve in the Garden of Eden. Augustine was not at all convinced that Lucretia, however chaste, was any more able to escape the effects of this sexual reflex than other mortals.[17]

There is a context for Augustine's doubts. *The City of God* was designed to reassure the Romans that the fall of the city of Rome into the hands of invading barbarians was not a disaster, because these Goths were also Christians. Augustine's argument in the early books juxtaposes Christian values with Roman paganism, and argues that Roman ethics were not up to the standard of Christian morality. But surely Lucretia's example showed that pagan values were at least as demanding? To justify his counter-argument, Augustine skilfully undermines Lucretia's status as an exemplary Roman matron, by calling in question the heroic account of her suicide. Why did she do it, he asks. After all, if she was innocent, she did not need to punish herself; since she took her own life, however, perhaps it was because – 'but she herself alone could know' – she succumbed to involuntary desire, and so committed adultery with Tarquin.[18]

Is *that* what Titian has depicted? A reflex, the disobedience of the self to the self, not just an assault against her will, but the response of her own body, as much against her conscious consent as the violation itself? What does Lucretia's face register? Tears, certainly. And in addition, fear? Or an incipient desire, as she holds her attacker so directly in her gaze?[19]

And is that also the source of the ambiguity I began with, the uncertain relationship in the position offered to the viewer between outrage and titillation? Does our doubt about how to read the image repeat Lucretia's contradictory response? Perhaps undecidability goes to the heart of the painting's appeal, as it offers to enlist the spectator in the enigma it also depicts.

(X)

What, then, does the painting show? Rape and resistance? Rape and consent under duress? Or a consent of the body which issues in adultery, not rape? *Tarquin and Lucretia* keeps its secret or, more exactly, demonstrates that there is no secret, no prior, separable intention diligently packed in, to be extracted by some equally diligent researcher as the final signified that would close the image. Instead, there are only multiple possibilities, intended or unintended, to be followed up and assessed in the light of what we can learn from the text itself in its relation of difference to the sources it cites. Could Titian have told us what he 'had in mind'? Possibly. But would we believe his account to be exhaustive, if the painting itself seemed to offer other options? If meaning is not at the disposal of the individual, can the artist ever have the last word?

I do not see any final way of resolving the questions the image poses. Mercifully, we do not need to. According to the theory of textuality I have drawn on, 'a text is made up of multiple writings . . . entering into mutual relations', including relations of 'contestation'. The painting does not have to make up its mind. And neither does its textual analyst. According to the theory of language I have invoked, there cannot be a final signified: no one true meaning can ever come to light. Although it remains an object of desire in all intellectual endeavour, the definitive truth is not available – now or at any time. An object of equal desire for all good cultural critics, the one proper meaning, the reading that would guarantee closure, is not an option. Meaning is not anchored in anything outside signification itself; and the signifying process supplants it. All we can be sure of, in other words, is the signifier, and this cannot be tied to any unique reading-to-end-all-readings. On the contrary, meanings are always ultimately undecidable.

Paradoxically, this is good news for PhD students in cultural criticism, and good news, too, for research in its entirety. There is literally no end to it. But there is a great deal of work to be done in the process of exploring all the possible avenues.

NOTES

1. I am grateful to Anne McMonagle for her astute comments on an earlier draft of this essay.
2. Susan Brownmiller, *Against Our Will: Men, Women and Rape*, New York: Simon and Schuster, 1975.
3. Laura Mulvey, 'Visual pleasure and narrative cinema', *Screen* 16, no. 3 (Autumn, 1975), pp. 6–18.
4. Roland Barthes, 'The death of the author', *Image, Music, Text*, trans. Stephen Heath, London: Fontana, 1977, pp. 142–8, 148
5. Barthes, 'The death of the author', p. 147.
6. Barthes, 'The death of the author', p. 147.
7. Michel Foucault, 'What is an author?', *Aesthetics, Method, and Epistemology*, ed. James Faubion, London: Penguin, 1998, pp. 205–22, 221.
8. Barthes, 'The death of the author', p. 148.
9. Jacques Derrida, 'Differance', *'Speech and Phenomena' and Other Essays on Husserl's Theory of Signs*, trans. David B. Allison, Evanston, IL: Northwestern University Press, 1973, pp. 129–60.
10. Jacques Derrida, *Limited Inc*, ed. Gerald Graff, Evanston, IL: Northwestern University Press, 1988, p. 40.
11. In anamorphic pictures, like Holbein's *Ambassadors*, painters play tricks with fixed-point perspective, sometimes including objects which are perceptible only from another position, like the elongated skull that floats unintelligibly in the foreground of that picture, until we move our line of sight to the side. But this is only another instance of the way a text offers to place the spectator. What makes *The Ambassadors* disturbing is that there are two distinct viewing positions, and from each of them the *rest* of the image is distorted.
12. Livy, I. 57–60 in Livy, *Books I and II*, trans. B. O. Foster, London: Heinemann, 1967, pp. 198–209; Ovid, *Fasti*, II. 725–852, Ovid, *Fasti*, trans. J. G. Frazer, revised G. P. Goold, Cambridge, MA: Harvard University Press, 1967, pp. 111–19.
13. Over fifty images of Lucretia survive from this period, and more commonly of her suicide than the rape. For examples see Ian Donaldson, *The Rapes of Lucretia: A Myth and its Transformations*, Oxford: Clarendon Press, 1982; Diane Wolfthal, *Images of Rape: The 'Heroic' Tradition and Its Alternatives*, Cambridge: Cambridge University Press, 1999. Shakespeare's narrative poem, *The Rape of Lucrece*, is one of a number of contemporary

texts in English on the subject. See also Stephanie Jed, *Chaste Thinking: The Rape of Lucretia and the Birth of Humanism*, Bloomington, IN: Indiana University Press, 1989.

14. William Shakespeare, *Hamlet*, ed. Harold Jenkins, London: Methuen, 1982, 2.1.80.

15. In fact, the Spanish support was not sustained, and Venice signed a treaty with the Turks in 1573.

16. Norman Bryson assumes that the painting depicts Lucretia's consent, but he ignores her resistance: see Norman Bryson, 'Two narratives of rape in the visual arts: Lucretia and the Sabine Women', in Sylvana Tomaselli and Roy Porter (eds), *Rape: An Historical and Cultural Enquiry*, Oxford: Blackwell, 1986, pp. 152–73, 168–70. Susanne Kappeler takes strong feminist issue with this account of the image. Instead, in her view, 'It is an unambiguous exhibition of force and defencelessness, of intimidation and fear, of violation of the woman's privacy, integrity, selfhood and will': see Susanne Kappeler, 'No matter how unreasonable', *Art History* 11 (1988), pp. 118–22, 121. Neither reading acknowledges the possibility of an unresolved ambiguity.

17. Discussing the rape of Christian nuns, too, he conjectures that this was for them 'an act that could perhaps not have taken place without some carnal pleasure' (Augustine, *The City of God Against the Pagans*, Books I–III, trans. George McCracken, London: Heinemann, 1966, I. 16 (p. 77)).

18. *The City of God*, I. 19 (trans. p. 87).

19. Bryson invokes Augustine in support of his case that Titian's depiction of Lucretia nude, in bed, in isolation from any surrounding domestic space, 'stresses themes which belong more to consent or seduction, than to forcible rape' (p. 170).

CHAPTER 10

Interviewing

Gabriele Griffin, University of Hull

INTRODUCTION

In a review of Diane Middlebrook's biography *Her Husband: Hughes and Plath – A Marriage*, Andrew Motion remarks that Middlebrook's text shows 'only a few signs of interviews with surviving friends' (Motion 2004). This remark forms part of a brief litany of omissions which Motion presents as an implicit criticism of Middlebrook's work. It highlights the assumption that, where possible, interview material should form part of the research conducted for a biography, and it functions in this introduction as an emblem of what has been referred to as 'the interview society' we now live in (Atkinson and Silverman 1997).

Interviews of various kinds, and not just with authors and their friends, are part of everyday life, so much so that some regard them as an extension of what human beings do 'naturally' as part of their everyday practices, that is talk (Rapley 2004: 16). Indeed, Tim Rapley suggests that 'interviewers don't need massive amounts of detailed technical (and moral) instruction on how to conduct qualitative interviews' (2004: 16), even as he proceeds to describe in detail how to conduct interviews. My own experience as both interviewer and interviewee in a variety of situations and research projects, and as a supervisor of research, suggests that researchers need to understand how the methods they choose – and that includes interviewing – impact on the results they obtain. Not everyone is equally competent at designing or asking questions, for instance, or at putting others at their ease, or at 'intuitively' understanding how the phrasing of questions impacts on the responses they receive. There is a big difference between a research student interviewing fellow students about their views on a particular novel and the same student interviewing a famous author. Katherine Borland (1991) tellingly describes the issues that arose when she conducted interviews with her grandmother who later maintained 'that's not what I said'. Selecting a research topic, finding appropriate interviewees, conducting effective interviews, and interpreting the material appropriately is not, then, 'natural' but achieved.

Although interviewing has been regarded as '*the* central resource' for contemporary social science (Atkinson and Silverman 1997), it is not a research method much discussed in English studies since the presumption is that English studies research is fundamentally textual. This is so despite the fact that the English Subject Centre's research report on *Postgraduate Training in Research Methods* (Williams 2003), which itself used 'face-to-face interviews with staff and postgraduate students' as 'the most appropriate methodology' (2003: 9), lists 'interviewing techniques for authors still alive' (2003: 57) as one of the research skills required for different fields of English. One might argue that considering 'authors still alive' as the only sources for interview data unnecessarily narrows the potential research areas explored in English studies. Rachel Alsop's chapter on ethnographic methods (see Chapter 7 in this volume), for instance, discusses the use of interviewing in research on readers. Penny Summerfield's chapter on oral history (see Chapter 4 in this volume) likewise deals with a particular kind of interviewing in order to understand how respondents view their past. It is the case, however, that a significant proportion of current interviewing in English studies research focuses on interviews with authors. Literary journals, for instance, abound with these. Below I shall therefore briefly comment on how interviews with authors have been conventionally presented, before suggesting other ways in which interviewing might be a useful research method for English studies. I shall then discuss the varieties of interview method, the issues that arise in the research process involved in interviewing, the interview itself, interview transcription and analysis, the integration of the material in the write-up of the research findings, and the ethical concerns raised by interviewing as a research method.

INTERVIEWING AUTHORS – THE CONVENTIONAL WAY

When reading volumes of interviews with authors – and I shall draw on two well established texts here, John Haffenden's *Novelists in Interview* (1985), and Heidi Stephenson and Natasha Langridge's *Rage and Reason* (1997) – one is struck by the way in which a certain format repeats itself: the focus is on an unproblematised 'substance' at the expense of reflection on process. Typically, the interviewer/editor provides an introduction summarising the views of the authors as expressed in the interviews. This introduction explains the editors' intentions behind the interviews: in Stephenson's and Langridge's case, to celebrate women playwrights' achievements, and to find out 'how they craft their plays, why they write, where they find their stories and why . . . they continue to be under-represented in mainstream theatre' (1997: ix); in Haffenden's case, to resurrect the importance of novelists' intentionality for the meaning of their work (1985: vii–xx). The introduction is followed by the interviews themselves, presented as chapters in which a brief introduction about each author precedes the textual reproduction of the interview. Whilst editors indicate why and how they chose the authors, they tend not to discuss how they secured the interview. Both the interviewer and the interviewee are presented as speaking in the well formed sentences that suggest a seamless interaction. Minimal, if any, reference is made to the interviewing process itself. In Stephenson's and Langridge's case, for instance, it is not made explicit who did the interviewing – did they both do it, or only one of them? Where did they do it? Clearly, they think this information irrelevant to their text. Haffenden makes slightly more reference to the process. Only in one instance, however, does he note an interviewee's engagement with the interview process *per se*, namely when Malcolm Bradbury asked him 'just one question about the proposed scope of the interview' and then 'appl[ied] himself to [Haffenden's] questions with rapt professionalism' (1985: 27). In two cases out of his fourteen interviewees, he comments on the latter's response to being interviewed: William Golding 'maintain[ed] a certain guardedness when submitting to a formal interview' (1985: 99), and Russell Hoban apparently proved to be 'carefully responsive to being interviewed with the proper proviso that to ask certain kinds of questions is "like asking the eggshells to explain the omelette"' (1985: 122). Haffenden may view Hoban's position as 'proper'; it does not lead him to engage more extensively with the interview process. He suggests, rather cryptically, in his introduction to the volume that he has 'not felt it necessary to be slavish to the writers' statements' (1985: ix) which may or may not refer to the way in which he edited the interviews for publication. But neither in his, nor in Stephenson and Langridge's volume, is the reader privy to the editing process and thus the considerations that went into the textualisation of the interviews. Yet, as I shall indicate below, there are many different ways in which one can transcribe interviews, and the transcription itself constitutes an interpretation of the process. Not explaining this interpretation means that transcription as interpretation is obscured by the author, implicitly suggesting that what is on the page is the only way to present the material.

The (intended?) impression is one of the interviewer's objectivity, neutrality, and invisibility; an invisibilisation of the interview process itself; and a sense of the editor's and authors' words speaking for themselves and presenting a, or the, truth. However, closer examination of the texts lays bare some of the effects of the process. In some of the introductions to the interviews, for instance, Haffenden describes in varying detail where and how his interviewees live, making comments both about the interiors of their working environments and/or homes, and on their conduct during the interviews. From this it becomes clear that he interviewed all the authors either in their homes or in their workspace. In other words, he went to *their* territory (rather than having them come to his space or to a third space 'owned' by neither interviewee nor interviewer), a fact which creates a particular dynamic that I shall discuss in greater detail below. He also says more about the circumstances in which some of the interviews took place than about others, though he does not explain this diversity. One gets a sense of his irritation during the Angela Carter interview where 'her baby Alexander consumes the room and threatens the interview with healthy hubbub'. This is only alleviated by the baby's father, admired for 'quietly and effectively tak[ing] control of the child', and ultimately by Haffenden 'escap[ing] to the street' (1985: 77). Similarly, he notes that his interview with Salman Rushdie was 'occasionally interrupted by telephone calls, builders calling at the door to talk about roofing and pointing, and Rushdie's own eagerness to check the Test match scores on teletext' (1985: 232). Such disruptions, which point to some of the issues involved in inter-viewing, are compensated for in other interviews through altogether more 'clubbable' activities: Haffenden notes approvingly that Russell Hoban 'encourages conversation with generous gins' (1985: 122); Martin Amis 'fetches me coffee and a generous drop of the hard stuff' (1985: 2). When Haffenden discusses the different lengths of his interview texts, he comments that this 'bears no relation to any judgement of relative merit or importance – only to the circumstances of the day and the time available for each recording' (1985: xix). Yet the interviews show that Rushdie, despite checking cricket scores, was much more prolix than Anita Brookner, for instance. One could, of course, argue that Rushdie is a more verbose writer than Brookner, and that the interviews simply attest to the different authors' different personalities and verbal predilections. But it also seems that Haffenden had to work much more at getting responses from Brookner (see, for example, p. 61 where Brookner gives repeated one-sentence responses) than from Rushdie. Haffenden, however, does not comment on this.

The question of how much one should engage with issues of process is a contested one. In research-specific contexts, the demand to be explicit regard-ing the research process has become increasingly pronounced, prompted by the recognition that the process itself exerts influence on the research outcome and therefore needs to form an articulated aspect of the research. Hence many dis-ciplines demand a method/ology section as part of their theses or research papers. On the whole, this is not as yet the case in English studies, but grant application processes increasingly demand that researchers engage explicitly with the process of their research, naming not only what they do but also how they do it (method) and what the rationale for it is (methodology).

Haffenden and Stephenson and Langridge do not discuss why they chose the interview method; they treat their interview material as a resource. Seale

(1998) distinguishes between two different kinds of use of interview data which reflect a common distinction between 'modern' and 'postmodern' interviewing:

1. *Interview-data-as-resource*, where interview data are regarded as (faithfully) reflecting the interviewees' reality outside of the interview.
2. *Interview-data-as-topic*, where interview data are viewed as reflecting a reality jointly constructed by the interviewee and interviewer (during the interview) (in Rapley 2004: 16).

Interview-data-as-resource is how Haffenden and Stephenson and Langridge treat their interview material. Hollway's and Jefferson's (2000) account of their interviews on fears about crime, on the other hand, treats the interview data as a topic in the sense of viewing the data as jointly constructed and not necessarily relating to an 'objective truth'. Similarly, Summerfield's account (in Chapter 4 of this volume) of her oral history interviews suggests the ways in which treating interview data as topics reveals much about the cultural constructions that inform how we talk about things. Whereas, broadly speaking, 'modern' interviews make the assumption that the speaking subject will produce a coherent account continuous with an actuality that exists independently of the interview, 'postmodern' interviewing (Gubrium and Holstein 2003) assumes neither such coherence nor such continuity. However, the latter is not regarded as therefore invalidating the interview data (that is, it assumes that subjects are contradictory, recall things selectively, are influenced by the interview situation, respond in accordance with the cultural context in which they operate, and so on). Rather, it is regarded as presenting a truth of the subject and her discourse – being and doing all the things just mentioned – that differs from the truth about the subject assumed for the interview-data-as-resource model. Within research-specific contexts, interview data should be treated both as resource and as topic but where one puts the emphasis depends on the individual research context.

INTERVIEWING FOR ENGLISH STUDIES

Apart from interviews with authors, there are many other contexts and projects in or for which one might want to conduct interviews. The key question is always, what information can be gleaned by adopting a particular research method that could not be gained in any other way? In-depth interviewing, for instance, lends itself to gaining an understanding of the perceptions of the interviewees, whether these be authors or readers. In fact, we have very little empirical knowledge of reader behaviour and perceptions. Much of what there is derives from the market research undertaken by publishers and booksellers. Such information could contribute significantly to our understanding of the importance of reading for individuals and groups of people. Whereas television and film research especially has done much to gauge audience responses, and significant research has been carried out to understand the impact of visual materials on individual behaviour (for instance in the context of pornography and violence), little importance has been attached to an investigation into the impact of reading books on readers' behaviour and views.

In the context of creative writing, authors themselves often conduct research, including interviews, from which to produce their work, whether this be books, articles, or web material. This is as true of documentaries as it is of investigative journalism as it is of biographies. It also applies to creative writers such as Jackie Kay, who in her novel *Trumpet* reports on interviewing (one of her characters is a journalist), and the playwright Anna Deavere Smith, who in performance pieces such as *Twilight: Los Angeles, 1992* and *Fires in the Mirror* draws on interviews conducted with people who have experienced race riots in order to 'reflect society' (Deavere Smith 1994: xxii).

VARIETIES OF INTERVIEWS

Interviews may be distinguished along three dimensions:

- *Interviewees involved*: one-to-one versus group interviews (the latter are predominantly discussed in terms of focus groups).
- *Format*: structured, semi-structured, or unstructured interviews.
- *Setting*: public or private space (interviewee's, interviewer's, 'neutral'); face-to-face, telephone, email, internet.

All three dimensions, as well as others such as interviewer skills in putting the interviewee at ease and asking appropriate questions, impact on the interview process and outcome. Thus, interviews with authors are more likely to be conducted on a one-to-one basis than interviews involving readers which might use focus groups. Bridget Fowler, for instance, conducted focus groups for *The Alienated Reader*. Group interviews may elicit a broader range of views and can be more resource- and time-efficient but, as Fontana and Frey (2003) point out, require a different set of interviewer skills from one-to-one interviews, in particular group management skills designed to reduce convergence of opinion among the group, encouragement of all members to participate rather than the group being dominated by one or two individuals and several members being silent, and retaining group focus on the topic (see also Cronin 2001). For this reason one needs to consider the size of any focus group carefully since the larger the group is, the more unwieldy it becomes. Groups of between three and six people are probably the best size to enable maximum participation within the quite common interview time framework of ninety to 120 minutes. Group management skills can be acquired through practice and observation of others conducting interviews but should not be assumed as intuitively present in any interviewer.

Structured interviews involve schedules where all questions, fully formulated, are pre-given, and asked in the same order, and ideally in the same manner, for every interviewee. This may involve closed questions requiring precise answers, often only 'yes' or 'no'. This is common in market research, and occurs where surveys are conducted with a view to creating data that can be subjected to statistical analysis so that one can assess, for example, how many interviewees gave a particular response. Typical examples in the field of literature include surveys to find out the best-loved British writer or, the best-loved poem, or interviews conducted to find out how many books respondents read on holiday. Such surveys might be conducted by questionnaire rather than by interview but response rates to questionnaires sent out randomly are notoriously low (Simmons 2001: 87) so interviews are often used to gain more responses.

According to Fontana and Frey, interviewers in these situations are required to 'treat all interview situations in a like manner' (2003: 68). They must 'never get involved in long explanations of the study; . . . never deviate from the study introduction, sequence of questions, or question wording . . . never let another person interrupt the interview . . . never suggest an answer or agree or disagree with an answer . . . never interpret the meaning of a question . . . [and] never improvise' (2003: 68–9). The idea is, obviously, to minimise interviewer impact. The situation involves a particular social dynamic, with the interviewer not engaged in a dialogue between equals, but in a stimulus–response mode (Fielding and Thomas 2001: 128) and in a 'neutral' manner, effaced in the process. This also, in some respects, 'obliterates' the individual respondent who has limited scope for 'free-range' answers, becoming a statistic in the process. This does not mean, however, that one may not elicit a variety of extreme and atypical views, for instance because of how one has chosen the respondents, or how the questions are worded. Structured interviews tend to use interview data as resource, and assume that respondents will answer truthfully. In this sense, they are positivistic. One advantage is that they generate comparable data.

Semi-structured interviews are less rigid in format, involving an interview guide rather than an interview schedule. The guide is designed as a prompt for the interviewer to ensure that all issues in the interview are covered. Interview guides may amount to no more than general headings (Fielding and Thomas 2001: 131), enabling interviewers to use their judgement in how to phrase questions, in what order to ask, and thus allowing greater responsiveness on the part of the interviewer to the interviewee and the interview situation as it develops.

Although the phrase 'unstructured interviews' is used in research methods literature, I doubt that there is such a thing as an 'unstructured interview' since interviewers always want to elicit a set of responses on a given topic (whether or not they have a good idea what these responses will be). However, in the extent to which the questions are determined by the interviewer prior to the interview and adhered to, the extent to which the questions are open or closed, and depending on what the interviewer wants to find out, interviews may be more or less structured, controlled by either the interviewer or the interviewee or both. Choosing the interview format is therefore a matter of research design, of what the researcher wants to discover.

The less structured an interview is, the more participatory it can become for both interviewer and interviewee. Unstructured interviews are commonly described as 'in-depth interviews' to suggest that such interviews are intended to produce '*elaborated and detailed* answers' (Rapley 2004: 15) or 'thick description' (Geertz 1973). Such elaborated answers are the aim of all interviews designed to elicit narratives from interviewees, whether these be in the form of oral histories, anecdotes or experiences. They may be conducted in either a facilitative and neutral manner, or in a facilitative and self-disclosing manner (Rapley 2004: 20). In the latter case, interviewers contribute narratives about their own experiences, a stance usually adopted when the interviewer and the interviewee share certain traits such as both being readers of romance fiction, for instance. The underlying idea is to create a situation of 'intimate reciprocity' (Rapley 2004: 23) where trust between interviewer and interviewee, an important factor in encouraging interviewees to give full and frank responses, is built out of the notion of shared experiences. One danger is, of course, that such disclosures on the part of the interviewer may become too dominant in the interview.

Interviews often begin with questions intended to put the interviewee at ease before moving on to more central aspects of the interview. Open-ended requests/questions such as 'tell me about your early reading experiences', or 'how did you come to be a reader of romances?' are more likely to result in extended answers than closed questions, and one of the skills an interviewer has to practise for unstructured or semi-structured interviews is how to phrase and ask such questions. A good way of 'testing' the openness of a question is to ask yourself if that question could be answered with one word such as 'yes' or 'no'. If it can, it is not very likely to elicit extended responses.

Feminist writers on interviewing in particular (see Järviluoma et al. 2003; Letherby 2003) have stressed the need for so-called participatory interviewing. This advocates a democratic ideal of exchange where interviewees are not simply 'milked' in a top-down fashion for the data they can provide but are involved on an equal basis in the research process, from helping to design the questions to involvement in the analysis of the data. Interviewers and interviewees are here matched in demographic terms (that is, black women interviewing black women; or women who enjoy reading detective novels interviewing other women who enjoy those texts), they contribute equally to the interview and equally disclose relevant aspects of their histories and experiences. This ideal is not always and/or entirely realisable. Researchers may, as Hollway and Jefferson did, interview people quite unlike themselves in many respects. Hollway and Jefferson speak of 'the defended subject' to explain that both interviewers and interviewees conduct themselves in interview so as to minimise and mask (unassuaged) anxieties they may have. Haffenden's text, for instance, betrays an acute awareness of his situation as a critic as opposed to a writer, a situation that, together with the fact that he was the interviewer and the authors the interviewees, produces an asymmetrical power relation between him and them. He describes his role in asking his questions as combining 'the critic and the reporter' (1985: ix) and, in an inadvertently condescending manner that is testimony to his unease about his status in interviewing 'great writers', states:

> I have tried to resist imposing my views on the interviewees, or in any sense putting words into their mouths, but there is actually little danger of that: the novelists are well able to dispute or refute opinions with which they disagree . . . a literary interview is above all else a service to the writer . . . and to the reader . . . (1985: ix)

Haffenden's interviews here emerge as a struggle over verbal territory and which opinions might or might not prevail; less famous than his interviewees and a petitioner since 'an interviewer cannot reach beyond what an author is prepared to present of his or her life and work' (1985: vii), he struggles between imposition and service to assert his equality within a culture in which to be a critic is always secondary to being an originator – in this instance, of literature. The very fact that he feels it incumbent upon him to state that in the interviews 'the most I could attempt was to press the novelists further to explore themselves and their works – *without thinking that I knew better*' (1985: xx; emphasis added) is indicative of this.

It would be interesting to know if any of Haffenden's interviewees – as sometimes occurs – demanded to see the questions he asked in advance, a request that must usually be complied with (since the interview is likely to be refused otherwise). This is, of course, another factor that impacts on the interview process since interviewees may require certain questions to be cut, for example. Pre-prepared questions required by the interviewee shift the power balance from interviewer to interviewee. But the notion that in some interviews (those that are not coerced) the interviewer automatically has more power than the interviewee, a common trope in interview literature, is clearly erroneous; in most interview situations both the interviewer and the interviewee stand to gain and both want something that the interview provides: data, a listening ear, or an opportunity to exchange views on a specific topic. The power structures involved in interviewing are thus complex and variable, and a key consequence for the interviewer is therefore to think through those structures and the relations s/he wants to create with the interviewee/s before embarking on the research – bearing in mind that this is always a two-way process between interviewer and interviewee. Awareness of possible issues is important. For instance, I had a postgraduate student who decided to interview famous Conservative women politicians; she had no public status compared to these women and, unlike them, was not well versed in interviewing. The interview transcriptions later showed that the interviewer was so in awe of these women that she found it difficult to manage the process. The politicians, in contrast, had plenty of practice in taking and repeating a line, irrespective of what was asked.

SELECTING APPROPRIATE INTERVIEW METHODS FOR A RESEARCH TOPIC

The type of interview (structured, semi-structured, unstructured; group or individual; face-to-face, telephone, email/internet; and so on) you choose for your research topic depends on the data you want to elicit. If you want to survey readers to arrive at quantifiable information about their reading habits, for example, you are likely to conduct structured interviews, possibly face-to-face or by telephone. If you want to elicit respondents' narratives, you will conduct semi-structured interviews, most likely face-to-face. Email/internet interviewing has become more frequent, particularly for respondents likely to use email lists or chatrooms. However, the much discussed issue of the unverifiability of respondents' identity (Stone 1996; Mann and Stewart 2003) in such contexts makes this kind of interviewing a contested method, especially where the purpose of the interview is to match responses with demographic data such as the sex of the interviewee.

A related issue is the question of the basis on which interviewees are selected, that is 'sampling'. Are the interviewees intended to be representative of a particular group of people, or does the research focus on them as individuals? Survey interviewing generally intends to achieve a degree of representativeness in its sample (Schaeffer and Maynard 2003), whilst in-depth interviewing is less intent upon generalising about a specific group of people than on understanding the views of a set of individuals.

FINDING RESPONDENTS

Haffenden's and Stephenson's and Langridge's texts suggest that they chose whom to interview in terms of their preferences. 'I chose the fourteen novelists in interview because of my interest in their individual achievements . . .' (Haffenden 1985: xix). This obscures the fact – known to anyone who has ever been approached in the street or at an airport by interviewers and refused to participate – that not everyone wants to be interviewed. Neither Haffenden nor Stephenson and Langridge indicate that anybody turned them down, yet it is unlikely that securing the interviews was straightforward. Famous, as well as not so famous, authors are busy people who may be selective about whom they speak to. Even prior to that, there is the question of how one accesses them, sometimes done through consulting references works such as *Who's Who* (which may or may not give private addresses, or the addresses of writers' agents), and sometimes done through writing to the authors care of the publishers that publish their work. Answers to enquiries may not be forthcoming or may take months. Haffenden interviewed his novelists over the course of more than a year, so it clearly took time to arrange matters.

Different issues arise when one wants to interview a specific group of people such as middle-aged theatregoers, women who read science fiction, or men who write diaries, in order to conduct research on that group. Often, these groups are found by locating one such person, described in anthropological literature as an 'insider', and then asking them if they know others like themselves. This technique of gathering interviewees or informants is known as 'snowballing'; it can be very effective in reaching one's target group but it also relies on the knowledge and social circles to which the insider has access, with all the specificities that that entails. In other words, a particular sample group will arise, and their views may not be representative of that kind of person (for example, men who write diaries) at large. However, this question of the generalisability of one's findings may not be the most important one when one is after individual narratives about a given experience. Another way of finding respondents is to advertise for them in publications or sites that the respondents one is aiming for can reasonably be expected to access. Newspapers, magazines, newsagents, libraries, websites, emailing lists are all useful sources of informants.

The number of interviews conducted, or the size of the sample, depends on the research topic (Arber 2001). The focus may be on a single interviewee, as in Borland's case, or on a number of people, as in Haffenden, and Stephenson's and Langridge's volumes. Overall, the sample size has to appropriate to the population being studied (Gobo 2004). In the context of a PhD, structured survey interviews may involve fifty to 100 or more interviews; unstructured interviews may include between twenty and forty interviewees. Conducting in-depth interviews takes time – the actual interview may last between ninety and 120 minutes. Additionally, travel to and from the place of interview may be involved, and the briefing and debriefing of the interviewee may take time. The demands on the interviewer, of which more below, are also such that, in my experience, it is difficult, especially where travel is concerned, to conduct more than two or three interviews in one day. The interviewing period therefore needs to be carefully planned, and might span six to nine months.

THE INTERVIEW PROCESS

Interviewing is demanding for both interviewer and interviewee. In-depth interviewing, in particular, demands a significant level of social and listening skills from the interviewer. One of the experiences many researchers have when they first interview is how difficult it is to keep focused during an interview. Haffenden, for instance, writes: 'If I have missed opportunities to challenge or follow up certain points, I must take responsibility for lack of skill and understanding' (1985: xx). One's attention may indeed wander; an interviewer's preoccupation with the next question or with what the interviewee has previously said may result in missing important clues in a response or not following up key points. Often, in reading transcripts of interviews, one finds something that might have been pursued further. But few interviews, other than ethnographic ones where researchers spend considerable amounts of time with their informants (see Chapter 7 in this volume), are repeat ones – mostly there is neither chance, nor opportunity, nor time nor other resources to go back and clarify what was meant. This has two implications. One is that attentive listening – not just as a researcher, so that one remains attuned to the details of what is said and can respond appropriately to these, but also to signal to the interviewee one's interest in what they have to say – is a crucial skill for interviewers. It is a skill that does not come 'naturally' but needs to be trained through practice interviewing. The other implication is that it is useful to conduct 'pilot interviews', sample interviews designed to enable the refinement of questions through an analysis of the interview experience and results they produce.

Both interviewer and interviewee need to be at ease during an interview. Where the interview takes place is one factor influencing that ease. If interviews occur in the interviewer's space (their office or home), this shifts the power balance towards the interviewer; where they occur in the interviewee's space, it shifts the power balance towards the interviewee. A 'neutral' space such as a seminar room or a café may be more appropriate, but every space has its own attendant issues regarding noise, disruption and so on. Ideally, interviews should be free from interruption and allow both parties to remain focused on what is said. As Haffenden's comments (see above) about his interview experiences with novelists show, such ideal scenarios may not always be achievable, and interviewers as well as interviewees have to be prepared to cope with this. The decision about where to interview is frequently a matter of negotiation with the interviewee. It should be appropriate to the interview situation and content: if the interview centres on a sensitive topic, for instance, the interview should be conducted somewhere where the interviewee is not overheard or likely to be disrupted.

These practical aspects are key to the success of an interview, measured in terms of the satisfaction both interviewee and interviewer feel about the process and the usefulness for the research of the data gathered. They include, critically, the use of appropriate equipment for the interview. Normally, interviews are recorded since one's memory of what was said is bound to be limited, and trying to make notes of what people say whilst interviewing is disruptive to the interviewing process (Fielding and Thomas 2001: 155). Interviewees need to be informed of the intention to tape their interview, and consent for this as well as the conduct of the interview has to be sought from them, preferably in advance of the interview. Interviewers must also ensure that the equipment is functioning, bearing in mind, for instance, that if their tape recorder works off mains electricity, they need to be somewhere with access to electricity, and may need an extension lead to place the recorder in an appropriate position. They need to ensure that they have sufficient tapes, that everything is working and that the recording will be audible. This should be tested, including immediately prior to the interview in the place where the interview will occur. This may seem obvious but I think that every research student I know who has conducted interviews has 'lost' at least one whole interview through technical hiccups such as low batteries or tapes not running, and has lost some data through lack of audibility because interviewees dropped their voices, or extraneous noise interfered.

As soon as possible after the interview, the researcher should make notes about the interview, highlighting everything both descriptive and analytic that was pertinent to that interview. These notes are extremely useful when one returns to the interview data at a later stage: they can augment the information one has, correct one's memory of the interview situation, and remind the researcher of aspects of the interview she may have forgotten. Such notes effectively form another source of data, and should therefore be done as soon after the interview as possible while one's impressions of the interview are still fresh.

Not only do interviewers influence the outcome of interviews but so of course do respondents. Adler and Adler's (2003) chapter on interviewing is significantly entitled 'The reluctant respondent'. This exemplifies a significant range of texts on this topic which articulate the *negative* effects interviewees can have on the interview. Fielding and Thomas (2001: 126) identify these negative effects as 'rationalization' (respondents trying to be logical and withholding judgements and emotional responses that may be very revealing); they may fear being 'shown up' (for example, regarding views they hold that they think are unacceptable) and therefore give answers that do not reveal their actual views; and 'over-politeness' to the interviewer (for example, telling the interviewer what they think she wants to hear). The potential discrepancy between interviewees' expressed views and their actual views and/or behaviours has been the object of some investigation (Hollway and Jefferson 2000; Fontana and Frey 2003: 91–4). Interviewees may state, for instance, that they go to the theatre much more frequently than they actually do. This may be due to their perception of the most acceptable answer in a given situation but may also be associated with the fact that interviewees' memory is not always accurate (see Chapter 4 in this volume). Understanding the potential partiality of what is imparted and/or understood does not therefore invalidate the findings (Rapley 2004: 29–30). It suggests instead the need for (self-)awareness and careful interaction with the research material in order for the researcher to remain sensitive to the specificity and scope of her findings.

TRANSCRIBING INTERVIEWS

Interviews can be transcribed in many different ways, either by the researcher herself or by professional transcribers. Especially in the early stages of a research career, it is always advisable for the researcher to transcribe interviews herself so that she immerses herself in the data and knows them well, in advance of their analysis (Fielding and Thomas 2001: 135). Professional transcription is expensive and has a significant error rate, requiring researchers to check systematically what has been transcribed against the original tapes, itself a time-consuming and frustrating process if error rates are high. In addition, transcription by others than the researcher means that the researcher loses the knowledge of the data provided through the transcribing process (Rapley 2004: 26–7). Transcribing interviews of ninety to 120 minutes' duration can take anything from five to eight hours, and is thus a lengthy process. Researchers therefore sometimes use a mixture of full and selective transcriptions of interviews, initially transcribing perhaps half the interviews fully, and then transcribing selectively from the second half. Selective transcription is a form of data interpretation since the researcher focuses only on particular parts of the interviews, deemed significant. Such transcription relies on the researcher having already decided what are the key issues she wants to focus on in her analysis of her data. Those key issues will already have been formulated at the research design stage when the researcher decided what to work on, whom to interview, and what to focus on in interview, and that process is further refined at the data analysis stage when the researcher selects from the data which themes emerging from the interviews to concentrate on in her write-up. How many interviews to transcribe fully and how many to transcribe selectively is a matter of the total number of interviews and of sample size. Fielding and Thomas suggest that if the researcher has twenty interviews or fewer, they should all be transcribed fully (2001: 135). PhD students must remember that interviews and their transcriptions must normally be available for inspection by the examiners at the point of thesis examination so that their claims can be tested against that material, and are in that respect no different from any other research source material.

There are many different conventions regarding how one might transcribe an interview, and each offers different views, interpretations and interpretive possibilities of the data. The following brief excerpt from Stephenson and Langridge's interview with Sarah Daniels provides one version:

But playwrights like Caryl Churchill started off something that was non-linear and different, that moved away from one central character.
Yes, in that respect Caryl Churchill is Picasso.

Why do you think you are accused of using improbable scenarios and dialogue?
It's difficult to answer this without knowing which scenes and what dialogue it refers to. The easy answer would be . . . (1997: 6)

Here interviewer (bold) and interviewee (not bold) are marked, with one question and answer separated from the next by a line between each question-and-answer unit, and the text produced in well-formed sentences. No indication is given of pauses, hesitations, bodily demeanour, or non-grammatical utterances. Yet all of these occur during interviews. The effect is to produce a streamlined, edited text in which the actual interview process is minimalised in favour of the semantic content of the questions and answers. When discussing a sensitive topic, however, your research interest may well be on how people responded to particular questions, and not just on what they said. So you may wish to notate pauses and hesitations, for instance, and also produce a *verbatim*, that is word-for-word, account, of what was said. Fontana and Frey cite Gorden's four basic modes of non-verbal communication in interview, all of which might usefully be noted in transcribing an interview:

Proxemic communication is the use of interpersonal space to communicate attitudes [for example, 'leans back' or 'leans forward'], *chronemics* communication is the use of pacing of speech and length of silence in conversation, *kinesic* communication includes any body movements or postures [for example, 'crosses legs', 'turns head away', 'faces interviewer'], and *paralinguistic* communication includes all the variations in volume, pitch and quality of voice. (2003: 87)

There are no standardised formats for transcriptions either regarding what is said or how it is said. Rather, the focus of the research determines what level of detail and how comprehensively it is recorded. Rapley (2004: 22–8), Poland (2003) and Edley (2001), for instance, provide examples and discussions of how one might transcribe effectively. The key consideration is to be consistent in the methods one uses (that is, always indicate pauses in the same way), and to produce an inventory of transcription decisions one has made (for example, '(.)' to indicate a pause) so that you as the researcher and others will be able to understand the notation in the transcriptions.

Finally, a distinction needs to be made between transcribing for research analysis and using transcriptions for publication purposes. Not all the data collected during interviewing will be reproduced either in a PhD thesis or in publications about the research. Often only fractions of the textualised interview will appear in published articles or books. It can be helpful to tell readers how and what kind of editing decisions were made, though if the focus of the published analysis is on interview content, this may be very limited. A second issue is how you incorporate interview material in your write-up. Mostly, this is done by seamlessly integrating interview material in the form of quotations into the body of the analytical text (see Chapter 4 in this volume for an example). The resultant fragmentation of the interview material means that the researcher has an obligation to the interviewees to present what they said as faithfully as possible to the spirit of what was said within the frame of the analysis. Integrating interview material in brief snippets into an analysis of that material means that the researcher overtly imposes her research frame onto the material. As Fontana and Frey put it: 'Traditionally, readers were presented with the researcher's interpretation of the data, cleaned and streamlined and collapsed in rational, non-contradictory accounts' (2003: 87). A different way of doing things is demonstrated in the transformation of interview material within creative writing, for example, a play or a biography, or in the theoretical writings of Pierre Bourdieu (1986; 1999), for instance, where interview material is separated out from analytical sections to allow contrapuntal voices to emerge, the words of the interviewees appearing in ways that may disrupt or query the analytical stance taken. This creates an intertextual dialogic dynamic which in some respects reduces researcher control over the argument in favour of a more open-ended textual stance.

Following on from the transcription of the interview recordings, a decision has to be made about what to do with them. Since these produce new data sets, the research councils are very interested in their deposit in one of the sound archives such as the Arts and Humanities Data Service or the National Sound Archive. There they may be utilised in future research. Interviewees' consent must therefore be obtained for such deposit.

ANALYSING YOUR INTERVIEW DATA

The analysis of the interview data will be determined by your research topic and the purpose of the write-up. If you conduct interviews with authors and your intention is to reproduce those interviews as Haffenden and Stephenson and Langridge did, then the main job after the interview will be the writing of the introduction (based on the notes you made before and after the interview), and the editing of the interview text, re-writing what was said into well formed sentences and eliminating repetitions, sometimes even inconsistencies, in what is said. If you want to extract particular bits of information from your data to generate an argument onto which these interview snippets throw additional light, you need to proceed through careful reading and rereading of the transcripts, accompanied by marking-up or coding either manually or electronically (see Seale 2003) themes and issues as they emerge and recur, which will then form the basis of your analysis (Rapley 2004: 27–9). The coding categories you apply will in part be predetermined by your original research questions and in part by what you find in the data. Ryan and Russell Bernard (2003) provide a useful description of the different ways in which one may approach the analysis of interview data, and indicate their interpretive effects on the interview analyses.

ETHICAL ISSUES IN INTERVIEWING

There are a series of ethical issues involved in interviewing (see, for instance, Chapter 4 in this volume) related to the fact that one is dealing with other people and the stories they choose to tell or information they choose to disclose. A key issue is gaining the trust of interviewees so that they will talk openly. Attempts at building such trust are often made through seeking to pair interviewers and interviewees in terms of similarities, through careful explanations of the purpose of the interview, and through explicitly stating that all information will be anonymous and treated confidentially. The latter assertions are, of course, not appropriate where authors are concerned since interviews are not least about publicising their work, but they will apply to the interviewing of readers and audiences, for instance. Authors may instead stipulate that their consent is required for the final write-up of an interview. Chapter 4 in this volume discusses the problems of showing transcriptions to interviewees, especially where these are *verbatim*, since we are acculturated into assuming that we speak in well formed sentences (after all, that is what most drama dialogue looks like and that is how most interviews in public circulation appear); interviewees may feel 'shown up' by not speaking in perfect sentences. More importantly, they may decide that what they said does not 'show them in a good light', and may ask for parts of the interview, which from the researcher's viewpoint are extremely valuable, to be cut. There is no easy answer to these issues. The most pragmatic solution is to ask for interviewees' consent in writing to use their comments at the time of the interview. This might be part of the process, prior to the interview, of explaining to them the purpose of the research in general and the interview specifically.

Additionally, the researcher should treat the interview material with respect. This means that no harm should come from the use of that material to those who offered it. This may seem like a vague definition but it is clear that slanderous or libellous uses of the material, for instance, are unacceptable.

Interviewers may decide, as has been argued by many feminist writers on research methods, to give back something to those whom they interviewed. One useful way in which this can be done for multiple interviewees – and it is something a number of PhD students I have supervised have done – is to organise a one- or half-day event either for, or including, interviewees, where the researcher presents her work, centring on the research findings, and invites the interviewees to comment. Interviewees frequently agree to be interviewed because they are interested in the topic; they will therefore also be interested in the findings. Organising an event for participants not only allows them to network among themselves but may also yield further insights for the researcher as a result of the comments made on the findings. It is a highly productive way of concluding an interview research process.

CONCLUSION

Interviewing is a useful research method for understanding people's views and perceptions as producers and consumers of literary texts. Its processes are complex and involve a number of important questions such as: what information do I hope to glean from the interviews that I cannot get through another research process? What questions do I need to ask? What kind of interviews should be conducted and with whom, how, where and in what manner? What resources will be needed for the interviews? What will I do with the interview material in terms of transcribing, analysing and archiving it? Rather than merely staying 'loose' and 'flexible' as Turkel (1995) proclaimed it, careful consideration of these questions will repay in the use of interviews as a research method.

REFERENCES

Adler, Patricia A. and Peter Adler (2003), 'The reluctant respondent', in J. Holstein and J. Gubrium (eds), *Inside Interviewing*, London: Sage, pp. 153–73.

Arber, Sara (2001), 'Designing samples', in Nigel Gilbert (ed.), *Researching Social Life*, London: Sage, pp. 58–82.

Atkinson, Paul and David Silverman (1997), 'Kundera's *Immortality*: The interview society and the invention of self', *Qualitative Inquiry* 3: 304–25.

Borland, Katherine (1991), ' "That's not what I said": Interpretive conflict in oral narrative research', in Sherna Berger Gluck and Daphne Patai (eds), *Women's Words*, London: Routledge, pp. 63–76.

Bourdieu, Pierre [1979] (1986), *Distinction*, trans. R. Nice, London: Routledge and Kegan Paul.

Bourdieu, Pierre et al. (1999), *The Weight of the World*, trans. P. P. Ferguson et al., Cambridge: Polity Press.

Cronin, Ann (2001), 'Focus groups', in Nigel Gilbert (ed.), *Researching Social Life*, London: Sage, pp. 164–77.

Deavere Smith, Anna (1993), *Fires in the Mirror*, New York: Anchor Books.

Deavere Smith, Anna (1994), *Twilight: Los Angeles, 1992*, New York: Anchor Books.

Denzin, Norman K. and Yvonna S. Lincoln (eds) (2003), *Collecting and Interpreting Qualitative Materials*, 2nd edn, Thousand Oaks: Sage.

Edley, Nigel (2001), 'Analysing masculinity: interpretative repertoires, ideological dilemmas and subject positions', in Margaret Wetherell, Stephanie Taylor and Simeon J. Yates (eds), *Discourse as Data*, London: Sage, pp. 189–228.

Fielding, Nigel and Hilary Thomas (2001), 'Qualitative interviewing', in Nigel Gilbert (ed.), *Researching Social Life*, London: Sage, pp. 123–44.

Fontana, Andrea and James H. Frey (2003), 'The interview: From structured questions to negotiated text', in N. Denzin and Y. Lincoln (2003), *Collecting and Interpreting Qualitative Materials*, Thousand Oaks: Sage, pp. 61–106.

Fowler, Bridget (1991), *The Alienated Reader*, London: Harvester Wheatsheaf.

Geertz, Clifford (1973), *The Interpretation of Cultures*, New York: Basic Books.

Gobo, Giampetro (2004), 'Sampling, representativeness and generalizability', in Clive Seale et al., (eds), *Qualitative Research Practice*, London: Sage, pp. 435–56.

Gubrium, Jaber F. and James A. Holstein (eds) (2003), *Postmodern Interviewing*, London: Sage.

Haffenden, John (1985), *Novelists in Interview*, London: Methuen.

Hollway, Wendy and Tony Jefferson (2000), *Doing Qualitative Research Differently*, London: Sage.

Holstein, James A. and Jaber F. Gubrium (eds) (2003), *Inside Interviewing*, London: Sage.

Järviluoma, Helmi, Pirkko Moisala and Anni Vikko (2003), *Gender and Qualitative Methods*, London: Sage.

Kay, Jackie (1998), *Trumpet*, London: Picador.

Letherby, Gayle (2003), *Feminist Research in Theory and Practice*, Buckingham: Open University Press.

Mann, Chris and Fiona Stewart (2003), 'Internet interviewing', in J. Holstein and J. Gubrium (eds) (2003), *Inside Interviewing*, London: Sage, pp. 241–65.

Motion, Andrew (2004), 'Any of his smells', *The Guardian*, 17 July: 15.

Poland, Blake D. (2003), 'Transcription quality', in J. Holstein and J. Gubrium (eds) (2003), *Inside Interviewing*, London: Sage, pp. 267–88.

Rapley, Tim (2004), 'Interviews', in Clive Seale, Giampietro Gobo, Jaber F. Gubrium and David Silverman (eds), *Qualitative Research Practice*, London: Sage, pp. 15–33.

Ryan, Gery W. and H. Russell Bernard (2003), 'Data management and analysis Methods', in N. Denzin and Y. Lincoln (eds) (2003), *Collecting and Interpreting Qualitative Materials*, Thousand Oaks: Sage, pp. 259–309.

Schaeffer, Nora Cate and Douglas W. Maynard (2003), 'Standardization and interaction in the survey interview', in J. Holstein and J. Gubrium (eds) (2003), *Inside Interviewing*, London: Sage, pp. 215–39.

Seale, Clive (1998), 'Qualitative interviewing', in Clive Seale (ed.), *Researching Society and Culture*, London: Sage.

Seale, Clive F. (2003), 'Computer-assisted analysis of qualitative interview data', in J. Holstein and J. Gubrium (eds) (2003), *Inside Interviewing*, London: Sage, pp. 289–310.

Simmons, Rosemarie (2001), 'Questionnaires', in Nigel Gilbert (ed.), *Researching Social Life*, London: Sage, pp. 85–104.

Stephenson, Heidi and Natasha Langridge (1997), *Rage and Reason: Women Playwrights on Playwriting*, London: Methuen.

Stone, Allucquère Rosanne (1996), *The War of Desire and Technology at the Close of the Mechanical Age*, Cambridge, MA: MIT Press.

Turkel, Studs (1995), *Coming of Age: The Story of Our Century by Those Who've Lived It*, New York: New Press.

Williams, Sadie (2003), *Postgraduate Training in Research Methods: Current Practice and Future Needs in English*, London: English Subject Centre, Royal Holloway College.

CHAPTER 11

Creative Writing as a Research Method

Jon Cook, University of East Anglia

The idea of creativity or creative writing as a research method may seem a contradiction in terms. Long-held beliefs about the nature of creativity identify it as something that is outside or beyond methodical thought. Plato presented his philosopher, Socrates, as charmed by poets but sceptical about the latters' capacity to be governed by reason: 'a poet is a light and winged thing and holy, and never able to compose until he has become inspired, and is beside himself, and reason is no longer in him'.[1] Romanticism is often taken to reinforce these beliefs in its account of the poet as the exemplary creative individual. Wordsworth's Preface to *Lyrical Ballads* is the source of one influential idea about the psychological and emotional process that goes into the making of a poem: 'poetry is the spontaneous overflow of powerful feelings'.[2] Whatever else may go into the process of composition according to Wordsworth – recollection and contemplation amongst them – the emphasis given to spontaneity here might seem at odds with the systematic labour and careful preparation associated with method. Another famous Romantic statement, this time from Keats, reinforces the idea that creativity and method are at odds: 'If Poetry comes not as naturally as leaves upon a tree, it had better not come at all.'[3] Poems, according to this view, occur as if by natural necessity. The poet may be the medium through which this natural necessity works, but no amount of method will either help or hinder the process.

One way of summarising this durable and still active constellation of beliefs is to say that an important dimension of creativity lies in its engagement with unconscious processes. The creative writer has some special relation with these processes, however defined, and this relation is what makes the writer valuable. All this happens beyond or outside established canons of reason and, since the idea of a method is an integral part of the development and the display of reason, method is at best irrelevant and at worst threatening to creativity.

There is another and opposite assumption about creativity that makes it difficult to reconcile with the idea of a method. In this case, creativity is assumed to be a particularly intense or prolonged kind of labour. Creative work is something like a vocation or religious calling. The person engaged in it is set apart from others, utterly absorbed by the demands of a particular work, oblivious to everyday divisions of time between work and leisure, getting and spending. Yeats, in one stanza of his poem 'The Long Legged Fly', presents Michelangelo's work in the Sistine Chapel in Rome in just those terms. The artist's imagination is trance-like, a state of utter absorption:

> Like a long-legged fly upon the stream
> His mind moves upon silence[4]

Yeats presents the moment-by-moment actions of the painter – 'His hand moves to and fro' – and the mental state that accompanies them. Out of this state, according to Yeats, comes the work that shapes how we imagine ourselves. But it is hard to see how this version of artistic work can be reconciled with the idea of a method for at least two reasons. First, what happens in the moment of artistic creation cannot be generalised as a set of rules or procedures of the kind that we associate with the idea of a method. Secondly, a method implies an economy. It is a way of working that will achieve results in a given period of time. But this presentation of Michelangelo by Yeats suggests that he is oblivious to time in this sense. Another example would be the novelist, James Joyce, who took seven years to write *Ulysses*, and another twenty years to write *Finnegan's Wake*. If he were working in today's research environment, he would not win good marks for time management.

These assumptions about creativity's recalcitrance to method still gnaw away at some recent attempts to assimilate the fact that an increasing number of universities and colleges are awarding PhDs for creative work. The English Subject Centre's publication on postgraduate training in research methods identifies a skill-set of research methods in English.[5] These include 'higher order analytic, critical and literary skills', 'domain knowledge', 'bibliographical knowledge', and so on. Understandably, this reflects the assumption that a doctorate in English will be a work of criticism and scholarship. Creative writing, as the document goes on to acknowledge, does not fit. In a section on MA degrees and their function in providing research training the document states: 'Creative Writing was seen to be an exception and to be unlike other Master's degrees' (2003: 14). This is followed by a quotation from one of the respondents in the survey that provided the basis of the report:

> In Creative Writing, [the skills] are being able to workshop a piece of writing and learn from peer responses, being able to feed this back into

creative projects . . . The practice of production of original research means that research and analysis may be presented differently from other aspects of English.

The last sentence is tantalisingly vague: how, in practice, is the difference expressed? Unfortunately, nothing more is said. The purpose of the document at this point is simply to acknowledge an exception.

The stress that creative writing puts upon established definitions of research is evident in another text from the English Subject Centre, *Creative Writing: A Good Practice Guide*. Section 9 of the guide, 'Research and research training', acknowledges the expansion of doctoral-level work in creative writing and affirms its value as a form of research. But there are clearly problems of alignment: the different actors in the research process are not working with the same script. The Research Assessment Exercise allows for a form of research based upon 'the invention and generation of ideas, images, performances and artefacts including design, where these lead to new or substantially improved insights'.[6] But some universities chose not to return the work of lecturers in creative writing in the 2001 Research Assessment Exercise, perhaps because it was felt to be too risky, given, again, the tantalisingly vague nature of the definition of creative research. What would be examples of new or substantially improved insight? Nothing is said in response to the question, either in the RAE documentation or in the Subject Centre's guide.

When it comments on research training in creative writing, the guide draws heavily on another report, *Research Training in the Creative and Performing Arts and Design*, published in 2001 by the UK Council for Graduate Education. This report takes as its starting point the model of research proposed by the Arts and Humanities Research Board. Research questions need to be identified, a research context defined, and appropriate research methods specified. This model is juxtaposed with a statement about practice-based research, where practice is defined as 'the exercise of appropriate skills in the creation of an original work in the field or fields of creative and performing arts and design (e.g. drama, dance, music, fine arts, graphics, fiction, poetry, design).'[7]

The report is wisely reticent when it comes to the question of research methods in practice-based research. Acknowledging the plurality of the arts it addresses, the report's authors suggest that 'an eclectic approach could be valuable' and they reject 'any attempt to agree a generic "curriculum" of research methods which could be applied across the field' (2001: 18, 19).

The difficulty of assimilating practice-based research in the creative arts to established models of research in the humanities surfaces in the responses to a questionnaire that informed the writing of the report. Two contradictory claims interpret the same absence in different ways. One asserts that the 'distinctively creative nature of CPAD [Creative and Performing Arts and Design] research is often at odds with formal training programmes'. The other asserts that 'traditional methodologies are lacking in many CPAD disciplines' (2001: 25). The first claim celebrates what the second claim seems to lament. In both cases the traditional tension between an idea of creativity and an idea of method is evident. The Platonic image of the poet lives on, if only as a hesitant flicker of resistance to the requirements of research councils.

Given these difficulties, it is no surprise that the report identifies 'the need for a continuing evolution of research methods in the arts through national debate' (2001: 20). The need remains pressing. The argument that follows about the practice of writing as a research method is intended as a small contribution to this debate, as well as a guide to writers who may be about to start or have already started doctorates in creative and critical writing. The reports cited in this introduction make a valuable prelude to the debate about research methods in the creative arts without actually getting the argument started. They are attempts to reconcile the different demands of research councils, academics, writers and artists, and students engaged in doctoral-level work based in a creative practice. The movement between bullet-point decisiveness and acknowledgement of a plurality of methods and individual procedures indicates how difficult it is to address these varied and often conflicting constituencies.

WRITING AS DISCOVERY

How might the practice of writing be identified as a research method? The question seems to contain a paradox. Writing is usually regarded not as a research method, but as a means of presenting the results of research. The quality of writing can, of course, affect the quality of presentation, an issue reflected in the English Subject Centre's account of the skills needed for doctoral work. These include 'how to marshall an argument, how to think critically, how to write clearly and cogently'.[8] What this implies is that writing presents something – an argument, a line of critical thinking – the identity of which has been determined apart from the act of writing itself. The rhetorical order of the sentence itself suggests a progression from marshalling to thinking and then to writing. We might assume that something similar holds true for creative work. Imagination gets to work, a character in a novel comes to mind, then more than one character, or a story structure is mapped out, or a poetic image, and then the process of writing sets down what the imagination has conceived.

I suspect this conception of writing is more a product of rhetorical habit than serious intellectual conviction. It will be readily conceded that writing is integral and not just secondary to marshalling an argument, thinking critically, creating a character, a story, a scene or an image. But what, then, might it mean to think about writing in this way?

One answer to that question, and one way of giving substance to the notion of writing as a research method, depends upon the idea that writing is a means of discovery. This in turn assumes that the kinds of discovery made are connected to the development of technique. To conceive of writing as discovery or technique implies the necessity of rewriting, and it also calls for a practice of writing informed by extensive reading. If these conditions are met, then I think it is appropriate to call writing a research method.

The idea that writing is a form of discovery can be interpreted in a number of different ways. In his essay 'Feeling into Words', Seamus Heaney makes a distinction between craft and technique. Craft is what 'you can learn from other verse'.[9] In the case of poetry, it may have to do with learning certain meters and verse forms. Well crafted poetry can be an exhibition of technical virtuosity, but not, in Heaney's sense, of technique. Technique is a moment in the evolution of a work and, perhaps, of a writer:

> Learning the craft is learning to turn the windlass at the well of poetry. Usually you begin by dropping the bucket halfway down the shaft and winding up a taking of air. You are miming the real thing until one day the chain draws unexpectedly tight and you have dipped into waters that will continue to entice you back. You'll have broken the skin on the pool of yourself . . . (Heaney 1980: 47)

Heaney's metaphor for writing combines a sense of the familiar and routine with a moment that is strange and unexpected. Routines of writing can produce unexpected outcomes. They can move from the known to the unknown, a movement Heaney describes later in the same essay as 'a discovery of the ways to go out of [the writer's] normal cognitive bounds and raid the inarticulate' (1980: 47).

Heaney's argument is that craft is transformed into technique in a moment of discovery. What is discovered has at least two aspects, both conditioned by his belief that romantic conceptions of the writer still constitute a living tradition. Writing reaches back into experience and forward into form. Both constitute kinds of discovery. Poems begin with something given – in Heaney's formulation, 'the first stirring of the mind around a word or an image or a memory' – and end with something made. The two processes of discovery – of a hitherto undisclosed dimension of experience in one case, and of the adaptation or invention of a form in the other – are connected to self-realisation. Craft, according to Heaney, can be 'deployed without reference to the feelings or the self' (1980: 47), but technique cannot. The discoveries initiated by technique can be summarised in a metaphor that often finds its way into discussions of writing, that of 'finding a voice'. What is meant by voice here is at once individual – a voice different from other voices because what can be heard in it is, in Heaney's words, 'your essential patterns of perception' – and comprehensible, saying something that is worth listening to because timely and needed (1980: 47). Voice is discovered in the encounter between literary tradition and non-literary speech. 'Finding a voice' in this sense is not a once-and-for-all matter. If it is the goal of what technique can discover, voice itself has to be reinvented under the pressures of changing individual and collective experience.

Heaney derives his account of writing as discovery from reflecting on his own development as a writer. Writing nearly thirty years before Heaney, the American critic Mark Schorer gave a different inflection to the relation between writing, technique and discovery. His essay 'Technique as Discovery' is concerned with the development of a critical concept, one that will distinguish between novelists who regard technique as a means of presenting subject matter and those, the writers Schorer approves of, whose technique discovers their subject. A novel's technique is something more than the application of a set of literary skills – the manipulation of point of view, the ordering of events in a story, the invention of dialogue and character – that can be learnt and applied to a given subject. Instead, technique in fiction is 'a deep and primary operation'.[10] It is, according to Schorer, the only means the writer has 'of discovering, exploring, developing his subject, of conveying its meaning, and, finally, of evaluating it' (Schorer 1972: 387).

Schorer's essay is an attempt to find a critical vocabulary that will be adequate to the technical innovations of modernist fiction. His exemplary novelists are writers such as Joyce, Conrad and James. One value of Schorer's essay is that it can be translated from its initial context and purpose, and used to build a concept of writing as a research method. Like Heaney, Schorer wants to make a division between two ideas of technique, one that corresponds to but is not expressed by Heaney's distinction between craft and technique. The limited conception of technique gives priority to content over form. It insists that the value of a novel lies in the relevance or scope of its subject matter. The manner of its presentation is secondary. For Schorer this distinction cannot be drawn in either the serious practice or the serious criticism of the novel. Subject matter is discovered through technique. The initial ideas or promptings for a novel are transformed into subject matter by the application of technique.

Schorer does not make clear whether his idea of technique can be thought of as something that takes place in the mind of the writer, independent of the practice of writing. But the implication of his essay is that technique is inseparable from the act of writing. At one point in the essay he argues that the 'resources of language' are part of the 'technique of fiction'; language, that is, is thought of as something to be worked on, even worked over: 'language, the counters of an ordinary speech, as forced, through conscious manipulation, into all those larger meanings which our ordinary speech almost never intends' (1972: 387–8). Writing as technique discovers these 'larger meanings' in language, bringing the force of an artistic will to bear on a kind of speech that is ignorant of its own possibilities. Schorer is attracted to the idea that the properly creative writer, one capable of using technique as a mode of discovery, is a 'manipulator'. In the art of fiction, language is not the only resource subject to manipulation. Point of view is, according to Schorer, another crucial technique; like language, it can be deployed in ways that discover significance in a subject or it can be deployed as an inert device.

The criteria that might distinguish between these different uses can seem elusive. Schorer argues that 'discovering' technique does two connected things to the subject of the novel: one is objectification, and the other, by way of objectification, is evaluation. Objectification identifies a process in respect of the writer, a disentangling of unconscious emotional attachments and fantasies invested in the subject matter of the novel. The consequence of this disentangling is the achievement of an objectivity appropriate to literary art. For Schorer, the creation of significant literary fiction is an ethical act, and the objectivity he has in mind is an ethical objectivity. But, as the examples he uses make clear, ethical objectivity does not mean the affirmation of one set of values over another. Technique as discovery is both process and *procès*, a testing of the limits of particular perspectives and values, and, on the part of the writer, a repeated questioning of the significance of a given subject.

Schorer writes out of strong convictions about the importance of the novel as a modern literary form. The value of a technique is related to what it can discover about a particular cultural epoch:

> The technique of modern fiction, at once greedy and fastidious,
> achieves as its subject matter not some singleness, some topic or thesis,
> but the whole of modern consciousness. It discovers the complexity of
> the modern spirit, the difficulty of personal morality and the facts of
> evil – all the intractable elements under the surface which a technique
> of the surface alone cannot approach. (1972: 399–400)

These sound lofty and quite possibly vacuous ambitions for a writer, especially in the face of understandable scepticism about a totality such as 'the whole of modern consciousness'. But the value of Schorer's analysis of technique as discovery does not depend upon acceptance of these ambitious claims. The relevance of these sentences comes from their verbs. Technique 'achieves' its subject matter; it 'discovers' complexity. The novel is not described as representation or expression; its techniques are not in the service of mimetic credibility or the

requirements of genre. The techniques that Schorer describes are not manifestations of underlying structured rules or effects of language. Technique, in
Schorer's sense, is emphatically the *work* of the writer, not a set of rules to be
applied but a potential to be developed.

What writers do when they write is differently described by Heaney and
Schorer. Heaney writes as a poet who believes in the credibility of lyric voice.
Schorer writes as a critic of the novel. Both have their versions of technique in
writing as a form of discovery. In Heaney's case, the discovery is of hidden
depths and a form adequate to them. In Schorer's case, it is the potential of a
subject once it is explored by technique. Both assume that writing that is
strongly creative will bring what is experienced as outside or beyond language
into language. In Heaney's formulation, technique enables the poet to 'raid the
inarticulate'.

These formulations raise questions about purpose and purposiveness that
are themselves connected to the idea of a method. To have a method implies
that you know what you are about, that your work will not be undermined by
accident, digression or irrelevance. To possess a method assumes a kind of reassurance about the future, even an insurance against it. Method promises results
and it promises them in good time. The seventeenth-century philosopher
Descartes is often taken as an exemplar of methodical analysis. In his
Meditations he formulated a research method – 'doubt everything' – and a
research goal – the discovery of absolute certainty. The opening page of the
Meditations bristles with purpose and preparation. Descartes' conclusion about
the one thing he can be certain of – 'I think therefore I am' – has become a cel-
ebrated philosophical slogan, something that can be solemnly questioned or
affectionately parodied. But Descartes' example is instructive in another way.
His selection of a method allows him to embark confidently, but it is not long
before he finds himself in trouble: 'It feels as if I have unexpectedly fallen into
a deep whirlpool which tumbles me around so that I can neither stand at the
bottom nor swim at the top'.[11]

The narrative of the *Meditations* becomes an allegory of method. It exhibits
a tension within the idea of a method itself between its imperative and its
exploratory character. A method implies a set of rules or procedures, a dicta-
tion to thought or imagination as to how either is to proceed. But it also implies
an exploration to be undertaken, something that may produce or discover what
is unexpected. A method may prove itself insufficient in the face of what it
discovers.

My argument so far about writing as a research method may seem to be
exclusively about method's exploratory character. The imperative requirement of method – 'do this and this will result' – seems to be only weakly met.
I want to exacerbate this problem by considering a third example of writing as
discovery, from Denise Riley's book *The Words of Selves*. Riley is both a poet

and a theorist, and *The Words of Selves* combines a version of the autobiographical questioning of practice that characterises Heaney's 'Feeling into Words' and a version of the analytic stance found in Schorer's 'Technique as Discovery'.[12] But the tone of her argument and its direction are radically different from both. She questions the idea that creative writing leads to the discovery of voice, and offers only qualified support for an idea of technique as manipulation.

Riley's reconstruction of the process of writing does not begin with an experience that awaits articulation. Language is there from the start, a kind of din in the head, coming not from within the self but outside it. Voices coming from the outside make the attempt to 'find a voice' into a quixotic search:

> Poetry in its composing is an inrush of others' voices, and in this respect it is no more than a licensed intensification of the very same property in prose. So, 'finding one's own voice' must always be a frustrated search, fishing around in a strange fry-up, or a *bouillabaise* in which half-forgotten spiky or slimy things bubble up to the surface. Words crowd in uninvited, regardless of sense, flocking not through the brain but through the ear . . . (Riley 2000: 65–6)

Creativity – a term that Riley dislikes – is vested in the workings of language, not in the originating self of the writer. Language endlessly interferes with itself: the same sound produces words and sentences with very different meanings; a phrase takes on an unexpected meaning because it contains an unrecognised quotation; voice is made up from the echo of other voices.

Riley is as much interested in the writer's passivity as her activity. The idea that creative writing emerges in masterful technique is displaced by a different idea, the writer who listens to language. Heidegger's account of the poet provides one precedent here:

> But the responding in which a man authentically listens to the appeal of language is that which speaks in the element of poetry. The more poetic a poet is – the freer (that is, the more open and ready for the unforeseen) his saying – the greater is the purity with which he submits what he says to an ever more painstaking listening . . .[13]

The elevated obscurity of this may seem to disqualify it from any further consideration. What might it mean to listen to language, as distinct from some specific voice in language? How might language make an appeal? To make language appear in this way Heidegger bestows upon it a god-like identity.

Heidegger's attention to poetic listening can be better understood by noting the immediate context of this quotation. Heidegger contrasts the 'listening' that speaks 'in the element of poetry' with an attitude to language that he takes as characteristic of modernity:

> Meanwhile, there rages around the earth an unbridled yet clever talking and writing and broadcasting of spoken words. Man acts as though he were the shaper and master of language, while in fact language remains the master of man. When this relation of dominance gets inverted, man hits upon strange manoeuvres. Language becomes the means of expression . . . (quoted in Cook 2004: 255)

This is Heidegger on a grand sweep, moving from an illusion of modernity – that language is an instrument to be manipulated – to some of that illusion's technological and social manifestations: language as a display of personality, as media update, and, tellingly for this argument, as 'expression', the manifestation of subjective depths.

Riley invokes Heidegger's precedent to indicate a tradition that informs her own thinking about the passivity of the writer. His utterances hover in her argument not as a truth to be endorsed but a speculation to be considered. Her own view of the process of composition is more ironic and comic than Heidegger's, but what he has to say points to a utopian possibility, that the agency of language in poetic listening is neither repressive nor coercive. The call of language in poetry is not a manifestation of ideological force. It works outside the familiar power of language to use words like brands that attempt to put people in place and keep them there: 'you're a Muslim', 'you're a white middle-aged male', and so on.

These arguments about the agency of language in writing may seem to draw to themselves some of the hallowed slogans of theory: 'the death of the author', 'the free play of the signifier', 'the materiality of language'. One value of Riley's argument is that it is prepared to take these slogans seriously and, at the same time, develop an account of the poet's practice that they may seem to preclude. What writing discovers in this tension between the work of language and the work of the writer is an irony: that 'I have written both above and beneath what "I really meant"' (Riley 2000: 68).

The dialectic between 'what I have written' and 'what I really meant' is not straightforward. What emerges in a completed piece of writing does not simply subvert an originating intention to mean something. There is, of course, a perpetual comedy of language that works according to this subversion. It forms the basis for the satire on media-speak in magazines like *Private Eye*. From commentary on the recent Olympic Games, we get 'And Kelly is not one for hiding her heart on her sleeve', or 'She has been a child prodigy since she was a youngster'. The eagerness to say something striking about the moment in the moment produces an effect opposite to the one intended. The cliché suddenly goes wrong or language starts to spin out tautologies. Riley does not keep these comic turns out of her account of writing:

> Writing, you can feel like a blindfolded sculptor slapped around the head by damp lumps of clay which you must try to seize and throw back at the haphazardly forming art object before it stiffens itself into some shape you never quite intended. (2000: 67)

The process may be open to chance. Language may be doing work that is falsely attributed to the writer's intention or creative power. But something does take shape nonetheless and it can be called an 'art object'. This directs us to what may seem a banal conclusion: what is discovered in the process of composition is a form of language, something with its own distinctive shape and presence. But the banality seems less stark if this process of discovering form is connected to a critical and philosophical reflection. Creative writing becomes a mode of research into the nature of literary form and language, testing itself against different traditions of thought. These traditions can be only briefly indicated here but they might include Platonic conceptions, including the recent renewal of interest in beauty as a manifestation of creative power; or Aristotelian thinking about form as an emergent property of matter; or the deconstructive critique sensitive to the discrepancies between form and meaning; or the formalist attention to the question of what it is that makes a verbal message into a work of art. The list could be readily extended. Its purpose is to indicate what a research context might look like for the practice of writing under discussion in this chapter.

The 'haphazardly forming art object' is not the only thing that emerges in the process of composition. Something else occurs as well: Riley describes it as 'a retrospective knowledge' (2000: 67). At first sight this may seem to be a manifestation in writing of a common experience. It is only after we have said something that we discover what we mean. But the continuum between writing and speaking here does need qualification. The relation between intention and utterance in the composition of a literary work is not identical with everyday conversation. One influential account of the logic of conversation by the philosopher H. P. Grice argues that discovering the meaning of what someone is saying depends upon understanding their intention in saying it.[14] This does not assume a ponderous process of formulating an intention and then finding the appropriate words to convey it. The moment that intervenes between intention and utterance may be minute: 'not this one, but that one', 'is this where I register', 'I hate you'. In these and an infinite number of other cases, Grice's argument is that understanding utterances entails an understanding of the intentions that shape them. There is no coded relation between speech and intention here. 'Pass the salt' may be a way of intending to say that I have power over you rather than a simple request. The process can be a hazardous and error-prone, but its temporality implies a world in which people intend to say things and then say them.

It is not that all kinds of writing turn this model of intention into an irrelevance. But the kind under discussion here does throw it into considerable doubt. Riley's poet, 'like a blindfolded sculptor', is engaged in a hazardous dialectic with her material: language throws something at the writer and the writer throws it back. The exchange may prove fruitless, but it does not always prove fruitless. Part of the value of the process for Riley is that it is not subservient to the initial intentions of the writer.

Thinking about the question of whether the novel is a form of communication, the novelist and critic David Lodge has given a similar account of the place of intention in the practice of writing:

> [A] difficulty with the idea of the novel as an intentional act of communication is that until the writer has completed it he doesn't know what it is that he is communicating, and perhaps doesn't know even then. You discover what you have to say in the process of saying it . . . What you have written already, and what you plan to write in the future are always open to revision . . . The future of a novel in the process of composition is always vague, provisional, unpredictable – if it were not so, the labour of writing it would be too tedious to bear.[15]

Lodge holds to the idea that the novel is a kind of communication. The novelist writes with an imaginary reader in mind. This requires a way 'of projecting the effect of what you write upon an imagined reader'. But projecting an effect is not the same thing as knowing exactly what you want to write in advance of writing it. What is telling in Lodge's account is that knowledge of this kind would make the process of composition unbearable.

REWRITING

The relation of writing to rewriting has been implicit in much of the argument of this chapter. The importance of rewriting in the research process of creative writing needs to be distinguished from two assumptions that help but do not fully define what is at issue. The first of these draws upon an idea about professional practice. The majority of professional literary writers regard rewriting as a necessity of their profession. If PhDs in creative and critical writing are to work to a professional standard, it follows that writers working towards this degree should be required to rewrite not just once but many times. The second assumption derives from doctoral work more generally in the arts and humanities. The completion of a thesis requires more than one draft. This process works in accord with the skill-set of research methods in English cited earlier. Putting a thesis through more than one draft is a way of ensuring that it displays the skills of writing 'clearly and cogently'.

Neither of these assumptions is simply irrelevant to the idea of rewriting that I want to sketch here, although it is not hard to imagine a context in which to praise a novel or poem for its clarity and cogency might seem strange. What both assumptions miss is the fact that in creative writing the first draft is itself material for further research. What is to count as a first draft may vary. With works of fiction it may be a novel written through from beginning to end, or some chapters, or a few pages; in poetry it may be a few lines on a page, the first stirrings of a subject, or something that seems complete. In every case the first draft calls for a further questioning of the adequacy of language and form to what is waiting to be written.

The first draft raises a 'research question' for the writer. The question may not be explicitly formulated or it may be very precise and technical. Heaney's account of composition in 'Feeling into Words' distinguishes clearly between a first and second stage in the making of a poem, and we may think of this as corresponding to different stages in the process of drafting. Heaney cites Robert Frost's account of the genesis of a poem: 'a poem begins as a lump in the throat, a homesickness, a lovesickness. It finds the thought and the thought finds the words'.[16] The transition here is from the preverbal to the verbal, from a feeling to something – a 'thought' recognised by the mind – and then to its utterance.

How writing and rewriting maps on to this process shows how difficult it is to draw a clear boundary between what is not words and what is. Heaney's version of technique, discussed earlier in this chapter, comes into play when the 'lump in the throat' finds 'the thought', and thus before the thought finds the words. Yet technique arises for Heaney in the process of writing itself and writing is made with words. This draws towards a paradox: there is a moment in writing when words in one condition come before words in another. The process of rewriting in this view takes them from one condition to another, from the written word as, relatively, mute and inchoate, to the written language as, relatively, articulate and accessible. Heaney describes this form of rewriting or revision as 'making'. The verb has a particular resonance. Heaney invokes the traditional idea of the poet as a 'maker', someone skilled in the craft traditions of verse making. For Heaney 'making' comes after the earlier work of technique and implies a revisionary act. As a description of rewriting, it suggests that rewriting is concerned with a heightening of rhetorical effects, an attention to shaping a form rather than to discovering a meaning.

The old distinction between form and content hovers temptingly around the discussion. The first draft establishes the content, the second the form. The distinction is helpful in that it brings out the central role that *research into form* plays in a PhD in creative and critical writing. It is less helpful in that it makes an oscillation of attention between what is written and how it is written into a simple chronological sequence. Schorer's argument about technique as discovery suggests that the novelist's work moves back and forth between the exploration of a subject and the discovery of techniques that will bring out its complexity. 'Technique as discovery' implies the discovery of techniques. Writing fiction is inherently experimental, and this conception of writing requires rewriting. Each draft will produce a set of discoveries with implications that need to be tested, rejected or refined in a subsequent draft.

Denise Riley's exemplary poet is similarly committed to rewriting. The writer is 'constituted by habitual self-checking', something akin to the situation of David Lodge's novelist where '[what] you have written already and what you plan to write in the future are always open to revision'.[17] A curious temporality is at work. It is not just what is written that can be revised but what might be written in the future. In her discussion of the deceptive character of the lyric 'I', Riley's account of writing as rewriting points towards retrospective discovery:

> Yet the lyric 'I' also advertises its simulacrum of control under the guise
> of form. It's a profound artifice, and the writer and reader both know it.
> There's a semblance of craft here, but craft of a strange sort since it can
> only be exercised retrospectively. Held by form, I work backwards,
> chipping away at words, until maybe something gets uncovered which I
> can acknowledge as what I might have to say. (Riley 2000: 66)

The writer 'chipping away at words' implies a recurrent metaphor for rewriting, that it is akin to sculpting the words, discovering the shape in the stone.

READING

If rewriting is intrinsic to the practice of writing outlined in this chapter, so are particular kinds of reading. The thought that a course of reading is necessary to a writer's attainment is not new. T. S. Eliot provided some demanding protocols of study in his essay, 'Tradition and the Individual Talent', first published in 1919:

> [Tradition] cannot be inherited, and if you want it you must obtain it by
> great labour. It involves, in the first place, the historical sense, which we
> may call nearly indispensable to anyone who would continue to be a
> poet beyond his 25th year; and the historical sense involves not only a
> perception of the pastness of the past, but of its presence . . .[18]

It is worth dislodging Eliot from his customary place – white, male, elitist – in order to hear the continuing relevance of what he has to say. Although 'Tradition and the Individual Talent' became a touchstone for a generation of critics, it is an essay about the education of poets. We do not have to agree with the content of Eliot's tradition – 'the whole of the literature of Europe' – nor subscribe to his weary tone to see the importance of his claim about the historical sense. Reading informs writing by providing a version of historical sense. And this sense is dialectical, working through a perception both of the 'pastness of the past' and of 'its presence'. It is this that gives Eliot's account of tradition its distinctive tension, caught between the desire for ordered inheritance and the understanding that tradition is inherently unstable, endlessly transformed by new work.

Reading provides writing with historical sense – that, at least, is the basic slogan advanced here. Exactly how that happens in the research process for a PhD in creative and critical writing will, of course, vary. It may call for an intent reading of particular authors, as Keats read Spenser, Milton and Shakespeare to build his own poetic style. It may be a matter of encountering what Harold Bloom has famously described as the 'anxiety of influence': the sense that writing in the present is overshadowed by powerful voices that need to be deflected or transformed.[19] The course of reading may not concern itself directly with individual authors, but engage in a study of narrative codes, poetic convention, or speech styles. The development of an 'historical sense' does not require a reverential attitude to writing drawn from the past. It can be mined for ideas about character, convention or trope; it can be quoted, echoed, or parodied. In creative writing legitimate theft is legitimate inheritance.

Each writer discovers the tradition specific to a work in the process of writing it. The kind of reading required need not be exclusively literary. It can, in a widely accepted sense of the term, be archival. The American poet Charles Olson invented bibliographies for writers who came under his tuition that included works of history, geography, anthropology and collections of sermons. Pat Barker's *Regeneration Trilogy* ends with an author's note giving information on some of the historical characters who inhabited her fiction about the First World War, and a short bibliography of further reading about them. Her note gives a hint of the range of research that can go into the writing of fiction.[20] The novelist or poet can work in ways that coincide with those of the historian. This research can contribute to the accuracy necessary for a convincing historical fiction. But it serves another purpose as well: not just the requirements of historical accuracy but the invention of a language and a literary form.

The sketch of a method presented in this chapter has a bearing on another and often vexed question about the requirements of a PhD in creative and critical writing. Any creative work submitted must be accompanied by a critical commentary. This can often produce consternation and anxiety. Creative writers feel they must submit their work to the alien discourse of theory. Criticism is construed as a kind of signing-up to a particular method or theoretical school. The need for inverted commas becomes pressing here. Many 'creative' writers have also worked quite happily as 'critics'. There are numerous examples of writers commenting on the nature of writing. Some work of this kind has informed my account of 'writing as discovery'. The work of those labelled as 'critics' can be equally helpful. Resources are not lacking. Nor are the terms of a debate that can be articulated in the critical commentary that accompanies a work of creative writing. These can include arguments about the writer's agency in the process of composition, the role of intention, the nature of tradition, and the nature of craft and technique. What is discovered in the process of creative writing will become evident in the work itself. But there is nothing sacred about this. Discoveries can be documented and analysed by way of critical commentary, but analysis need not have the last word. The excitement in this research field arises when the findings of practice challenge the authority of critical concepts.

NOTES

1. E. Hamilton and H. Cairns (eds) (1961), *The Collected Dialogues of Plato*, New Jersey: Princeton University Press, p. 220.
2. W. Wordsworth and S. T. Coleridge (1963), *Lyrical Ballads*, ed. R. L. Brett and A. R. Jones, London: Methuen, p. 260.
3. John Keats (1958), *The Letters of John Keats*, 2 vols, ed. H. E. Rollins, London: Cambridge University Press, vol. 1, pp. 238–9.
4. W. B. Yeats (1965), 'The Long Legged Fly', in *Collected Poems*, London: Macmillan, p. 381.
5. S. Williams (2003), *Postgraduate Training in Research Methods: Current Practice and Future Needs in English*, London: English Subject Centre, Royal Holloway College.
6. S. Holland et al. (2003), *Creative Writing: A Good Practice Guide, Report Series No 6*, London: English Subject Centre, Royal Holloway College, p. 9.
7. UK Council for Graduate Education (2001), *Research Training in the Creative and Performing Arts and Design*, London: UK Council for Graduate Education, p. 10.
8. Williams, *Postgraduate Training in Research Methods*, p. 10.
9. Seamus Heaney (1980), 'Feeling into words', in *Preoccupations: Selected Prose*, London: Faber and Faber, p. 47.
10. Mark Schorer (1972), 'Technique as discovery', in D. Lodge (ed.), *Twentieth Century Literary Criticism: A Reader*, London: Longman, p. 391.
11. R. Descartes (1986), *Meditations on First Philosophy*, ed. and trans. J. Cottingham, Cambridge: Cambridge University Press, p. 16.
12. Denise Riley (2000), *The Words of Selves: Identification, Solidarity, Irony*, Stanford: Stanford University Press.
13. M. Heidegger (2004), 'Poetically man dwells', in J. Cook (ed.), *Poetry in Theory*, Oxford: Blackwell, p. 255.

14. H. P. Grice (1975), 'Logic and conversation', in P. Cole and P. Morgan (eds), *Syntax and Semantics 3: Speech Acts*, New York and London: Academic Press.
15. David Lodge (1996), 'The novel as communication', in *The Practice of Writing*, London: Secker and Warburg.
16. Heaney, 'Feeling into words', p. 49.
17. Riley, *The Words of Selves*, p. 71; Lodge, 'The novel as communication', p. 195.
18. T. S. Eliot (2004), 'Tradition and the individual talent', in J. Cook (ed.), *Poetry in Theory*, Oxford: Blackwell.
19. H. Bloom (1973), *The Anxiety of Influence*, New York: Oxford University Press.
20. Pat Barker (1996), *The Regeneration Trilogy*, London: Viking, pp. 591–2.

CHAPTER 12

ICT as a Research Method

Harold Short and Marilyn Deegan, King's College London

INTRODUCTION

The research practices of scholars in the humanities have been greatly changed over the past twenty years by the widespread adoption of information and communication technology (ICT). New practices now possible include different modes of communication and collaboration, use of the internet for information seeking and dissemination, use of computational text mining and analysis techniques, the ability to present and interrogate primary source materials, use of large-scale reference materials such as dictionaries and encyclopaedias, complex textual editing, the use of hypertext in literary theory, use of visual imaging and image enhancement, the use of databases and structured modelling techniques. Sometimes the use of ICT is ancillary to the main purpose of the work, with the resultant work itself being little different from how it might have been without ICT; sometimes it is transformative and results in new resources, new structures and new knowledge. We have come to refer to the second of these uses of ICT as 'digital scholarship'.

The academic study of English is an extensive area, and all aspects of literary, linguistic and historical methods can be enhanced by the use of advanced ICT research approaches. This chapter presents a brief overview of the diverse uses of ICT in the study of English. It is not possible to cover any topic in depth here, and so the reader is referred to further sources for more extensive coverage.

AN INTRODUCTION TO TEXTUAL COMPUTING

The development of the stored program computer (originally conceived of by Charles Babbage as the analytic engine in the nineteenth century) was a consequence of the code-breaking machines developed in the Second World War. Its first use was for large-scale number crunching, but its value in processing large volumes of text was perceived early. Father Roberto Busa, a Thomas Aquinas scholar, was one of the first humanists to produce electronic text in the late 1940s, laboriously entering texts on punched cards and constructing huge lexical and morphological databases. The use, and more importantly the re-use, of electronic texts has grown exponentially since then. Early textual computing was largely mechanistic and concerned more with scientific analysis than with imaginative reading; linguistic applications reliant upon the analysis of large quantities of data were the most popular. Stylostatistics, which offers analyses of textual corpora for authorship attribution or dating was, and still is, a common technique, but one which was not taken up by mainstream textual scholars or literary critics. Easier forms of input via keyboard, and better screens, first of all encouraged widespread use of word processing, and then the use of email. Now textual scholars use ICT in many different ways. The availability of more user-friendly technologies and their broad uptake encouraged textual scholars to begin speculating upon the nature of text and textuality in the new fluid media, and allowed discussions on these matters across space and time on electronic discussion lists. The development of cybernetic hypertexts and multimedia has excited attention from a broader range of scholars, both for their abilities to map complex textual spaces and integrate non-textual materials, and for the theoretical illuminations possible when conceptualising textual theories. This includes the ability to present intricate textual traditions in new forms of editions, delivered on CD-ROM or, increasingly, on the world wide web.

Important, too, in any discussion of the use of new technologies for research in English studies is the recent increase in technical capacities of processing power and bandwidth that mean that text expressed symbolically can be analysed and transmitted. High-quality images of texts and manuscripts can be captured and shared. Increasingly we can access and produce sound and video online. These developments are driven primarily by other concerns than the scholarly, deriving in large part from the entertainment industry. Advancements in technical capabilities allow greater and more flexible access to our source materials, but certain problems ensue from the ownership by large and powerful corporations of both the technologies and the source materials.[1]

What is interesting for scholars of English in the extension of computational methods into the realms of visual- and time-based media is that this happens at a time of concomitant developments in English which study a whole range of media alongside the textual, and which set store by the actual materiality of a text as well as its underlying meaning. So studies of the physicality of textual witnesses are desirable adjuncts to scholarship, and are made much easier by the use of digital technologies. Studies of other visual manifestations of the oeuvres of writers are also easier in the digital world (for instance, the use of Blake's paintings alongside his poetry in the Blake Archive, discussed later). Film and audio, important in the current study of English, can be expressed digitally with increasing ease, and integrated with other media, as well as annotated and linked to other sources.

PRIMARY SOURCE STUDIES

Most scholars and students of English are likely to be consumers rather than producers of digital primary source materials, but an understanding of some of the key issues in digital production is useful. Digital capture of manuscript and early printed materials has some significant benefits for the scholar. Digital facsimiles of astonishing fidelity are now being produced, such as the 'Turning the pages' resources at the British Library, including the Lindisfarne Gospels and the Sherborne Missal.[2] This means that access to fragile or rare originals can be restricted, ensuring their preservation for the long term. It is also possible to carry out enhancement of digital images of originals, making lost readings visible again. The Electronic Beowulf project is a good example of this, recovering readings through the use of digital imaging techniques developed by the space industry and medical science. This project, a collaboration between the British Library and the University of Kentucky, has used advanced imaging techniques for the recovery of letters and fragments obscured by clumsy repair techniques, and has demonstrated the use of computer imaging to restore 'virtually' the hidden letters to their place in the manuscript.[3] Another benefit of the digitisation of primary source materials is that they become amenable to a kind of cross-interrogation that was not formerly possible. Early English Books Online (EEBO), for example, offers access to page images of around 100,000 books printed in English between 1475 and 1800, together with bibliographic information, and the EEBO Text Creation Partnership (TCP) is creating searchable full text of around 25,000 of these.[4] The study of English writings of this period could be transformed by access to such a resource. Primary source materials can be provided by libraries in digital form as straightforward surrogates for their analogue originals, or they can be integrated as part of electronic textual editions, which are dealt with in more detail below.

Many libraries, archives, galleries and museums worldwide have embarked on significant digitisation programmes of primary source materials, and this has resulted in a large amount of high quality content becoming available for scholarly use. Indeed, one of the concepts that is now discussed is that of the 'global digital library': content from many different sources that is created according to the best standards (see below) so that it can be accessed 'virtually' from anywhere and interchanged, shared and incorporated into different systems. The data is said to be 'interoperable' when it adheres to these standards and can be manipulated using common tools. Interoperability is the *sine qua non* of the digital scholarship of the future.

While the availability of a critical mass of high-quality content at the touch of a button is a huge leap forward, the usefulness of this content is somewhat constrained by the limited availability of sophisticated tools for its exploitation. However, projects led by the Graduate School of Library and Information Science at the University of Illinois at Urbana-Champaign[5] and by the Centre for Computing in the Humanities (CCH), King's College London,[6] are beginning to develop tools for the analysis, manipulation and presentation of digital content. The CCH project is developing tools for the addition and organisation of complex annotations to textual and image content, and for the extraction of keywords from full-text content, as well as for sophisticated textual analysis. The LEADERS project (Linking EAD to Electronically Retrievable Sources), a collaboration between the School of Library, Archive and Information Studies (SLAIS) at University College, London and the National Archives is also creating tools for the exploitation of digital content. It is doing so by developing a generic computer-based toolset that will enable the creation of an online environment which integrates finding aids encoded in Encoded Archival Description (EAD) format with Text Encoding Initiative-encoded transcripts and digitised images of archival material in order to enhance remote user access to archives.[7]

TEXTUAL ANALYSIS

Given the computer's original function as a manipulator of symbols, its use in the analysis of text is a natural one. Although many critics question an approach to textual analysis that is mathematical or statistical, many such valuable studies have been carried out on English texts, on authors and works from all periods and genres. When embarking upon this kind of textual analysis, it is vital to be clear about the kinds of questions that can be asked of the texts, and to understand how (or, indeed, whether) the computer can assist in this. Text analysis tools can be relatively sophisticated, and the statistical models that can be applied to the output are complex; this is outside the scope of the brief overview offered here. If scholars wish to engage in advanced text analysis, training in the analytical techniques and statistics is needed. However, it is possible to carry out useful analyses without an in-depth knowledge of statistics, and with the use of relatively simple tools. Given the widespread availability of text in electronic form, some knowledge of computerised text analysis is useful for the English scholar.

Computers can help scholars search through large bodies of text very fast. Especially if that text has been indexed by a text analysis program, they can look for complex patterns of words, and they can present results of complex searches in contextualised or graphic formats that make understanding the results relatively straightforward. An early use of computerised text analysis was the production of concordances. The concordance itself is not a new tool. There have been great nineteenth-century concordances of the Bible, Shakespeare's and other writers' work. But having the ability to produce a customised concordance on the desktop in minutes, and then analyse the results, gives powerful new tools to the critic.

One area of textual analysis that is of great interest to the literary scholar is that of stylostatistics. It began in the 1960s with the work of researchers such as Frederick Mosteller and David Wallace who solved the knotty problem of who had written some of the Federalist Papers. It was not taken up more widely because of the difficulties of capturing the volumes of electronic text needed, and the difficulties of learning the statistical techniques. In the 1980s these methods were taken up by scholars such as John Burrows with his seminal work on Jane Austen's style, and many studies have now appeared on Shakespeare and other Renaissance authors, on modern poetry, and on the *Wizard of Oz*, among many other texts and types of text.[8]

Ebooks and Electronic Text

The world is now awash with electronic text but most of it is not suitable for text analysis without some explicit work in adding mark-up and encoding that makes it structurally and intellectually amenable to computational manipulation. Mark-up and encoding (see also Chapter 6 in this volume) are dealt with in the next section of this chapter: here, we deal with sources of already available and marked-up text, as well as the preparation of text from printed originals. But first we discuss the curious rise and partial fall of ebooks. Ebooks have been an interesting development in the history of electronic text for, as originally designed, the ebook was first produced and marketed as a kind of electronic text that could only be read on a dedicated ebook reader, controlled by publishers and libraries to prevent unchecked proliferation of singly purchased copies. The dedicated readers were relatively expensive, and it is probably the success of palm computers, sub-notebook computers and tablet PCs with their more interchangable formats that have driven them off the market. Ebooks *have* been successful (though after some commercial difficulties) in the large-scale production of ebook libraries such as Questia, which describes itself as the world's largest online library,[9] and netlibrary, which describes itself as the world's leading provider of ebooks.[10] Both these extravagant claims are actually borne out by volume: Questia provides fully-searchable access to over

49,500 books and 392,000 journal, magazine, and newspaper articles, and netli-brary has more than 70,000 complete titles currently available in ebook form. These can be enormously useful research resources, and contain much primary and secondary material for the English scholar.

Ebooks have been developed to give searchable and flexible access to large volumes of texts for reading and research, aimed at the educational market.[11] The texts, however, are not really amenable to detailed manipulation by text analysis programs outside their 'reading' contexts. But there are sources of elec-tronic text that *are* amenable to such manipulation, and the good news is that many of them are free. The UK's Arts and Humanities Data Service (AHDS) Centre for Literature, Languages and Linguistics[12] makes good-quality elec-tronic text available for downloading (subject to certain legal restrictions) and currently has some 2,000 resources in a number of different languages.[13] The Electronic Text Center at the University of Virginia also provides electronic texts freely for scholarly purposes, and currently claims to have tens of thousands of texts available.[14] The Humanities Text Initiative, University of Michigan, has offered online access to full text resources since 1994, and it too has many thou-sands of texts available, many free both within and outside the university.[15] However, a word of caution is warranted in relation to all online materials: the texts that are included may have been selected mainly because they were out of copyright rather than because they were judged to be the 'best' texts.

It is often the case that the scholar or student of English pursuing a research topic may not find what they need among existing resources, and so will need to create, or have created on their behalf, the texts they wish to analyse. This can be a straightforward process, but is likely to be time-consuming and even costly, especially if large volumes of text are needed or if the texts are compro-mised, complex, or difficult to read in some way. Small volumes of text can be keyed into the computer by the scholar. Large volumes may require some kind of intelligent computer manipulation (Optical Character Recognition or OCR), or re-keying by third-party companies, expert in text capture. OCR works well on good, clean, modern text, and less well on older or damaged text. The output from OCR usually has to be corrected in some detail and if there are many errors, the correction process can be more time-consuming and expensive than having the texts re-keyed in the first place. OCR output 'usually' has to be checked. Some software offers certain kinds of 'fuzzy' matching for texts captured by OCR and left uncorrected, but this is *not* intended for use where the texts are to be subjected to rigorous analysis and where accuracy is key. Instead, it is used for the preparation and presentation of large bodies of printed materials (such as newspaper pages) where retrieval of the individual articles is important, but where instances of individual words are not. See the British Library Newspaper Pilot[16] and a recent article on news-paper software for examples of this.[17]

Where re-keying is chosen, the texts are usually re-keyed by two different operatives and then the resultant texts matched using software to pick up errors. Re-keying can give around 99.995 per cent accuracy, sometimes better, even on difficult texts. The best way to find out about different methods of capture of electronic text is to access the AHDS Guide to Good Practice on the topic.[18]

For scholars working intensively on an individual text, there is probably no substitute for transcribing the text directly onto the computer and adding appropriate tagging and metadata according to a standardised framework. This can be done using almost any standard word processor or text editor, though there are specialist packages like XMetaL which allow the easy production and validation of text marked up in XML (eXtensible Markup Language), as we discuss in the next section.

TEXT ENCODING

In applying computing tools and techniques in humanities research, the question of technical 'standards' – that is, the choices made in relation to hardware, software and methodology – has always been important. A particular concern of scholars working with texts in the late 1970s and early 1980s was how to ensure that electronic files produced by one scholar/editor could be passed to another without having to undergo complicated transformations, which was the norm unless both were using more or less the same hardware and software. Increasingly, individuals and projects defined their own standards for structuring textual materials which meant that useful text might be locked into some local system and be unusable elsewhere – this is both uneconomic and wasteful of scholarly effort.

These concerns led to a major international project, the Text Encoding Initiative (TEI), sponsored by the three professional associations in 'humanities computing': the Association for Literary and Linguistic Computing (ALLC),[19] the Association for Computers and the Humanities (ACH),[20] and the Association for Computational Linguistics (ACL).[21] It was largely funded by the European Commission and the US National Endowment for the Humanities. During its life, the project involved hundreds of scholars from all humanities disciplines and many countries. It is certainly the largest collaborative project ever undertaken in the humanities.

The purpose of the project was to produce guidelines that would help to ensure that electronic textual materials could be passed from one scholar to another, now and in the future, in a form that is independent of any particular hardware or software. The first set of guidelines was published in 1994.[22] In 2000 the project came to an end, and was replaced by the TEI Consortium, hosted at the universities of Bergen (Norway), Oxford, Virginia and Brown. The goal of the consortium is to maintain the international collaborative framework within which scholars can work together to specify and adapt a common technical standard for the encoding of texts in scholarly work. The basis of this standard is XML (eXtensible Mark-up Language), which is now widely used in preparing documents for publication on the internet across all domains. Details of the consortium and a wealth of information about text mark-up, including tutorial and reference material, can be found on the TEI Consortium website.[23]

The reasons for marking up text have now gone far beyond the initial basic 'data interchange' goal. It is important to distinguish at least three kinds of mark-up (or 'encoding'):[24] descriptive, structural, and content. Descriptive (or 'metadata') mark-up is used to record important information about the text, such as author, title, publisher and publication date. This is the type of information we expect to find in the front matter of a printed volume as a matter of course, but which was conspicuous by its absence in many early online publications. Structural mark-up is used to identify the structural components of a text: poem, stanza, line in a verse collection; act, scene, line in a play; chapters in a novel. Content mark-up is necessary if any aspects of the text content are to be processed in some systematic way, for example to create an index. It is quite common to mark up names – of persons, places or institutions – and dates, and linguists routinely encode parts of speech, but it may also be useful for certain types of research to encode other matters of scholarly judgement, for example stylistic devices. In scholarly editions a key use of content mark-up is to encode the matters of editorial judgement usually presented in the critical apparatus.

An important underlying principle of mark-up is the separation between the text itself and any particular rendition of it. An encoded text can be processed in many different ways. One common type of processing is to prepare it for publication, when instructions are given about how particular mark-up elements are to be rendered, for example chapter headings to be printed or displayed in bold, titles in italics, names underlined, the critical apparatus to be printed or displayed in a particular format, and so on. It is axiomatic that the tags themselves are not rendered, other than in exceptional circumstances. Any encoded elements can be processed, and such processing is not limited to rendition. The production of indices has already been mentioned. It becomes a simple matter to generate an index for any encoded element, for example an index of persons, places, institutions, stylistic devices, and so on. Similarly, it is possible to provide 'structured' searches on any encoded element, so that, for example, one may search for 'brown' specifically as a person, an institution, or a colour.

The degree and type of encoding will vary from text to text depending on the purpose of the research. 'Shallow encoding' generally includes basic metadata and structural mark-up, and is likely to be sufficient where the most common type of manipulation is to be 'free text' searches either within the text itself, or across a set of similarly marked-up texts. 'Deep encoding' encompasses the part-of-speech mark-up needed for linguistic analysis, and other detailed content mark-up.[25] As the number of electronic texts available online continues to increase, there is growing interest in the potential for systematic searching, and other types of analysis and manipulation, across large numbers of texts. To realise the full potential of such developments, it is particularly important that the encoding of all the texts involved has been done to a common standard – hence the continuing importance of standards initiatives such as the TEI Consortium.

TABULAR DATA: DATABASES

In text encoding, the text itself is the starting point, and the mark-up provides a mechanism for additional information to be embedded in the text. Subsequent processing can exploit the tags or it can ignore them, depending on what is required. In some cases, however, it may be more effective to create sets of data elements in tabular form, and to use well established spreadsheet or relational database software for recording and analysing the data. If the data sources, for example, are disparate in character, and drawn from many different locations, the effort involved in marking up all the different texts might be disproportionate to the analytical benefits to be gained; it may be more effective to extract and summarise or categorise the source data, and place it in a set of database tables. A well structured academic database will, in any case, always include references to the underlying data sources.

A database approach is most likely to be effective where the data to be stored and manipulated is already in a relatively structured form – as in parish baptism records, for example – or where it is appropriate to shape it in this way – for example recording basic information about an author's publications, or key biographical events, or managing data collected as a supplement to the research, such as a set of digital images. The important point is that database software is designed to help with manipulating very regularly structured data, and since most humanities source data is irregular, this approach needs to be used with due caution.

It is now quite common to encounter digital research resources that have been created using a range of technical methods and techniques: marked-up texts; images and maps; databases; even sound and video. The Blake Archive, mentioned earlier, is a good example of a digital resource in which the marked-up texts and the images are equally important, with underlying databases to manage the integration of the materials.[26]

MODELLING HUMANITIES DATA

Formal research methods in the humanities are very different from those in the sciences, and often the methods used by humanists are internalised and implicit to such a degree that they do not feel like 'methods' at all, but are seen rather as natural approaches that all scholars are bound to take as starting points for research. 'Modelling of data', then, may initially seem a foreign concept for humanists. However, all research is the process of applying some kind of structured investigative method to a body of materials, and in order to apply those methods, a model must be created. This model may not be made explicit, but it is there nevertheless.

When embarking on advanced computational research on humanities data, the data must be modelled explicitly as computers only operate on explicit and detailed commands. The effectiveness of the model depends on the quality of the analysis and design process that underlies it. It needs to be understood first that a formally structured analysis and design exercise is needed, which takes account of the complexities of the source data and the potentialities of the technical approaches, and maps one to the other.[27] Where text mark-up is involved, a formal 'document analysis' process is recommended.[28] In setting up relational databases, there are well established methods of analysis and design which lead to an 'Entity-Attribute-Relationship' model, the type of data model the software was designed to manipulate. This modelling process can be greatly revealing to the scholar as it forces him or her to think very hard at a meta-level about what exactly is to be modelled in order to obtain the desired results.

USE OF TEXTUAL CORPORA

The computer has given new dimensions to the study of the English language in the last twenty years with the building of large linguistic corpora. A corpus is here understood as a body of naturally occurring data in electronic format that can be used for linguistic research. A collection of machine-readable texts is not a corpus, as a corpus will usually have some unifying function: a corpus is created for a *purpose* and is sytematically designed and marked up to fulfil that purpose. Corpus linguistics is the study of language on the basis of text corpora. Its aim is to understand how language works by reference to extensive real-world examples of both written and spoken language. There are four main characteristics of a modern corpus:

1. Sampling and representativeness
2. Finite size

3. Machine-readable form
4. A standard reference

There is a growing number of extensive corpora of English, modern and historic, spoken and written, large and small.[29] Corpora can be used for many different kinds of linguistic study, and the use of corpora in the analysis of language and meaning can often result in some surprises. Corpora can be used for lexical studies, for semantics and pragmatics, for grammatical analysis, for socio- and psycho-linguistics, for stylistics, and so on. McEnery and Wilson offer an excellent introduction to the use of corpora in linguistics.[30]

TEXTUAL CRITICISM AND ELECTRONIC SCHOLARLY EDITIONS

Underpinning much work in the study of English (and of course, many other languages and literatures) is the work of bibliographers and textual critics in the production and deep analysis of scholarly editions. Computerised methods as applied to textual criticism were initially intended to assist the scholar in the production of the conventional end-product: a printed critical edition of the text with the base text printed in full and the variants from other texts at the foot of the page or at the end of the work. Over the centuries the critical edition has reached a high level of sophistication in the organisational principles that allow a flat, linear, printed book to present information which is not linear, and part of the research training of the editor is in the arcana of presenting multiple texts for publication, as much as in understanding the relationship of textual witnesses and their contribution to the history and meaning of the work. Now, however, developments in textual presentation software using structural mark-up and hypertextual linking mechanisms mean that critical editions are increasingly generated and published in electronic form. Indeed, very few scholars would embark upon an editing project today without using ICT methods in the preparation, production, and delivery of major editorial works. Electronic editions have many benefits, but may also raise controversial issues. They offer a plenitude of materials that represent a work in all its different states of being. They also allow the situating of works within a nexus of social, contextual and historical materials, all of which contribute to the meanings. However, one of the traditional goals of editing is the presentation of a fixed and stable text according to well understood and explicitly stated principles. The traditional format preserves the fixity generally expected of editions, the electronic does not do so unless specific steps are taken.

There are now many scholarly editing projects in English that one could point to as exemplars. One seminal project is the Canterbury Tales Project, which has established a system for including digital facsimiles and transcriptions of all manuscripts of the Canterbury Tales, along with a wide range of analytical and contextual material.[31] The project has experimented successfully with new technologies for the collation and analysis of complex textual traditions, including the use of the techniques and software used in evolutionary biology for tracing descent.[32] Currently, certain of the individual tales are available in this new format.[33]

The new Cambridge edition of the works of Ben Jonson proposes an interesting relationship between conventional and electronic editing. The plan is to produce simultaneously a six-volume traditional edition and a networked electronic edition, the second of which will grow and change as scholarship develops and will 'distribute editorial power among the users'.[34] This is an interesting approach as the reliable and stable text that is so important to establish will be at the core of a conventional edition at the same time as being at the centre of a highly fluid, 'rhyzomic' network of hypertext links. Fixing the text in one form and therefore being assured of its stability can perhaps allow for more experimentation in the electronic medium. It will be interesting to see in what way and over what period the editions diverge, and at what point, if ever, there is felt to be the need for a new printed edition. If there ever *is* a new printed edition, no doubt it will differ profoundly from the first, given its electronic 'after-life'.

Editing poetry in the electronic medium has particular challenges, as poetry is a visual as well as a verbal form. Structures like line breaks, stanzas, letter shapes as defined by the authors need to be maintained as per the original. As Fraistat and Jones suggest,

> Because poetry, with its enhanced self-consciousness of the physique of
> texts, expresses itself inextricably through particular interfaces, any
> editor of poetic texts in the digital medium must be centrally
> concerned with the interface, with matters of textual display and
> appearance.[35]

The Romantic Circles website houses hypertext editions of Romantic poetry with different versions transcribed, page images of a variety of sources, collations, annotations and so on.[36] Fraistat and Jones suggest that electronic editions of poetry might offer a 'potentially infinite expansion of the traditional editorial apparatus', and that users might be able to have their own customised version of the edition, based on their behaviour while interacting with the materials. They also suggest that an important feature of online poetry could be the 'contextural' relation of multiple texts on the internet within hyperlinked clusters, where the poem interacts with many other kinds of information. This is an exciting but problematic concept, as it means that a text could change constantly, and therefore calls into question the notion of the fixed edition and the stable referent that scholars have long relied upon.

One result of the advent of computers in textual criticism is the re-definition of the notion of what is an edition, with a move towards providing archives of textual materials instead of heavily edited definitive editions. An exemplary project demonstrating the archive potential of new kinds of editions is the William Blake Archive. The editors of the archive describe it having been conceived as

> an international public resource that would provide unified access to major works of visual and literary art that are highly disparate, widely dispersed, and more and more often severely restricted as a result of their value, rarity, and extreme fragility.[37]

This is a very different notion from that of the scholarly edition with its interpretation included as part of the presented work, and its necessarily high degree of selectivity. From the conventional view that more is selected out than left in, we move to the electronically facilitated view that everything is left in, and it is for the reader to choose what is relevant to a particular need in the work of an author. This is claimed to be a process by which power is devolved from editor to reader, giving the reader access to all the resources used by the editor. While this can be empowering for the reader, it requires a greater degree of skill and experience in interpreting editorial materials, and so might, on the contrary, prove disempowering for the less experienced.

A recent development in France concerning the writings of more modern authors is the use of hypertext systems to study the genesis of works of literature: so-called 'genetic criticism'. This is seen by its exponents as a form of literary criticism, giving primacy to interpretation over editing, though the editing and preparation of sources is a key part of genetic criticism. Where possible, all the working papers and drafts that an author produces as part of the creative process are presented, linked together hypertextually. The key focus of genetic criticism is the reconstruction and analysis of the writing process. Working papers have complex relationships with finished and published works of literature, and publishing them in facsimile does not always allow this complexity to be presented in a meaningful way. Presenting them through hypertext systems allows their non-linear nature to be shown in a way more congruent with their original composition and permits different media types to be integrated and linked.[38] Works of genetic criticism on a number of writers, including Flaubert, Proust, Joyce, and Zola, are in progress.[39]

ELECTRONIC TEXTUALITY

Of particular interest to theorists is the ontology of electronic text, for the key and crucial difference between electronic text and written text is that electronic text exists not as words on surfaces, but as electrical impulses. The written text is fixed, and the electronic text is fluid. With the advent of printing, the written text became fixed in multiple copies of essentially the same work and could be widely disseminated. The electronic text can be even more widely disseminated, given that it does not rely on a stable medium to convey it. This has positive and negative consequences. However often an electronic text is copied, it does not degrade. The hundredth copy is exactly the same as the first. As Richard Lanham puts it, 'Unlike print, the electronic text defies conventional wisdom. You can have your cake, give it away, then eat it, and still have it'.[40] Electronic text also has the property of simultaneity: one text on a (connected) machine anywhere could be accessed by 1,000 machines throughout the world, 1,000 virtual texts on 1,000 screens. But the minute the screen is switched off, the text vanishes and has to be recreated from the stored copy for further access. Conversely, the text could be displayed on the same screen as a number of other texts from diverse locations, compared, contrasted, even integrated with them. The boundaries of texts are consequently more permeable. Texts can thus be exchanged, proliferated, transmitted across the world in seconds, integrated with other media, and linked into complex interpretive networks of variants, editions, illustrations, and so on. As Kathryn Sutherland points out, the dispersion of location, identity, and appearance of electronic text is making a significant contribution to our understanding of textuality.[41] We have become so used to the book as textual mediator that for the most part we scarcely notice its artefactual state and how it imposes its 'machinery' on what we read; we accept a kind of synonymity between text and book. There is some sense in this, since the book (individually as well as generically) has proved a robust machine for text dissemination, while one of the current anxieties about electronic storage media is their rapid obsolescence: note the discussion above about ebook readers, which came and went in just a couple of years.

For textual critics, this new textual world is a liberating environment: some kinds of works still function well in book form, others (dictionaries, encyclopaedias, scholarly editions) have outgrown the bounds of the codex and are enriched by their cybernetic presentation. For other scholars, the theories of cybernetic hypertext prove illuminating in their consideration of multi-layered, multi-plot novels: Patrick Conner's analysis of *Huckleberry Finn*[42] and Kathryn Sutherland's study of Dickens' *Little Dorrit*[43] are good examples. The underlying paradigm of hypertext is simple: it is a means of linking together textual materials using what have become known as 'nodes' and 'links'. Its manifestation can soon become highly complicated, however, as nodes and links multiply very quickly, until there are often millions of links. The complexity of hypertext systems (something we all become more familiar with daily as we negotiate the world wide web) means that there is an almost limitless number of paths the reader/user can take through a cybernetic system. Each decision to move in a certain direction, while limiting some choices, also offers a vast number of possibilities for the next move. Interactive games, which make the routes to success or failure contingent upon certain right or wrong choices, exploit these ever multiplying links to create rich fictional structures which have been attracting the interest of narratologists.[44] On the world wide web there are numerous sites for hypertext and interactive fiction: one that is of particular note is the StorySpace web site Eastgate Systems.[45] This offers a well established tool for the composition of hypertext narratives (StorySpace), as well as a large number of hypertext narratives and fictions for sale and available on CD or online.

The problem with trying to discuss interactive books and fiction is that for many the opposition is printed word equals linear and static, electronic word equals non-linear and dynamic, and this is, of course, a false notion. Very few printed products are strictly linear, some novels and poetry perhaps (though even there authors play a good deal with the presentation of non-linear or simultaneous events in book form), but periodical publications (newspapers, magazines, journals) defy linearity, as do reference works and complex works of scholarship. And every text is 'interactive', changing according to a particular reader at a particular hour in a particular place. All readers create their own text while reading, and every new reading is an act of re-creating, just as every new access to an electronic text is a process of creating a human-readable version afresh on the screen. However, the use of the electronic medium in order to understand how fictions and narratives work is a valid one, and experimentation with new forms of creativity in writing and reading technologies brings new possibilities to the world of ideas. A useful introduction to hypertext criticism and hypertext fictions is the special issue of the *Journal of Digital Information* on hypertext criticism, in particular the essay by Jill Walker which is a critique of a hypertext poem written as a hypertext.[46] One of the leading figures in assessing textuality in the electronic age is Jerome McGann; see in particular his Rossetti project,[47] his book *Radiant Textuality*,[48] and his essay 'The Rationale of Hypertext',[49] among numerous other publications.[50]

Altogether, the scholar of English has a great many more tools available for interpretation, analysis and presentation of critical work. If you are writing on *Pride and Prejudice*, you can rent DVDs of the various film and TV adaptations as well as reading critical books, you can cut and paste 'quotes' into the article and publish online. Writing on *King Lear*? Use the Cambridge CD-ROM of the play with multiple texts and facsimiles (including a hypertext edition), a database of performance information, images, essays, and much other supplementary material. Look at the 'Three Lears' project that has created virtual reality models of three modern performances[51] and check out some playbills.[52] Pass a query into Questia and you will get more than 3,000 more or less relevant hits.

BEYOND INDIVIDUAL RESEARCH

Two other aspects of applying technological methods in humanities research are worth at least brief discussion. First, not only do most of the projects to create new digital research resources involve multiple technologies, they are also likely to involve modes of collaboration that are new in the humanities. Large research teams of scholars distributed around the world have been able to work together across institutional, national and international boundaries, and truly interdisciplinary and multi-disciplinary work has been enabled. An increasing number of major research projects, too, depend on bringing together discipline and technical specialists to work in collaborative frameworks that are new, and that have resulted in major new advances. Increasingly sophisticated and flexible technologies are making possible new kinds of interdisciplinary work and the creation of truly multi-disciplinary digital resources.

Thus, the Blake Archive project involves a number of academic specialists drawn from many disciplines, several geographically dispersed institutions, and a number of technical specialists to cover the range of technologies and technical methods involved; the collaborators also include eight galleries and a private collector. There are practical implications in this, regarding technical infrastructure and management methods. More important perhaps are the implications for institutional research cultures, which will involve mechanisms for peer review of the research resources created in such projects, and the political will as well as the practical basis for giving due academic recognition to those who invest their intellectual capital in this way. The Arts and Humanities Research Board (AHRB), the principal UK funder of research in the humanities disciplines, is keenly aware of the range of issues, including peer review and academic recognition, related to research work in the digital arena. In October 2003 it launched a three-year 'ICT in Arts and Humanities Research' programme, directed by Professor David Robey, University of Reading. As a major part of this programme, a 'Methods Network' is to be established, starting at the beginning of 2005.[53] Jerome McGann's NINES project (Networked Interface for Nineteenth-Century Electronic Scholarship) is an example of a specific project aiming to establish a new framework for publications and peer review in a particular domain.[54]

Finally, it is worth considering the broader infrastructure to support digital scholarship in the humanities. In the UK, the Arts and Humanities Data

Service (AHDS) was established in 1996. It is funded by the Arts and Humanities Research Board (AHRB) and the Joint Information Systems Committee (JISC) of the Higher Education Funding Councils. Its role is to advise on technical standards in creating digital resources across the range of arts and humanities disciplines, and to establish metadata standards such that it can provide a cross-domain catalogue of digital resources. In its work on standards it is also concerned about inter-linking between resources and 'inter-operability' – that is, being able to manipulate data from different resources using common tools. The AHDS also has responsibilities in relation to the long-term preservation of digital resources. The AHRB and AHDS have a strategic partnership, in which the AHDS acts as a technical reviewer of applications for AHRB funding and in which successful AHRB applicants are required, as a condition of grant, to deposit their digital materials with the AHDS. It regularly publishes guides to good practice, case studies and other information useful for scholars engaged in or considering the creation of a digital research resource.[55] In the US, the work of the Commission on Cyberinfrastructure for the Humanities and Social Sciences established by the American Council of Learned Societies (ACLS) is an initiative to assess the research infrastructure needed for humanities scholarship.[56] Many similar institutions and projects have been created across the globe, in Europe, Asia, Australia and New Zealand. While these all have broad remits across the humanities, they are creating and shaping the technological framework for the English scholarship of the future, nationally and internationally.

FURTHER READING

The major journal for digital scholarship is *Literary and Linguistic Computing: The Journal of Digital Scholarship* (Oxford UP). Also of interest is *Computers and the Humanities* (Kluwer), renamed from 2005 *Language Resources and Evaluation*. This will be the first publication devoted to the creation, annotation and exploitation of language resources for use in language processing applications, corpus linguistics and linguistic studies.

Many of the publications of the Office for Humanities Communication (OHC) at King's College London are relevant to research in English, in particular those produced in partnership with the Institute for English Studies:

Chernaik, Warren, Caroline Davis and Marilyn Deegan (eds) [1993] (1997), *The Politics of the Electronic Text*, London: OHC.
Chernaik, Warren, Marilyn Deegan and Andrew Gibson (eds) (1996), *Beyond the Book: Theory, Culture, and the Politics of Cyberspace*, London: OHC.
Chernaik, Warren and Patrick Parrinder (eds) (1997), *Textual Monopolies: Literary Copyright and the Public Domain*, London: OHC.
McKitterick, David (ed.) (2002), *Do We Want to Keep Our Newspapers?*, London: OHC.

General

Buzzetti, Dino, Giuliano Pancaldi and Harold Short (eds) (2004), *Augmenting Comprehension: Digital Tools and the History of Ideas*, London: OHC.

Schreibman, Susan et al., (eds) (2004), *A Companion to Digital Humanities*, Blackwell: Oxford and New York.

Databases

Benyon, D. (1997), *Information and Data Modelling*, New York: McGraw-Hill.

Bowers, D. S. (1988), *From Data to Database*, Chapman and Hall (new edition forthcoming from Wiley, 2005).

Date, C. J. (1983), *Database – A Primer*, Reading, MA: Addison-Wesley.

Date, C. J. (1999), *An Introduction to Database Systems*, 7th edn, Reading, MA: Addison-Wesley.

Greenstein, D. I. (1994), *A Historian's Guide to Computing*, Oxford: Oxford University Press.

Hernandez, M. J. (1997), *Database Design for Mere Mortals: A Hands-on Guide to Relational Database Design*, Reading, MA: Addison-Wesley.

Mark-up and metadata

Deegan, Marilyn and Simon Tanner (2002), *Digital Futures: Strategies for the Information Age*, London: Facet Publishing.

Tommie Usdin, B. and C. M. Sperberg-McQueen (eds) (1998–2001), *Markup Languages: Theory and Practice*, Boston, MA: MIT Press.

Sperberg-McQueen, C. M. and L. Burnard (eds) (1994), *TEI P3: Guidelines for Electronic Text Encoding and Interchange*, Oxford and Chicago.

Textual analysis and stylistics

Bradley, John (2004), 'Tools to augment scholarly activity: an architecture to support text analysis', in Dino Buzzetti, Giuliano Pancaldi and Harold Short (eds), *Augmenting Comprehension: Digital Tools and the History of Ideas*, London: OHC, pp. 19–47.

Burrows, John (1987), *Computation into Criticism: A Study of Jane Austen's Novels and an Experiment in Method*, Oxford: Clarendon Press.

Burrows, John (2002), ' "Delta": a measure of stylistic difference and a guide to likely authorship', *Literary and Linguistic Computing*, 17, pp. 267–87.

Burrows, John (2003), 'Questions of authorship: attribution and beyond, the Roberto Busa Award Lecture (2001)', *Computers and the Humanities*, 37, pp. 5–32.

Holmes, David I. (1998), 'The evolution of stylometry in humanities scholarship', *Literary and Linguistic Computing*, 13, pp. 111–17.

Holmes, David I., Lesley J. Gordon and Christine Wilson (2001), 'A widow and her soldier: stylometry and the American Civil War', *Literary and Linguistic Computing*, 16, pp. 403–20.

Hoover, David L. (2001), 'Statistical stylistics and authorship attribution: an empirical investigation', *Literary and Linguistic Computing*, 16, pp. 421–44.

Textual editing and electronic text

Deppman, Jed, Daniel Ferrer and Michael Groden (2004), *Genetic Criticism: Texts and Avant-textes*, Philadelphia: University of Pennsylvania Press.

'Editing for a New Century' (2000), ed. Peter M. W. Robinson and Hans Walter Gabler, special issue of *Literary and Linguistic Computing*, 15.

'Electronic Scholarly Editing – Some Northern European Approaches' (2004), ed. Mats Dahlström, Espen S. Ore and Edward Vanhoutte, special issue of *Literary and Linguistic Computing*, 19.

Burnard, Lou, Katherine O'Brien O'Keefe and John Unsworth (eds) (2004), *Electronic Textual Editing*, New York: Modern Languages Association.

Hockey, Susan (2000), *Electronic Texts in the Humanities: Principles and Practice*, Oxford: Oxford University Press.

Lanham, Richard A. (1993), *The Electronic Word: Democracy, Technology, and the Arts*, Chicago: University of Chicago Press.

Shillingsburg, Peter (1996), *Scholarly Editing in the Computer Age: Theory and Practice*, 3rd edn, Ann Arbor: University of Michigan Press.

Shillingsburg, Peter (1997), *General Principles for Electronic Scholarly Editions*, New York: Modern Languages Association.

Sutherland, Kathryn (1987), *Electronic Text: Investigations in Method and Theory*, Oxford: Oxford University Press.

Hypertext

Bolter, Jay D. (1990), *Writing Space: The Computer, Hypertext and the History of Writing*, Hillsdale, NJ: Lawrence Erlbaum. See URL: http://www.eastgate.com/people/Bolter.html

Delany, Paul and George P. Landow (eds) (1990), *Hypermedia and Literary Studies*, Cambridge, MA: MIT Press.

Landow, George P. (1992), *Hypertext: The Convergence of Contemporary Critical Theory and Technology*, Baltimore: Johns Hopkins University Press.

Journal of Digital Information (2000), special issue on hypertext criticism, 7.

Corpus Linguistics

Biber, D., S. Conrad and R. Reppen (1998), *Corpus Linguistics: Investigating Language Use*, Cambridge: Cambridge University Press.

Kennedy, G. (1998), *An Introduction to Corpus Linguistics*, London: Longman.

McEnery, T. and A. Wilson (2001), *Corpus Linguistics*, 2nd edn, Edinburgh: Edinburgh University Press and http://www.ling.lancs.ac.uk/monkey/ihe/linguistics/contents.htm

Sinclair, J. M. (1991), *Corpus, Concordance, Collocation*, Oxford: Oxford University Press.

Useful websites

AHRB centre for British film and television studies, http://www.bftv.ac.uk/

Annotated Bibliography for English Studies, http://abes.swets.nl/abes/

British Fiction, 1800–1829: A Database of Production and Reception, http://www.cf.ac.uk/encap/ceir/research/database.html

Centre for Editing Lives and Letters, http://www.livesandletters.ac.uk/

The Complete Writings and Pictures of Dante Gabriel Rossetti: A hypermedia research archive, http://www.iath.virginia.edu/rossetti/

Donne Variorum Project, http://www.donnevariorum.com/

Electronic Literature Organization, http://www.eliterature.org/

Electronic Text Centre at Virginia, http://etext.lib.virginia.edu/
Humbul Humanities Hub, http://www.humbul.ac.uk/
Hyperizons, http://www.duke.edu/~mshumate/hyperfic.html
The Internet Poetry Archive, http://www.ibiblio.org/ipa/
Literature Compass, a new literature resource from Blackwell Publishing,
    http://www.literature-compass.com/
Literature On-Line, http://lion.chadwyck.co.uk/
Luminarium: early English literature and literary history, http://www.luminarium.org/
Michael Best's Home Page, research resources on Shakespeare,
    http://www.engl.uvic.ca/Faculty/MBHomePage/
Middle English Compendium, http://ets.umdl.umich.edu/m/mec/
Modernist Journals Project, http://www.modjourn.brown.edu/
The Paperback Revolution, http://www.crcstudio.arts.ualberta.ca/paperbacks/index.php
Perseus Digital Library (Renaissance materials, electronic edition of the works of Christopher
    Marlowe), http://www.perseus.tufts.edu/
Piers Plowman electronic archive, http://www.iath.virginia.edu/seenet/piers/piersmain.html
Postmodern Culture, http://www.iath.virginia.edu/pmc/contents.all.html
Renaissance women online, http://www.wwp.brown.edu/texts/rwoentry.html
Romantic Circles, http://www.rc.umd.edu/
Romanticism on the Net, http://users.ox.ac.uk/~scat0385/
The Victorian Web, http://www.victorianweb.org/
Voice of the Shuttle, http://vos.ucsb.edu/
William Blake archive online [UK Mirror], http://www.blakearchive.org.uk/
Women Writer's Project at Brown University, http://www.wwp.brown.edu/
York Doomsday project, http://www.lancs.ac.uk/depts/yorkdoom/intro.htm

NOTES

1. This was the theme of a keynote address by Derek Law, Librarian and Director of
   Information Resources Directorate, University of Strathclyde, at the 1999 Digital
   Resources for the Humanities Conference. Derek G. Law (2000), 'The Mickey Mouse
   world of humanities scholarship', in Marilyn Deegan and Harold Short (eds), *DRH 99:
   Selected Papers*, Office for Humanities Communication, London 2000, pp. 1–24.
2. For these and other British Library digitisation projects, see http://
   www.bl.uk/collections/treasures/digitisation1.html
3. See www.bl.uk/collections/treasures/beowulf.html for a general description. The project
   published two CD-ROMs: Kevin Kiernan et al. (eds) (2003), *Electronic Beowulf*, London:
   British Library Publications. An online guide to the publication, including a great deal of
   background information about the manuscript and the project, is at:
   http://www.uky.edu/~kiernan/eBeowulf
4. http://www.lib.umich.edu/eebo
5. http://alexia.lis.uiuc.edu
6. http://www.kcl.ac.uk/cch
7. http://www.ucl.ac.uk/leaders-project/
8. See Erica Klarreich (2003), 'Bookish math: statistical tests are unraveling knotty literary
   mysteries – stylometry', in *Science News*, 20 December, for a fascinating account of
   modern stylostatistics. Many articles on stylostatistics are published in *Literary and
   Linguistic Computing*.

9. http://www.questia.com

10. http://www.netlibrary.com/Gateway.aspx

11. The AHDS Centre has published an excellent guide to sources of free ebooks: Ylva Berglund, Alan Morrison, Rowan Wilson, Martin Wynne (2004), *An Investigation into Free eBooks: Final Report*, at http://www.ahds.ac.uk/litlangling/ebooks/report/FreeEbooks.html

12. http://www.ahds.ac.uk/litlangling

13. http://www.ota.ahds.ac.uk

14. http://etext.lib.virginia.edu

15. http://www.hti.umich.edu

16. http://www.uk.olivesoftware.com

17. Marilyn Deegan, Emil Steinvel and Edmund King (1992), 'Digitising Historic Newspapers', *RLG DigiNews* at http://www.rlg.ac.uk/preserv/diginews/diginews6-4.html#feature2 This approach is also an important element of the Nineteenth-Century Serials Edition (NCSE) project, a study of print culture in the nineteenth century focused on runs of six serials, carried out by Birkbeck College and King's College London, funded by the AHRB. See http://www.ncse.ac.uk

18. Alan Morrison, Michael Popham and Karen Wikander (2000), *Creating and Documenting Electronic Texts: A Guide to Good Practice*, at http://ota.ahds.ac.uk/documents/creating/

19. http://www.allc.org

20. http://www.ach.org

21. http://www.aclweb.org

22. C. M. Sperberg-McQueen and L. Burnard (eds) (1994), *TEI P3: Guidelines for Electronic Text Encoding and Interchange*, Oxford and Chicago.

23. http://www.tei-c.org

24. The terms 'mark-up' and 'encoding' tend to be used almost interchangeably. Encoding is done with 'tags', usually distinguished by being enclosed in chevron brackets, e.g. <title>A Tale of Two Cities</title>, and usually paired, as in the example, so that the computer knows unambiguously where the encoded material begins and ends. In order to be processed at all by computer, text must be encoded in some way. In many computing applications, for example word processors, the encoding itself is usually hidden; for example, when a piece of text is italicised, the text is shown on the screen or on paper in italics, but the basis for this are tags – 'begin italics' and 'end italics' – embedded in the text but hidden from view.

25. Our colleague Willard McCarty is preparing an 'Analytical onomasticon to Ovid's *Metamorphoses*', in which a single word in the poem often has several tags associated with it. This is 'deep encoding' indeed, but needs a very specific purpose to justify the time involved – more than ten years in this case. See http://www.kcl.ac.uk/humanities/cch/wlm/onomasticon-sampler

26. The Blake Archive was initiated and is based at the Institute for Advanced Technology in the Humanities at the University of Virginia (http://www.iath.virginia.edu). The website has a 'mirror' in the UK, at http://www.blakearchive.org.uk Among many other academic projects in which texts, images and databases are integrated are the medieval stained-glass project Corpus Vitrearum Medii Aevi at http://www.cvma.ac.uk and the Corpus of Romanesque Sculpture in Britain and Ireland, at http://www.crsbi.ac.uk, Both are based at the Courtauld Institute of Art. In both projects the scholarly analyses and other text materials are marked up in XML following the guidelines of the Text Encoding Initiative, and relational database software is used to manage both the database of digital images and the integration of the texts and images in the web sites.

27. The intersection between the rich and varied complexities of humanities data and the systematic rigour required for computation, and both the limits and the intellectual consequences of this intersection, are specific research interests of groups such as the Institute for Advanced Technology in the Humanities at the University of Virginia (http://www.iath.virginia.edu), and the Centre for Computing in the Humanities at King's College London, where the authors are based (http://www.kcl.ac.uk/cch).

28. The Women Writers Project at Brown University (http://www.wwp.brown.edu) is a particularly good example of a project with a broadly based and systematic approach to text encoding, based on the TEI guidelines, with very useful documentation. For their guidance on 'document analysis', see http://www.wwp.brown.edu/encoding/training/DocAn.html. Other reference and training materials of this kind can be found on the TEI Consortium website.

29. The main ones include: the Brown Corpus: a corpus of written American English from 1961, compiled at Brown University; the LOB Corpus: (Lancaster–Oslo–Bergen Corpus): written British English from 1961; the London–Lund Corpus: spoken British English from the 1960s and early 1970s which was recorded and transcribed at the Survey of English Usage (University College London) and Lund University (Sweden); the Helsinki Corpus: a diachronic corpus consisting of a selection of texts covering the Old, Middle, and Early Modern English periods which can be accessed through ICAME at http://helmer.aksis.uib.no/icame.html; BNC – the British National Corpus – a huge corpus of 100 million words which can be searched from http://escorp.unizh.ch/. A password is required, but can be obtained by accessing the same address. Also of interest is Wordnet, an online lexical reference system whose design is inspired by current psycholinguistic theories of human lexical memory. English nouns, verbs, adjectives and adverbs are organised into synonym sets, each representing one underlying lexical concept. Different relations link the synonym sets (http://www.cogsci.princeton.edu/~wn/). ELRA, the European Language Resources Association, whose missions are to promote language resources for the Human Language Technology (HLT) sector, and to evaluate language engineering technologies, lists a number of useful corpora of English from different genres (http://www.elra.info/). The SCOTS project (Scottish Corpus of Texts and Speech) is the first large-scale project of its kind for Scotland. It aims to build a large electronic collection of both written and spoken texts for the languages of Scotland with an initial focus primarily on the collection of Scottish English and Scots texts (http://www.scottishcorpus.ac.uk/).

30. T. McEnery and A. Wilson (2001), *Corpus Linguistics*, 2nd edn, Edinburgh: Edinburgh University Press, and http://www.ling.lancs.ac.uk/ monkey/ihe/linguistics/contents.htm

31. http://www.cta.dmu.ac.uk/projects/ctp

32. Peter M.W. Robinson and Robert J. O'Hara (1996), 'Cladistic analysis of an Old Norse manuscript tradition', in *Research in Humanities Computing 4*, ed. Susan Hockey and Nancy Ide, Oxford, pp. 115–37.

33. See http://www.cta.dmu.ac.uk/projects/ctp/publications.html

34. David Gants, 'Drama case study: the Cambridge edition of the works of Ben Jonson,' *Electronic Textual Editing*, ed. Lou Burnard, Katherine O'Brien O'Keefe and John Unsworth, forthcoming 2004.

35. Neil Fraistat and Steven Jones, 'The poem and the network', in *Electronic Textual Editing*, ed. Lou Burnard, Katherine O'Brien O'Keefe and John Unsworth, forthcoming 2004.

36. http://www.rc.umd.edu

37. http://www.blakearchive.org.uk/public/about/glance

38. Daniel Ferrer (1995), 'Hypertextual representation of literary working papers', *Literary and Linguistic Computing*, 10, pp. 143–5.

39. See http://www.item.ens.fr

40. Richard A. Lanham (1993), The *Electronic Word: Democracy, Technology, and the Arts*, Chicago: University of Chicago Press, p. xii.

41. Kathryn Sutherland (1997), *Electronic Text: Investigations in Method and Theory*, Oxford: Oxford University Press.

42. Patrick Conner (1997), 'Lighting out for the territory: hypertext and ideology in the American canon', in Kathryn Sutherland (ed.), *Electronic Text: Investigations in Method and Theory*, Oxford: Clarendon Press, pp. 67–105.

43. Kathryn Sutherland (1990), 'A guide through the labyrinth: Dickens's *Little Dorrit* as hypertext', *Literary and Linguistic Computing*, 5 pp. 305–9.

44. Andrew Gibson (1996), 'Interactive fiction and narrative space', in W. Chernaik et al. (eds), *Beyond the Book: Theory, Culture and the Politics of Cyberspace*, London: Office for Humanities Communication Publications.

45. http://www.eastgate.com/Storyspace.html

46. Jill Walker (2000), 'Child's game confused: reading Juliet Ann Martin's oooxxxooo.', *Journal of Digital Information*, http://jodi.ecs.soton.ac.uk/Articles/vo1/io7/Walker/

47. Jerome J. McGann, *The Complete Writings and Pictures of Dante Gabriel Rossetti. A Hypermedia Research Archive*, http://jefferson.village.virginia.edu/rossetti

48. Jerome J. McGann (2001), *Radiant Textuality. Literary Studies after the World Wide Web*, New York, Basingstoke: Palgrave/St Martins.

49. 'The Rationale of hypertext', in Kathryn Sutherland (ed.) (1997) *Electronic Text, Investigations in Method and Theory*, Oxford: Oxford University Press, pp. 19–46.

50. http://www.engl.virginia.edu/faculty/mcgann.html

51. Christie Carson (2004), 'A report on Virtual Reality (VR) in theatre history research: Creating a spatial context for performance', *Early Modern Literary Studies* Special Issue 13 (April): 2.1–12 <URL: http://purl.oclc.org/emls/si-13/carson>

52. http://www.playbill.com/multimedia/search/3524

53. See http://www.ahrb.ac.uk/ahrb/website/apply/research/strategicinitiatives/ict_in_arts_hu manities_research.asp. Information on the Methods Network and other programme activities will be added to the website from time to time.

54. http://faustroll.clas.virginia.edu/nines

55. The AHDS web site is at http://www.ahds.ac.uk. The AHDS has a distributed structure. There is a co-ordinating Executive, based at King's College London, and five separately based 'service providers', each with specific responsibility for a group of arts and humanities discipline areas and for a group of most relevant technical standards.

56. http://www.acls.org/cyberinfrastructure/cyber.htm

Notes on Contributors

Rachel Alsop lectures in Gender Studies at the University of Hull where she has taught research methods to postgraduates at both Masters and PhD level. She is co-author of *Theorizing Gender* (Cambridge: Polity, 2002). Both as a theorist and as an empirical researcher, she has utilised and written on ethnographic methods.

Catherine Belsey is Distinguished Research Professor of English at Cardiff University. Her books include *Critical Practice* (London: Methuen, [1980] 2002), a classic on textual analysis; *The Subject of Tragedy* (London: Tavistock, 1985); *Desire: Love Stories in Western Culture* (Oxford: Blackwell, 1994); and *Shakespeare and the Loss of Eden* (Basingstoke: Macmillan, 1999). In 2002 she published *Poststructuralism: A Very Short Introduction* (Oxford: Oxford University Press), which does exactly what it says on the cover. She has extensive experience of teaching postgraduates at MA and PhD level.

Jon Cook is Dean of the Faculty of Arts and Humanities at the University of East Anglia (UAE). His recent publications include *Poetry in Theory* (Oxford: Blackwell, 2004) and an essay on 'Relocating Britishness and the Break-up of Britain' in *Relocating Britishness* (Manchester: Manchester University Press, 2004). A biography, *Hazlitt in Love*, is forthcoming. He has supervised writers on the University of East Anglia's PhD in creative and critical writing since the degree's inception in 1986. From 1986 to 1994 he was convenor of the Creative Writing MA at UEA. He has taught at universities in Europe, India and the United States.

Marilyn Deegan is Director of Research Development at the Centre for Computing in the Humanities (CCH) at King's College London, and editor of *Literary and Linguistic Computing*. She was formerly Director of Forced

Migration Online at Oxford University, where she is still a Special Consultant, and she has been working in humanities computing and digital libraries for the last fifteen years. She has published widely in the field, and is co-author with Simon Tanner of *Digital Futures: Strategies for the Information Age* (London: Facet Books, 2002). She has co-edited *The Politics of the Electronic Text* (London: OHC, [1993] 1997) and *Beyond the Book: Theory, Culture, and the Politics of Cyberspace* (London: OHC, 1996).

Mary Evans is Professor of Women's Studies at the University of Kent, Canterbury. A renowned feminist straddling English and the social sciences, she is one of the leading experts on auto/biographical methods. Her publications include *The Woman Question* (London: Sage, [1982] 1994) which has become a standard textbook; *Jane Austen and the State* (London: Tavistock, 1987); *An Introduction to Contemporary Feminist Thought* (Cambridge: Polity, 1997); and *Missing Persons: The Impossibility of Auto/biography* (London: Routledge, 1999). She has taught both postgraduates and research methods for many years.

Gabriele Griffin is Professor of Gender Studies at the University of Hull where she teaches a research training course on research methods for English and Gender Studies postgraduates. Her publications include *Contemporary Black and Asian Women Playwrights in Britain* (Cambridge: Cambridge University Press, 2003); *Thinking Differently: A Reader in European Women's Studies* (co-edited with Rosi Braidotti; London: Zed Books, 2002); and *Who's Who in Lesbian and Gay Writing* (London: Routledge, 2002). She is co-founding editor of the academic journal *Feminist Theory* (London: Sage). She is co-ordinator of an EU-funded research project (2004–07) on 'Integrated Research Methods in the Humanities and Social Sciences' (www.hull.ac.uk/researchintegration).

Pat Hudson is Professor of Economic History at the University of Wales, Cardiff University. She is President of the Economic History Society, and author, among others, of *History by Numbers: An Introduction to Quantitative Approaches* (London: Edward Arnold, 2000), which offers a excellent introduction to the uses and meanings of numbers for non-numerate students. Other publications include *The Industrial Revolution* (London: Edward Arnold, 1992); *The Genesis of Industrial Capital* (Cambridge: Cambridge University Press, 1986); and she co-edited, with W. R. Lee, *Women's Work and the Family Economy in Historical Perspective* (Manchester: Manchester University Press, 1990).

Gillian Rose is Professor of Cultural Geography at the Open University where she has taught and developed research methods courses for postgraduates, a project begun at the Graduate School of Social Sciences at the University of Edinburgh. She is author of *Visual Methodologies* (London: Sage, 2001). She has also published extensively on the female subject and space.

Harold Short is Director of the Centre for Computing in the Humanities (CCH) at King's College London, and Chair of the Association for Literary and Linguistic Computing. He is responsible for the development of masters and undergraduate courses at King's College London in Applied Computing in the Humanities, and in Digital Culture and Technology. He has extensive experience of the application of computing in humanities research, and is technical director of a number of humanities research projects based in CCH. Marilyn Deegan and Harold Short are co-directors of the Office for Humanities Communication, which supports workshops and conferences, such as the annual Digital Resources for the Humanities conference, and has a publication series on issues related to the application of computing methods and techniques in the humanities.

Carolyn Steedman is Professor of History at the University of Warwick. Working at the interface of literature and history, her *Landscape for a Good Woman* (London: Virago, 1986) made her one of the leading feminist historians in the UK. Her recent volume *Dust* (Manchester: Manchester University Press, 2001) centres on archival methods and is a rebuttal to Derrida's article 'Archive Fever'. She has extensive experience of teaching both postgraduate students and research methods.

Penny Summerfield is Professor of Modern History at the University of Manchester and, apart from being an authority in oral history methods, has worked across various forms of cross-cultural production. She has significant experience of teaching postgraduates including in interdisciplinary settings. Her publications include *Reconstructing Women's Wartime Lives: Discourse and Subjectivity in Oral Histories of the Second World War* (Manchester: Manchester University Press, 1998); and she has co-edited, with T. Cosslett and C. Lury, *Feminism and Autobiography: Texts, Theories, Methods* (London: Routledge, 2000).

Index